THE ADVENTURE GUIDE
TO
BAJA CALIFORNIA

The Adventure Guide to
BAJA
CALIFORNIA

Wilbur H. Morrison

HUNTER
PUBLISHING, INC

Hunter Publishing, Inc.
300 Raritan Center Parkway
Edison NJ 08818
(908) 225 1900

ISBN 1-55650-590-6

Revised edition © 1993 Wilbur H. Morrison
First edition published 1990

Cover photograph:
El Arco de Cortez, Cabo San Lucas
Bernard Bansse/Superstock

Regional maps: PhotoGraphics
City maps: Instant Mexico Auto Insurance Services

For
Mabel who shared many of my
travels to Baja California

Contents

FOREWORD

For more than 35 years I have been traveling to Baja California on fishing trips or just to relax. It is an ideal place for either pastime.

Each year more than 50 million people cross the United States border with Mexico's Baja California at Tijuana, making it the busiest border crossing in the world. Few of these people ever go beyond the border cities, thereby missing the extraordinary experience of traveling into Baja's interior. Other tourists fly to the peninsula's southern cities, again failing to realize that it is the interior that holds the most enchantment.

It is my hope that this book will inspire more people to go beyond the border cities and enjoy the pleasures of a land still largely unspoiled by man.

There are few books about Baja California, and many of them are inaccurate. In exploring the peninsula's past, I used original sources wherever possible and cross-checked facts to assure accuracy. I have either been to all of the places described in this book, or I've interviewed Mexican friends who have been there recently.

Wilbur H. Morrison
Fallbrook CA 92028

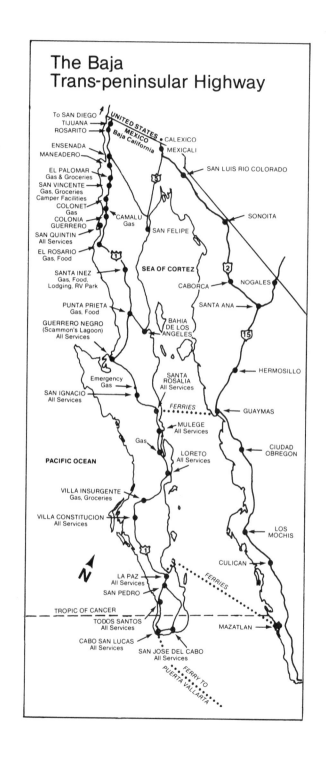

The Baja
Trans-peninsular Highway

To SAN DIEGO
UNITED STATES
TIJUANA
MEXICO
ROSARITO
Baja California
CALEXICO
MEXICALI

ENSENADA
MANEADERO

SAN LUIS RIO COLORADO

EL PALOMAR
Gas & Groceries
SAN VINCENTE
Gas, Groceries
Camper Facilities
COLONET
Gas
CAMALU
Gas
COLONIA
GUERRERO
SAN QUINTIN
All Services

SONOITA

SAN FELIPE

EL ROSARIO
Gas, Food

SANTA INEZ
Gas, Food,
Lodging, RV Park

SEA OF CORTEZ

NOGALES

CABORCA

PUNTA PRIETA
Gas, Food

SANTA ANA

GUERRERO NEGRO
(Scammon's Lagoon)
All Services

BAHIA
DE LOS
ANGELES

HERMOSILLO

Emergency
Gas

SANTA
ROSALIA
All Services

SAN IGNACIO
All Services

FERRIES

GUAYMAS

MULEGE
All Services

Gas

PACIFIC OCEAN

LORETO
All Services

CIUDAD
OBREGON

VILLA INSURGENTE
Gas, Groceries

VILLA CONSTITUCION
All Services

LOS
MOCHIS

CULICAN

N

LA PAZ
All Services

FERRIES

SAN PEDRO

TROPIC OF CANCER

TODOS SANTOS
All Services

MAZATLAN

CABO SAN LUCAS
All Services

SAN JOSE DEL CABO
All Services

FERRY TO
PUERTA
VALLARTA

Introduction

Tourist Cards & Passports

American and Canadian citizens who restrict their visits to border areas as far south as Ensenada, and who remain in Mexico not more than 72 hours, need not obtain a tourist card. All others must procure one, and it is free.

There are two types of cards. The single-entry card is valid for 90 days. It will be picked up by border authorities at the end of your trip. (Single-entry tourist cards become automatically invalid if they are not used within 90 days of their issuance.) Multiple-entry cards provide unlimited entry into Mexico for 180 days. For these cards two frontal photographs are required. They are available in the United States from Mexican Consulates or any Mexican Government tourism office. Single-entry tourist cards are available to American and Canadian Automobile Association members who are United States or Canadian citizens. Airlines and travel agencies routinely provide tourist cards for their clients. They can also be obtained at the border from Mexican immigration authorities, but this is not advisable because it can result in time-consuming delays. Those applying for tourist cards must have either a valid passport, or a birth certificate issued by the government office in that person's birthplace. Naturalized United States citizens must present a valid passport, a Certificate of Naturalization or Certificate of Citizenship. Whatever the validation, it must be brought with you on the trip. Wallet-sized naturalization cards or other documents are not acceptable. Canadian citizens must have a valid passport or birth certificate. Citizens of other countries should contact their nearest Mexican Consulate for regulations governing their visit to Baja California. Children under 18 years of age, who wish to enter Mexico without both parents, must have a notarized copy of a form entitled "Permission for a Minor to Travel in Mexico." This can be obtained at any Mexican tourism office. If a child's parents are divorced or separated, the signed form must be presented when a tourist card is requested, along with the parent's divorce or separation papers. If one of the parents is deceased, the death certificate must accompany the form and the surviving parent must sign the form. If a child is under legal guardianship, the guardian must sign the form and provide guardianship papers. If both parents are dead, death certificates are required.

Currency Exchange

Since 1982, Mexican currency has been sharply devalued. In 1992, the exchange rate between Mexican and United States money averaged 3,050 pesos to the dollar but the peso fluctuates almost daily. Most Baja businesses are eager to accept American dollars because of their stability, and normally this is to the advantage of visitors, but it is advisable for tourists traveling into Baja California's interior to have Mexican money as well. For example, some gasoline stations and smaller businesses only accept pesos. In general, tourist-oriented cities pose no problem in cashing American money. But if you pay dollars, insist upon change in dollars and vice versa; otherwise you'll lose money. International currency exchanges are located in most California cities, and on both sides of the border. In addition, American currency can be converted into pesos at most Mexican banks. Travelers checks are readily accepted at most hotels, or can be cashed at Mexican banks, but they are not readily accepted by most businesses.

The Mexican Government continues to order sizable increases in the cost of all accommodations, restaurants, places of entertainment and services in Baja. The prices listed in this book do not cover the increase in taxes (at least 15 percent) that are applied to your bills. Some places will charge an additional fee of up to 15 percent as a service charge.

Medical Facilities

Baja California's medical facilities are excellent in the major cities, with well-equipped hospitals, clinics and pharmacies. In rural areas, such facilities are scarce but emergency critical care air transport services are available throughout the peninsula with in-flight physicians and nurses. They are on call 24 hours a day. Critical Air Medicine, Inc. is in San Diego at (619) 571-0482 or toll-free in the US (800) 247-8326. Within Mexico, call toll-free 95-800-010-0268.

Avoiding Medical Problems

In general there is no more reason to become ill in Baja California than there is at home, but changes in environment – different food and water – can cause intestinal disturbances. Mexicans who visit the United States have the same problem. Tap water can be a problem in most places, and it should be avoided. Bottled water, soft drinks or Mexico's excellent beer make good substitutes. But over-indulgence in alcohol, food and activity can add to your discomfort if "Montezuma's Revenge" should strike.

Smallpox and other vaccinations are no longer required for travel into any part of Mexico.

The Language Barrier

By and large the Mexicans you will meet speak and understand some English, and in the larger resort areas bilingual personnel predominate. A Spanish-American phrasebook, readily available in most bookstores, can help surmount the language problem.

Telephoning Mexico

To call Mexico from another country, dial 011 52, then the area code and number.

Time

Baja California Norte – the top half of the peninsula – observes Pacific Standard Time from the last Sunday in October to the first Sunday in April, and Pacific Daylight Time during the rest of the year. Baja California Sur is on Mountain Standard Time all year, which means that its clocks are an hour ahead of California's during the winter months, but the same during the summer.

Crime

Baja, particularly in its rural areas, has far less crime than the United States but it is wise to observe the same precautions as at home, keeping your car locked at all times, carrying a minimum of cash and never leaving valuables in your car or room.

What To Do In An Emergency

If, despite all precautions, you should encounter problems or require emergency services, contact the State Tourism Department or the local police. In Mexico, government authority is vested in the *delegado*, an elected official who handles emergencies and civil or legal disputes. In rural areas, where crime is rare, an appointed citizen has this responsibility. The Attorney General for the Protection of Tourists has offices in Tijuana, Ensenada, Mexicali and San Felipe. At Tijuana it is located in the State Tourism Department in Plaza Patria on Boulevard Díaz Ordaz; (66) 81-9492 or 81-9493. In Ensenada the office is located at Avenida López Matéos 1360;

(667) 6-2222. In Mexicali, it is in the Tourist and Convention Building at Calzada López Matéos 1360; (667) 6-2222. In Baja California Sur, Tourist Protection is located at La Paz: State Tourist Office, Paseo Alunta Obregón at 16 de Septiembre; (682) 2-5939.

In northern Baja California, the United States Consulate is on Calle Tapachula near Agua Caliente Racetrack in Tijuana. He will assist Americans Monday through Friday from 8 a.m. to 4:30 p.m. at his office, or he can be reached by calling (66) 81-7400 during these hours. When the Tijuana Consulate is closed, call (619) 585-2000.

Car Permits

No car permits are required unless you take one of Baja's ferries to mainland Mexico. Then a car permit/tourist card combination is needed for the principal driver, while other occupants need only the standard tourist card. These car permits are issued at all points of entry into mainland Mexico, including Baja's ferry ports. They are free and are valid for 90 days. If you need a car permit, the usual proof of citizenship is required, plus the original registration or a notarized bill of sale for each vehicle (including motorcycles). For vehicles still under finance contracts you must have written, notarized permission from whoever holds the lien stating that the driver has permission to take it into Mexico. A notarized affidavit of authorization is required if the owner (such as a company or another person) is not the same as the driver.

Motorhome and motorcycle drivers are further restricted because only one permit can be issued to a person. This can be a problem for some people because one person can not enter mainland Mexico, or board a ferry in Baja California, with a motorhome *and* a motorcycle even if he or she owns them. You can get around the regulation by registering one of the vehicles to a passenger, or obtain a car permit for one of the vehicles by using a notarized affidavit of permission from the owner. But there can be permits only for the number of qualified drivers in your group, and they must be 18 years of age or older.

Mandatory Mexican Insurance

Mexican law does not recognize insurance policies other than those issued by Mexican-licensed companies. It is essential, therefore, that you obtain a separate Mexican insurance policy prior to driving in Baja. Throughout Mexico a person involved in a traffic accident, who does not have a valid Mexican policy, can be detained by the police regardless of the type of accident, and incarceration can go on for months in serious cases. Insurance policies are written by the day, month or year, and are issued upon application. Offices of the American Automobile Association can provide policies in California. Or you can stop at Instant Mexico Auto Insurance Services, whose main office at 223 Via de San Ysidro, San Ysidro CA 92073 is open 24 hours a day. You can call toll free within California at (800) 345-4701 or in the rest of the United States at (800) 638-0999. There is easy access off Route 5. In addition to insurance, they also provide tourist information, tourist cards, Mexican fishing licenses, and boat permits. There is also a notary public on hand to issue affidavits for those who forgot to bring their birth certificates.

Trailer Limitations

Trailers must not be more than 8 feet wide and 40 feet long, unless a special permit is authorized by the Federal Highway Police Road Office in Tijuana. Baja California's roads are the limiting factor. Compared to American highways, they are quite narrow. Even main roads are only 19 to 25 feet wide and they rarely have any shoulders. There are few places to turn around on inland roads and many roads have high crowns that force a car to drift to the right. This takes some getting used to so as not to over-correct while steering. High winds are a problem in many areas, offering the usual difficulties encountered everywhere under such conditions by recreational vehicles, trucks and passenger cars pulling trailers. Speeds are lower in Baja than in the United States and it is wise to observe the posted limits of 40 to 50 miles per hour (half that in hilly or mountainous country). Outside the main cities night driving should be avoided. Range land is rarely fenced so you need to watch for cattle and horses wandering on the roads.

Police Roadblocks

Armed police or Mexican military personnel set up occasional roadblocks to search vehicles for arms or drugs. Unless you are apprehended for possession, you'll be treated courteously. Otherwise you'll learn that Mexico's jails are among the world's worst. If you have broken no laws, and you feel that you have not been treated with common courtesy, by all means report unfair treatment to the United States Consulate or the Mexican Attorney General for the Protection of Tourists in Tijuana, or the State Tourism Department in La Paz.

Car Repair

Prior to your trip to Baja's interior make sure your car and other vehicles are in top mechanical condition. In the cities, most repair work can be accomplished, but outside them it's problematical. Carrying along extra engine fluids – oil, water, brake fluid and anti-freeze – may save you a great deal of frustration. The government of Mexico controls the types of automobiles sold and parts available are limited to those makes. Even in the cities, a serious breakdown of an important part can force you to wait for days or even weeks. In local villages, mechanics rarely have the expertise to work on modern cars. It's not worth the risk to visit any part of Mexico without having your car checked thoroughly before you leave home.

Green Angels

If you do get in trouble, stay with your car and wait for "The Green Angels." These are government-operated vehicles that provide free emergency service to tourists. They are pledged to pass any spot on any particular road throughout Baja California at least twice a day. The cars of The Green Angels are driven by mechanics, but not all are bilingual. They carry a limited range of parts and provide gasoline at cost. Most importantly, if there is a serious condition beyond their control, they are able to summon help by radio.

Fuel Availability

Gasoline is readily available throughout Baja on its major highways, but if local shortages develop you may not be able to get the type of gasoline you require. Never let your tank get below the half-filled mark! Unleaded gasoline is normally not available along the 344-mile portion of Highway 1 between San Quintín and San Ignacio. Diesel fuel is more readily available everywhere except for the 104 miles between La Paz and Cabo San Lucas on Highway 19. There are two grades of gasoline. "Magna-Sin" is unleaded with a Mexican rating of 92, but equal to 81 on the American scale, while "Nova" is listed with an octane rating of 81, although United States standards would give it only a 79. You can improve the octane rating by mixing the two gasolines or using a gasoline additive to stop the "pinging." Gasoline is relatively cheap. Magna-Sin premium is approximately $1.25 per gallon, the leaded Nova is $.91, and diesel is $.72 per gallon. Mexican gasoline occasionally has water or other impurities in it and some drivers insist upon straining the fuel through a chamois cloth. Don't expect attendants at any station to wash your windows, so be prepared to do your own. In those cases where it is done for you, expect to pay a tip.

ROAD SIGNS

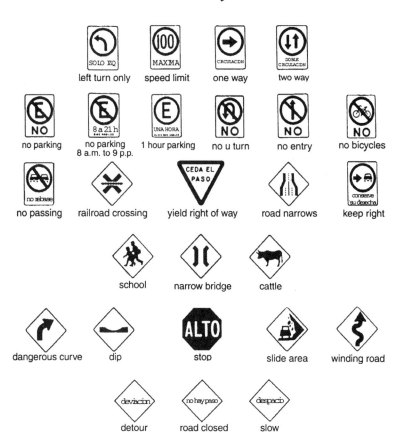

left turn only   speed limit   one way   two way

no parking   no parking 8 a.m. to 9 p.p.   1 hour parking   no u turn   no entry   no bicycles

no passing   railroad crossing   yield right of way   road narrows   keep right

school   narrow bridge   cattle

dangerous curve   dip   stop   slide area   winding road

detour   road closed   slow

Pemex stations have a monopoly in Mexico and some of its stations in rural areas are unclean. Restroom facilities are often filthy and without paper towels or even toilet paper. Carrying your own paper may save you an embarrassing problem.

Traffic Signs

All of Mexico's highways use the uniform traffic sign system of pictographs, and they are self-explanatory even when they are in Spanish.

Hazards Off The Main Highways

There are special problems for travelers who leave the main highways and roam through the countryside. Delightful surprises await the adventuresome, along with some unpleasant ones. Much of the interior is wild and incredibly rugged in the deserts and mountains. With proper high-clearance vehicles and personal equipment, and if you are able to dispense momentarily with the routine comforts of civilization, such trips will reap a bounty of unimaginable beauty and adventure. But be prepared, because this land of empty spaces and lonely beaches that seldom see the footprints of man is so isolated that help may not be forthcoming if you need it. Plan well ahead so you'll have the proper equipment for desert travel and can subsist largely on your own, with an occasional isolated rancho to offer help in time of need. Don't go anywhere alone! Stay with a group. Be sure someone knows where you have gone and when you are expected to return. Off-road vehicles should have at least 50-60 gallons of extra fuel, and at least five gallons of water per person, plus non-perishable food that will last at least two weeks. There are few places in the interior with surface water because the heat is omnipresent. Some areas get almost no rain in the course of a year. Protect cameras, food and other possessions with plastic bags – not only from the heat but from the dust.

If you're not an experienced desert or mountain traveler, and no one in your party is so experienced, hire a guide. The vastness of Baja's interior can be overwhelming, and you'll be on your own as in few places on earth. People have died from thirst and/or heat exhaustion because they failed to take a few elementary precautions. Learn all you can about surviving under such circumstances before you leave home, or else stick to the main roads. Dirt roads should not be traveled in most of today's passenger cars. Even trucks should have high clearances because the roads can be spine-jarring and rough enough to break even the toughest axle if driven too fast. These off-the-beaten-track roads are not signed properly – rarely ever in English and sometimes not at all – so know in advance where they lead, or stay off them.

Citizens' Band Radios

Mexico now provides three channels – 9, 10, and 11 – for use of citizens' band radios by tourists. Channel 9 is restricted to emergencies, 10 can be used by tourists to communicate with one another, while 11 is used to obtain directions and receive information. You must have valid permits issued only by Mexican Consulates. They can be obtained at Ensenada and La Paz in Baja, but it is advisable to procure them in the United States. Each permit is about $3 and you must prove citizenship and provide the make, model and serial number of your CB radio. Only Channels 1-22 can be used without amplification beyond five watts transmission power. You must surrender the permit when you leave Mexico.

Camping Out

Outside of the cities, where RV sites usually double as tent sites, you can camp almost anywhere. High winds pose a problem for all but the most sturdy tents, and nights can be downright cold, particularly on the Pacific side of the peninsula. Flash floods during the rainy season make camping on the bottom of arroyos or ravines almost suicidal. Wood is scarce in Baja so cooking and/or heating fires must rely on cactus skeletons. And, don't be a litterbug! It's getting to be a problem, even in the backcountry. Burn your litter, or pack it out.

By Air Or Bus

Air and bus services throughout Mexico are cheaper than the United States and generally first rate. Bus service is an inexpensive way to travel if you don't have an automobile.

Air travel to Baja has been erratic in recent years due to the bankruptcy of some airlines, the merger of others, and the frequent changing of flight schedules. You can only make connections to travel into Baja from Los Angeles and San Diego in California, or from cities on the Mexican mainland. Mexicana Airlines provides direct service from Los Angeles to San José del Cabo, and nonstop service from Tijuana to La Paz. Its jetliners also fly from Los Angeles, Tijuana, Mexicali and La Paz to cities on the mainland. Mexicana makes daily flights from Mexico City to Cabo San Lucas and Tijuana, but it does not have service between Cabo San Lucas and Tijuana. For further information, call (800) 531-7921. Aero California has daily flights from Los Angeles to Loreto, La Paz, and San José del Cabo; from San Diego to San José del Cabo; and from Tijuana to San José del Cabo and La Paz. For details, call (800) 237-6225. Gunnell Aviation, Inc. has charter aircraft that service communities with airports in Baja from any Southern California airport. For details, call (213) 870-3778.

Aero Mexico operates daily flights from Los Angeles to La Paz and from Tijuana to La Paz. Call (800) 237-6639. Mexican airlines have the same high standards as all other carriers, and their service is excellent. If you depart from Mexican cities on these airlines there is a substantial saving on fares.

Fishing Licenses

Baja California's surrounding waters provide some of' the world's finest salt-water fishing. Fresh-water fishing is confined primarily to mountain areas but even there it is limited. Non-resident aliens 16 years or older must purchase a

Mexican sport-fishing license that covers all types of fishing everywhere, including fishing from private boats in Mexican waters. Licenses are issued for a day, a week, a month or a year and are effective at 12:01 a.m. of the starting date listed on the license's application. They vary according to changes in the value of the peso but currently run about $13.60 per week, $20.20 per month, and $27 per year. Application may be made at the Mexico Department of Fisheries at 2550 5th Ave., Suite 101, San Diego CA 92103 from 8 a.m. to 2 p.m. Monday through Friday. Only cash or money orders (no personal checks) are accepted. Their phone number is (310) 233-6956. Licenses may also be obtained at resorts where fishing is part of their schedule, from boat charter organizations or from Southern California Automobile Club Offices if you're a member. Ten fish can be caught per day, but no more than five fish of the same species. Only one full-grown marlin may be taken and two tarpon, halibut or sailfish. Use of nets and explosives is forbidden. Skin and scuba divers may only fish with hand-held spears or hand-powered spearguns. It is illegal to trade or sell the fish you catch, and a patch of skin must be left on to permit identification. Mexican law prohibits the taking of abalone, lobster, shrimp, pismo clams, cabrilla, totuava, oysters and sea turtles. These species can be purchased at designated public markets or fishing cooperatives.

United States Customs permits the importation of fish, but only an amount for personal consumption. Anyone bringing fish into the United States must have a valid Mexican fishing license or a Mexico Department of Fisheries form covering purchase of the fish.

Private boats fishing in Mexican waters must first obtain a boat permit. It can be purchased by the month or for periods up to 12 months. Fees are based upon the boat's length, and the number of months it will remain in Mexican waters. Applications must be submitted to Mexico's Department of Fisheries at 2550 5th Ave., Suite 101, San Diego CA 93103; (310) 233-6956. Auto Club members may use one of their offices. The Mexican office is open between the hours of 8 a.m.

and 2 p.m., Monday through Friday. Applications must include the boat's registration number issued by the State Department of Motor Vehicles in California, or the U.S. Coast Guard certificate number, with the boat owner's full legal name, home address and telephone number. Fees must be paid by cashier's check or money order for the exact amount. For mail orders, a stamped, self-addressed return envelope must be enclosed.

Hunting & Firearms

Baja is not noted for its hunting, but waterfowl are plentiful on both coasts and in the Colorado River Delta, while ducks can be found in lagoons and marshes. There are rabbits, quail and doves throughout Baja as well as a few deer – rbut they are scarce and special permits are required to hunt them. Most open seasons are from mid-September to the end of February.

If you want to bring your own gun, four documents are required including a multiple-entry tourist card, a consular certificate, a gun permit and a hunting permit. Only weapons brought into Mexico on an approved basis for the hunting season are permitted, and then only two sporting firearms and 50 rounds of ammunition for each gun are permitted. All military and .22-caliber rimfire guns and pistols are strictly prohibited.

Hunting in Baja isn't worth the trouble, but some people insist on going through the lengthy process. The procedure is as follows: Each applicant must present a letter of good conduct from his local police department or sheriff's office, with two front-view passport-size photographs. Then the applicant receives a consular certificate that authorizes him to enter Mexico as a hunter. This is required when applying for a gun permit and contains a description of each firearm, including type, make, serial number, caliber or gauge and number of cartridges.

At the Mexican border, the hunter leaves his guns and ammunition on the American side until he presents his consular certificates and makes written application for a hunting permit. State Tourism Offices in Tijuana and Mexicali can direct hunters to agents who handle these permits. They are issued by the Department of Wildlife for processing between 9 a.m. and 2 p.m. Monday through Friday. Hunters must purchase permits for each Mexican state in which they plan to hunt, and each permit costs at least $35. It is non-transferable and valid only for the current season.

For a gun permit there are two Southern California organizations who handle the paperwork and furnish information on hunting conditions and government regulations. They are: The Mexican Hunting Association, Inc., 3302 Josie Avenue, Long Beach CA 90808, (213) 421-1619; and Wildlife Advisory Services, P 0. Box 76132, Los Angeles CA. 90075, (213) 385-9311. Permits can run up to $300 or more, depending on what is to be hunted.

What You Can Bring Out Of Mexico

A United States resident is permitted to bring back articles with a retail value up to $400 without paying a duty if they are for that person's use and personally transported by that person. Couples and families, including children, can pool their exemptions to acquire possessions of considerable value. There is no minimum time for your stay in Baja California to qualify, but the exemption can be used only once during a 30-day period. In addition, duty-free and tax-free gifts that do not exceed $50 in value may be sent by tourists while in Mexico to a friend in the United States. The package should be marked "unsolicited gifts" with the value written on the outside of the package. However, you are forbidden to send alcoholic beverages, tobacco products or perfumes valued at more than $5, although a liter of liquor can be personally brought across the border by each adult 21 or older. Returning travelers need not declare their mailed gifts and they do not apply against the $400 exemption. Most fresh fruits and vegetables, and certain other agricultural products, are strictly forbidden to be brought into the United States. Also forbidden are the importation of dangerous drugs, unsafe toys, obscene materials, seditious writing and explosives such as fireworks. Purchases above the duty-free limit, and below $1,400, will be taxed at a fixed rate of 10 percent.

Those who travel in Mexico might consider registering their foreign-made goods with United States Customs before crossing the border. Cameras and binoculars would be good candidates, particularly if they are new, unless you have the original receipts for their purchase. Otherwise, you may have an argument about paying duties above the allowable $400 permitted for each visit.

What You Can Bring Into Mexico

There are only a few restrictions on what you can bring into Mexico. As a tourist, you can take one still camera and one 8 mm. or 16 mm. movie camera with you, plus 12 rolls of film. A video camera, and six blank cassettes, is also permitted if your picture taking is solely for pleasure and not for commercial purposes. Oddly, tripods are prohibited.

Pets

Dogs and other pets can be a problem and it's advisable to leave them at home. Some hotel operators refuse to allow pets, and there are special inspections and health certificates required for pets that are brought along. Before you leave home you must obtain a vaccination certificate for rabies, and the official Interstate and International Health Certificates for Dogs and Cats from a veterinarian. Then these documents must be approved by a Mexican Consul who charges at least $20. The visa for your pet is good for six months. If your pet is out of the United States more than 30 days, you must present these certificates when you return to the United States.

Take Normal Precautions

Traveling in Baja is an adventuresome and enjoyable experience, but only if you strive to make it so by taking normal travel precautions and respecting the land and its people. It is wise to make reservations well in advance to avoid the possibility of finding no available accomodations. If you prepare for your trip properly, it will be unlike any other trip you have taken. Baja California, the land of eternal summer, is truly a land of enchantment and one that you will never forget.

The History of Baja

The interior of Baja California is one of the least-traveled places on earth, despite its 450 years of recorded history. It begins only a hundred miles south of the western border of the United States and Mexico. Until the Trans-Peninsular Highway from the Mexican-American border to Baja's tip at Cabo San Lucas was opened in December 1, 1973, it was a largely undiscovered land of cactus-covered deserts. The sole previous highway was a meandering dirt road that only the intrepid dared, and seldom even then without special cars or trucks.

The irregularly-shaped 800-mile peninsula has more than 1,000 miles of Pacific Ocean coastline. It varies in width from 30 to 145 miles, has approximately 6,000 square miles more area than the state of New York and is 100 miles longer than the boot of Italy. More than half of its population lives in the border cities, and much of the 55,000 square miles of its wilderness interior is virtually uninhabited. Most of this interior is desert, an area that receives less than 10 inches of rainfall each year.

Sierras, or mountain ranges, form an almost unbroken chain from Baja's 145-mile border with Alta California and Arizona in the United States to the peninsula's tip at Cabo San Lucas, where the earth plunges to one of the Pacific Ocean's greatest depths. The highest mountain is Picacho del Diablo, or Devil's Peak. It is part of the Sierra San Pedro Mártir (Saint Peter martyred) and from October to May is often snow-capped. It can be seen from mainland Mexico 140 miles to the east, and from far out in the Pacific Ocean in the west. This range of mountains lies in the north-central part of the peninsula. The tallest peaks are difficult to climb, as are some of the southern mountains, except through a few mountain passes.

Through the years, infrequent torrents of rain from tropical storms have carved canyons below these mountain ranges, and formed alluvial plains on the desert floors below them. The ranges in the far south are not as impressive as those in the north, and the land tends to flatten out at their bases – particularly where the peninsula narrows to a width of 30 miles just above La Paz. Mountains rise again in the region of Cabo San Lucas, and the slopes of the Sierra de la Laguna are covered with forests.

Baja California might not have been discovered until many centuries later if it had not been for the persistence of Christopher Columbus. From 1483, he devoted all of his efforts towards the establishment of an expedition to seek a shorter route from the Old World to the Far East, rather than the customary one of sailing around the tip of Africa from the south Atlantic Ocean to the Indian Ocean.

Columbus's explorations in 1492 and later were so successful in opening up the New World for Spain that his adopted country soon dominated the region. This was fortunate for Spain because her internal wars during and after the ouster of the Muslims from the Iberian peninsula had drained most of her wealth. It was hoped that Columbus's voyages of discovery would replenish the royal treasury at small cost to the government.

By the 16th century Spain had taken title to almost half of the known world, while Portugal had taken much of the remainder. Spain now claimed Mexico, Central America, the Caribbean Islands, half of South America, and much of what

Until the mid-18th century Baja was considered an island, as shown on this map published in England shortly before the first mission was founded in San Diego.

is now the United States. By 1531, Spain ruled more of the world's surface than Great Britain ever did in later years.

Spain's colonies were overseen by the king and his counselors, but they delegated authority to viceroys or "vice-kings," who were appointed for a one-year term, and who were responsible for civil, religious and military affairs. Rules were established in advance because of the great distances separating the homeland from its far-flung colonies and the difficulty of making necessary changes that often took months to implement. At first, members of the clergy and the military worked closely together to subdue lands and set up colonies. The clergy was given initial authority, but civil authority was established at a later date.

Columbus's voyages for the Spanish Crown sparked strong interest in further explorations and conquests. Hernán Cortés, after conquering Emperor Moctezuma's Aztec empire between 1519 and 1521, quickly opened trade routes with Guatemala to the south, and north to Mexico's central plateau. Once these routes were established, he constructed a cobblestone road to Guadalajara and on to the tropical port of San Blas that today is part of the state of Nayarit.

The farther west his forces moved to the Gulf of California, the more rumors Cortés heard of a fabulous island with a lake filled by pearls, with mountains of pure gold guarded by beautiful Amazon women who lured men to their destruction. Such tales fired the imagination of this redoubtable conquistador. With equal ardor for the beautiful women of this strange land, and the fabulous riches supposedly available in such abundance, Cortés made plans to send an expedition from the mainland side of the Gulf of California.

Cortés was a striking figure, taller than most men of his time, with dark eyes flashing out of a pale face. He dressed in the best of clothes; particularly those that emphasized his slender, well-muscled figure with its broad shoulders. A man of military genius who excelled in fencing and horsemanship, Cortés had a natural dignity and commanding presence that made him beloved by his followers.

Cortés, and other literate men of his time, were aware of a popular medieval romance entitled *Las Sergas de Esplandián* by García Ordóñez de Montalvo that was published in 1510. In this book, *The Exploits of Esplandián*, the author describes a fictional assault upon Constantinople by a Sultan Radiaro of Persia and his lords, who were considered infidels by the city's Christian defenders. A work of pure fiction, written 60 years after Constantinople actually fell into the hands of the Turkish sultans, it is memorable only because the book describes a mythical island called California. This island supposedly was near the terrestrial paradise that Christopher Columbus hoped to find. The author describes California as an island peopled by beautiful black women, living as Amazons without men, whose courage in battle was legendary. The island was said to have steep cliffs and rocky shores that made it almost impregnable because the Californians lived in caves carved out of solid rock.

In extolling the courage of these women, the author said their arms were made of gold, as were the harnesses of the wild beasts that they tamed and rode into battle. To further excite the avarice of would-be conquerors, the author stated that gold was used because it was the only metal on the island.

The Californians relied upon their large fleet of ships, the author claims, to raid other countries, and they were aided by an air force of griffins who were half-eagles and half-lions. These griffins supposedly were captured in traps when they were small by women dressed in thick hides. While caring for the griffins in their own caves as they grew up, the Californians fed them the bodies of men whom they had taken prisoner, including the boys to whom they gave birth. The author doesn't explain who the fathers were. Presumably they were the prisoners before they were fed to the griffins. Ever afterwards, the author relates, every man who made the mistake of landing on the island was fed to the griffins.

Appropriately, these Amazons were led by a Queen Calafia who was large in stature and incredibly beautiful. Bored at home, with no nearby countries to conquer, Calafia longed for new worlds beyond her island empire to subdue. When she heard about the gathering of sultans in the Near East to besiege the Christians in Constantinople, she set out in her fleet of ships to offer her assistance. Her eager subjects applauded the adventure, and she ordered that her largest ship be equipped with stout gratings to house 500 griffins. Once the ship was ready, she set sail with her armed Amazons and, after an uneventful voyage, joined the assembled sultans and their armies outside Constantinople. In defiance of historical truth, the Christians emerged victorious after several great battles, and Esplandián, son of King Amadis of Gaul, married the Greek emperor's daughter after the monarch conveniently abdicated his throne in Esplandián's favor.

Queen Calafia had fallen in love with the handsome Esplandián and was desolate. She was now held prisoner by the Christians, although she was monarch of a great kingdom. In the end, Emperor Esplandián took pity on her and, after she renounced paganism and became a Christian, he permitted her to marry his handsome cousin Prince Talanque and they lived happily ever after.

Whether this fanciful tale resulted in the naming of California will never be known. It certainly must have intrigued Cortés and the soldiers of his army and whetted their appetites for the exotic women who lived on such an incredibly rich island. The author of the novel claims that the word California was derived from the Greek words "kalli" for beautiful, and "ornis" for bird – because the island had so many griffins. Quite possibly the term "callida fornax" – hot furnace in English – used to describe the sweat baths of the aborigines, and also applied to one of Baja California's ports by Cortés, may be the true origin of the name.

At first, Cortés believed that what later became known as Baja California was an island, and that its riches, real and imagined, were worth exploring. He was convinced that by sailing north in the Gulf of California ships would reach the Atlantic Ocean. Actually, as late as the 18th century, there were men who believed there was such a passage from the upper gulf to the north Pacific Ocean.

Cortés's first attempt at exploration of the gulf ended in failure when one of his two ships was captured by an enemy, Nuño de Guzmán, in the Bahía de Banderas. This bay now opens to Puerto Vallarta. The other was stranded at the port of Ahome in Sinaloa province.

Despite this initial failure, Cortés was stimulated to greater endeavors as he personally traveled to the Isthmus of Tehuantepéc to supervise the construction of two more ships. The *Concepción* and the *San Lázaro* sailed for Baja California October 19, 1533. Although Captain Diego Becerra of the *Concepción* was murdered by his crew, the ship's pilot Fórtuno Jiménez took the ship to a bay later known as La Paz. Tragedy struck again when the pilot and 22 of his crew were slain by Indians, possibly for violating some of their women, while they tried to replenish the ship's water supply. The surviving mutineers hastily sailed to a port in Sinaloa. Meanwhile, the *San Lázaro,* under Captain Hernando de Grijalva, sighted islands in the Pacific and, without further exploration, returned to Acapulco.

During their brief stay in Baja California, the crew of the *Concepción* noted that the Indians had beautiful pearls. Intrigued by this disclosure, Cortés financed and led a third expedition. His fleet included three ships with 500 Spaniards, including soldiers, family members, priests and slaves. Cortés hoped to colonize the land. Arriving at the place where Jiménez and 22 members of the *Concepción's* crew were slain by Indians May 3, 1534, he named his new colony Santa Cruz, and remained there for two years. Eventually the hostility of the Pericué and Guaicura Indians, the sickness of many of his people, and the chubasco winds that periodically swept the area destroying everything in their path convinced him of the futility of maintaining a colony, despite the many advantages of the place. This settlement, where La Paz later was established, had been started 86 years before the Pilgrims landed on Plymouth Rock in Massachussetts, and it had to contend with far worse conditions.

In 1537, Cortés tried again by dispatching Captain Francisco de Ulloa to explore the gulf then called El Mar Bermejo – the Vermillion Sea. Some thought it received its name because it resembled the Old World's Red Sea. It is more likely that its name was derived from the discoloration caused by the Río Colorado or Red River that empties into it. Ulloa reached as far north as the mouth of the Colorado, and returned along the coast of the mainland. Next, this excellent navigator sailed around Cabo San Lucas and reached Cedros Island before returning to the mainland. Everywhere Ulloa was discouraged by the barrenness of the land and the poverty of its aboriginal occupants. Before he returned to Mexico City to report on his voyage, he named the gulf the Sea of Cortéz in honor of his benefactor. Ulloa was murdered by one of his men near Guadalajara. He had kept a diary of his findings to give to Cortés, but the latter never saw it. It was lost for a hundred years.

Despite his great contributions to the expansion of the Spanish Crown in the New World, Cortés was constantly beset by financial problems and jealous rivals repeatedly tried to have him removed. He returned to Spain in 1541 determined to seek redress for the many wrongs done to him. He was vindicated and received personal compensation for his long service to the crown. His pleas for additional funds to continue explorations in the New World were denied, however, and he never returned to Mexico.

The "Dourado Map." This may have been based on information brought back by Cabrillo's pilot, Ferrelo, and is thought to have been used by Sebastian Vizcaíno when he charted the California coast in 1602-03. It was made in 1570 and shows the Pacific coast from San Blas, Mexico to Cape Mendocino, California.

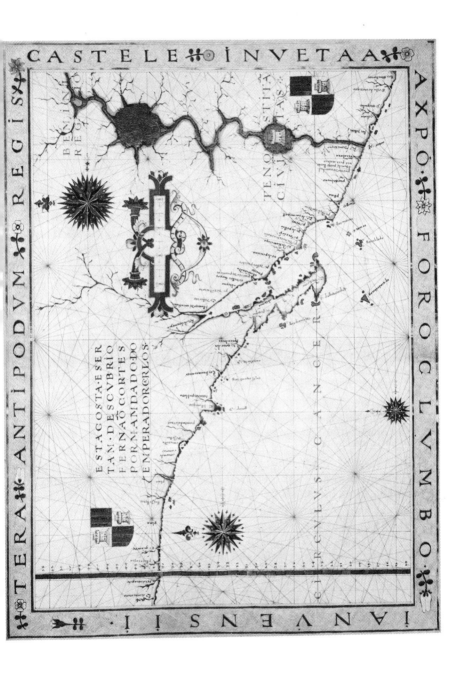

The military might of Spain had failed to subdue the aborigines, and now men armed only with a cross and a Bible hoped to succeed where others had failed. While further colonization attempts were held in abeyance, explorations continued. A Portuguese navigator, Juan Rodríguez Cabrillo, flying the Spanish flag, sailed in 1542 to what later became known as La Paz before turning south to round the peninsula's tip. Then he sailed north and charted the bays and islands on the west coast. En route, he rested his crew from September 17th to the 23rd in a bay he named San Matías, now known as Bahía de Todos Santos at Ensenada. Later, he discovered the bay at present-day San Diego and named it Bahía de San Miguel for the Archangel Saint Michael. Cabrillo died from a fall after his ship reached the Channel Islands off Santa Barbara. It is believed that he was buried on San Miguel Island. After his death, Cabrillo's ships continued to sail north, though missing San Francisco Bay, before turning back.

The voyage was successful because several bays were located to shelter Spanish galleons from British and Dutch privateers on their way home from the Spice Islands in the Orient.

In circumnavigating the globe in 1521, Captain General Ferdinand Magellan had discovered what later became known as the Philippine Archipelago as well as the Spice Islands to the south between what is now the Indonesian Island of Celebes and New Guinea. In late 1542, the viceroy of Mexico authorized his nephew Ruy López de Villalobos to lead an expedition of six ships and approximately 370 men to the Far Eastern islands first explored by Magellan. Villalobos discovered dozens of islands that were missed by Magellan. He changed its name to Las Islas Filipinas after the Infante who later became Philip II of Spain.

This Spanish explorer later was forced to surrender to Portuguese authorities when his ships ran short of food. He died in the Philippines, but the survivors of his expedition were returned to Portugal, and eventually to Spain.

Sir Francis Drake also explored the west coast of the New World 24 years later and, unaware of Cabrillo's voyage of exploration on behalf of Spain, Drake took possession for England and named the country New Albion.

Another Englishman, Sir Thomas Cavendish, in July, 1586, sailed from Plymouth, England, with a fleet that he equipped at his own expense to carry the war between his country and Spain into the Pacific Ocean. The wealthy Cavendish hoped to emulate Sir Francis Drake who earlier had circumnavigated the globe. Cavendish's ships included the *Desire*, the *Content* – half the size of the flagship – and the much smaller *Hugh Gallant*. The ships were manned by 123 men and boys.

The captain-general's fleet sailed around Cape Horn and sacked towns along the coasts of Chile, Peru and Mexico. During these raids, Cavendish captured several Spanish ships, some heavily laden with treasure. The *Hugh Gallant* had to be scrapped because she proved so unseaworthy, but Cavendish converted one of his prizes for duty with his own ships, naming her the *George*. This ship disappeared later en route to Baja California.

Cavendish was most anxious to capture the annual Manila galleon en route home from the Philippines at this time of year. A captured French pilot, who hated the Spaniards, gave him precise details of the galleon's expected route. Armed with this valuable information, Cavendish's ships *Desire* and *Content* arrived off Baja's Cabo San Lucas on October 14, 1587 and lay in wait. Three weeks passed before the *Santa Ana,* a large galleon captained by Don Tomás de Alzola, made her appearance November 4. The *Santa Ana* was caught by surprise with most of her guns stowed in her hold. The crew of the Spanish ship repelled a boarding party of Cavendish's men with small arms fire and "a sort of great stones which they threw at our heads." Cavendish ordered his ships to withdraw out of range, and used his guns against the *Santa Ana* for five or six hours until the captain on the Spanish ship hoisted a white flag and surrendered.

Cavendish's fleet was enriched by the acquisition of 122,000 pesos of gold, and 40 tons of Oriental goods such as spices and silks. The whole cargo probably was worth two million pesos in Spain. The English captain-general burned the Santa Ana to the waterline in a harbor a few miles east of Cabo San Lucas, and freed most of the 190 members of the *Santa Ana's* crew and passengers. Some passengers were women, and they had a difficult time in this primitive land until the *Santa Ana* was rebuilt and they all made their way to Acapulco. There, the Mexican viceroy received the first word of the loss of the Manila galleon with its valuable treasure.

Cavendish retained several of the *Santa Ana's* passengers and crew to assist him in sailing to the Philippines. Two were young Japanese men, one was a Portuguese citizen who had traveled in the Orient, and the other was the *Santa Ana's* Spanish pilot who agreed to navigate. The two English ships sailed November 19, but the *Content* and the *Desire* were soon separated. The *Content* was never heard from again, and its gold and silver were lost.

Cavendish cruised the Orient with *Desire,* but he had to hang the former Spanish pilot when he tried to communicate with his countrymen in Manila. After rounding Africa's Cape of Good Hope, Cavendish returned to Plymouth 25 months after he had left the English port. He was only 28-years old at the end of his voyage. During his long foray against the Spanish his small fleet had burned 19 ships, and sacked many towns and villages among Spanish possessions in the Pacific.

Dutch and English privateers continued to operate extensively during the Protestant Reformation that shattered Christendom, and led to further wars against Spain. In a series of raids, Dutch and British freebooters frequented the coasts of Peru, Mexico and the Philippines, causing great damage to Spanish settlements. Spanish ships, en route home from the Philippines, routinely stopped at Cabo San Lucas or in the bay at present-day La Paz to replenish their water and provisions. They were prime targets. Millions of dollars worth of ships and treasure were taken from them.

To protect their ships in the Pacific Ocean, King Philip II of Spain directed the Viceroy of Mexico to continue exploration of the coasts of North America, and to found settlements near Cabo San Lucas and other Baja sites that were suitable. The king also hoped to find a place in Alta California along the northern coast to replenish the Manila galleons and refit them if necessary. The galleons routinely sailed down the west coast of North America each year. Along with the settlements, the king commissioned the viceroy in Mexico City to Christianize the Indians and to determine whether some of the unknown northern lands might be rich in minerals – particularly above the 40th degree of latitude. Each explorer was made responsible for seeking the so-called Straits of Annian. They had long been rumored to pass through the continent, creating a passage from the South Seas to the Atlantic Ocean in the vicinity of Newfoundland.

Admiral Don Sebastian Vizcaíno set sail from Acapulco in 1596 for the peninsula's tip. After a brief stop in the bay at Cabo San Lucas, he sailed north to the bay where Cortés had tried to found a settlement. Vizcaíno was well treated by the Indians, who gave him pearls and the fruit of the pitihaya. These fruits were particularly welcome because they are high in vitamin C and were effective in curing the ravages of scurvy. After leaving the area, Vizcaíno explored the west coast of the Baja peninsula as far as Cape Mendocino in the extreme northwestern part of Alta California. He named the cape in honor of Viceroy Don Antonio de Mendoza. His ship also discovered the harbor at Monterey, named in honor of his patron Don Gaspar de Zuñiga, Count of Monte Rey. So detailed were the charts that he made of the west coast of North America that they were used for 200 years. Like many explorers before him, once Vizcaíno lost favor at the Spanish court his explorations ceased, and he ended up as a minor Mexican port captain.

*Baja's Indians were not noted for their craftsmanship,
though they made beautiful baskets for storing, carrying, and
even cooking food. George Langsdorff drew these typical
handcrafts during a visit in 1803, including necklaces and a
bow and arrow.*

For years viceroys of New Spain had heard of the magnificent pearls that Indians gathered in the bays of this new
land. Captain Juan de Iturbi in 1615 was granted the pearl
fishing rights in the gulf. His first ship was lost to Dutch
privateers, but he was more successful with his second ship

and succeeded in founding several pearl fisheries. Some were beyond the 28th parallel that roughly divides the peninsula at its mid-section.

In 1615 Captain Alonzo Gonzáles explored the cape and, with strict control over his men, the Indians at Cabo San Lucas remained friendly. In the past, they had turned violent only when their women were molested. In his report to his superiors, Gonzáles said some of the Pericué Indians had light-colored hair, and painted their bodies in various colors. For many years some seamen from the Spanish galleons, and others from Dutch and English privateers, had jumped ship and settled among the Indians. Thus mulattoes were common. Also, it was the practice of many coastal ships to use black slaves. Due to harsh treatment, or merely to escape slavery, many blacks deserted their ships and went to live with the Indians.

In 1683, the Royal Council of the Indies sent an expedition to the peninsula in the charge of Admiral Isidoro Atondo y Antillón. It included three Jesuit padres, one of whom was Eusebio Francisco Kino, who was destined to make a name for himself. The others were Father Matias Gogni and Father Alegre.

The admiral led his three ships from the mainland port of Chacala to the site where Cortés had endeavored to establish a permanent settlement, the place now known as La Paz. They encamped at a spring surrounded by palm trees and, on April 2, 1683, they raised a cross. Two days later their efforts to procure food were rewarded when they netted a great quantity of fish in the bay. The next day, April 5, a church and a small presidio for the soldiers were started.

The Indians, seeing that their new visitors planned to make a permanent settlement, massed for an attack. While the aborigines were donning their war paint and threatened the settlement with bows and arrows, the soldiers prepared to defend themselves. The Jesuit fathers intervened, convincing the soldiers that such tactics had proved self-defeating in the past. They sought to placate the Indians without resort to arms. The soldiers agreed reluctantly and watched suspiciously as the padres gave presents to the Indians and invited them to join in a meal of porridge and fish.

The truce was short-lived. A few days later, the Indians attacked in strength. This time the soldiers ignored the padres' pleas and fired at the Indians, killing a number of them. Admiral Atondo y Antillón later sent forces into the interior but they too were attacked. He became so discouraged by the Indians' enmity that he withdrew his forces to the mainland.

Father Kino, the foremost pioneer priest in Baja California, refused to acknowledge defeat. An Italian by birth, Kino had been educated in Germany as an astronomer, navigator and cartographer. He had been a professor of mathematics at Ingolstadt, and had been a favorite of the ruling house of Bavaria. When he left Europe for the New World he vowed to devote his life to the conversion of the heathen. Kino also had some knowledge of farming and medicine that he put to good use among the aborigines, slowly gaining their respect and loyalty through his leadership. For Kino and the Society of Jesus, the attempt to colonize this new land and convert the savages, was a hallowed cause, and he believed that the Society was under the protection of heaven. Kino's genius for organization quickly became evident. He asked Father Juan María Salvatierra to direct the next colonizing attempt while he remained in Mexico to obtain the necessary funds. Religious orders in New Spain, and wealthy citizens, made substantial contributions. Their assistance was fortunate because the Spanish Government reneged on its pledge to advance funds on a regular basis.

In May, 1683, Kino and Admiral Atondo y Antillón made another attempt to increase Spanish influence on the peninsula by establishing a small settlement at the Indian village of Londo, 18 miles north of present-day Loreto. The admiral later decided that this area – San Bruno – was unfit for farming, and therefore unsuitable as a permanent settlement. He

Christianity never quelled the Indians' passion for gambling. The artist of the Russian ship Rurik *drew this sketch in 1816 of a popular game in which handfuls of sticks were tossed into the air. Betting was on whether the number that fell was odd or even.*

ordered the site abandoned, and it was not until 1699 that the mission of San Juan Bautista Londo was established.

When the Spaniards first started to explore Baja there were 40,000 to 50,000 Indians living on the peninsula. There were several tribes, and most of them spoke different languages, having little contact with one another. These Indians were the most primitive of any in the Western Hemisphere. The men were tall, dark brown in color, and wore their hair below their shoulders. Like most Indians, their bodies were not covered with much hair. Men wore little or nothing, but the women wore skirts that were held in place by thongs around their waists. These skirts covered the front of their bodies to their knees, and were made of strands of grass or tree twigs. A cross-weave held the strands together. In back, the women draped animal skins.

The northern Indians apparently were the only ones who used pottery for cooking and storing water. Normally, water was carried in animal bladders. All Indians used tightly-woven baskets for roasting acorns, jojoba and piñon nuts. Sand was placed in baskets in such a manner as to protect them from catching fire. Metates were used to grind seeds.

For fighting and hunting, the Indians used bows and arrows and spears made of wood. Arrowheads fashioned of stone were used to tip their spears and arrows. For fishing, they made lines and nets from agave fibers. Primitive stone knives also were widely used.

Cochimí Indians controlled the peninsula from Loreto north to the Colorado River. The remainder of the northern area, or approximately 10 percent of the peninsula, was inhabited by several tribes of Cocopah, Típai, Paipái, Santa Catarina and Kiliwa Indians.

South of Loreto, three tribes included the Guaiacura above La Paz, and the Hutchiti and Pericué tribes below it. Most of today's Indians are descendants of Yaquis who started to emigrate from the mainland when the Spanish first began their voyages of exploration. In the north, a few of the Kiliwa Indians still survive. Some own their own land, but most of the others work on mountain ranches as cowhands. The Kiliwas are strong, good-looking people, and good-natured. Some still retain age-old superstitions of their tribe. For instance, an all-black animal is viewed as a bad omen, signifying that something unpleasant will happen.

In the mountain areas where cattle now roam the high, grassy meadows, Kiliwa and other northern tribes once gathered nuts from the Parry piñon trees that exist only in northern Baja and parts of the state of California across the border. Early Indians ground the piñon nuts into a meal by using metates – hollowed depressions chipped in flat granite boulders. They also ate an edible mescal plant after baking the hearts in a fire pit heated by hot stones. Of course, the waters of the gulf provided them with fish of all kinds, plus

The botanist with the Russian ship Rurik *described Baja's male Indians as well formed, tolerably tall, and of dark brown complexion. He called the women "short and ugly."*

bird's eggs gathered on the islands or along the shore. The flesh of birds, rabbits and deer were also highly prized.

Evidently the majority of early Indians cremated their dead, because burial sites are rare.

Early Indians used simple words to describe basic necessities, so they found it difficult to understand Christian ideas. Mathematics was never developed among them beyond the fingercounting stage.

Each Indian tribe had a different concept of a supreme being. The Guaicuras believed that the sun, moon and planets were men and women who each night fell into the sea, emerging again at morning. Stars, they said, were torches lit by the spirit Guamongó and had to be relit each night after being extinguished by the sea.

The Cochimí believed there was a great man who lived in the sky and who created all plants and animals, including human beings. They held a feast each year in his honor. A gaily-appareled youth, known for his fleetness of foot, first appeared at the top of the highest mountain in each area. He came running into the valley at the appointed time to join a feast that had been prepared by the women but that only men were permitted to eat. The guamas, or medicine men, took advantage of the gullibility of tribal members by providing spiritual counseling and receiving special food and clothing in return.

Prior to the time that the Indians were exposed to the diseases of white men, some of them evidently lived to be quite old. Father Johan Jakob Baegert, pastor of Mission San Luis Gonzaga, wrote extensively of the Jesuit period, and he claimed that the Indians could thrive on anything. Although to him and his fellow white men all Indians were the most pitiable of God's creatures, even he had to admit that they seemed incomparably happier than those who lived in civilized countries. He wrote, "A native Californian sleeps as gently and as well on the hard earth, under the open sky, as any European in his soft feather bed."

"In all his life the native Californian never seems to have anything to distress him, to destroy his joy for life, to make death desirable. No one to plague or persecute him, to throw a lawsuit about his neck; no hail, or army, to lay waste his land, no fire or lightning to burn his farm. There is no hate, no jealousy, no taxes."

"These Californians seem to have nothing, yet at all times they have what they need. It is no miracle that hardly a one among them has gray hair, and then only very late in life. They are always in good spirits. They laugh and joke continuously. They are always contented, always joyful, which without doubt makes for real happiness – what all in the world are striving for and few achieve."

His major regret, he said, was that few of them could be convinced of the bliss to be gained by acknowledging the true faith and conducting themselves as Christians.

Father Kino died in 1710, and his loss to the missions was great. He had been the prime promoter of colonization from the beginning, defending the rights of the Indians, and seeking their spiritual salvation.

Father Salvatierra devoted the remaining years of his life to the establishment of a system to govern the missions, and it was put into effect in 1716 – the year before he died. It provided positive controls over missionaries, soldiers and the Indians.

Father Juan de Ugarte fortunately had 13 more years of life to devote to his flock. He was later appointed procurator for the missions that the Jesuits hoped to establish. He lived a year more than Father Francisco Piccolo who had helped to establish Loreto. In particular, Ugarte devoted his efforts, in between exploration trips, towards the establishment of peace among the warring tribes, while Piccolo concentrated his energy on the education of the younger members of the tribes.

Two unarmed Spanish soldiers from Santiago, 80 miles south of La Paz, were killed by hostile Indians October 1, 1734, when they went in search of beef to slaughter for the mission. The rebels next went to Father Carranco's house where they brutally dragged him outside, filled his body full of arrows and beat him with clubs and stones. A young Indian who sought to intervene was quickly killed. They built a fire, stripped the bodies of clothes, and burned them. The church and house were ransacked and the buildings burned.

Padre Tamaral was next to die in a similar manner at San José del Cabo. Father Taraval at Todos Santos was warned that the Indians were heading for his mission, and he left immediately for La Paz with two soldiers. There, during the absence of Padre Gordon at Loreto, the La Paz mission was burned to the ground. The padre and his escort took a canoe to Espíritu Santo Island, and then sent word to Loreto of their plight. They were soon rescued and taken to the Dolores del Sur mission between La Paz and Loreto.

With the southern missions largely destroyed, Padre Jaime Bravo, mission president with headquarters at Loreto, wrote authorities in Mexico City and the governor of the Province of Sinaloa for help. He asked for 60 Yaqui warriors to put down the rebellion, but when the ship was ready to sail 500 Yaquis volunteered to go. The ship would hold only 60 so the others could not be accommodated.

At Loreto, Spanish soldiers joined the Yaquis, along with a large number of Christian Indians, and they marched south under Captain Esteban Rodríguez Lorenzo. The rebels fled before them and an uneasy peace settled around the missions once the work of rebuilding began.

So concerned was President Jaime Bravo about the rebellion that he suggested to the padres at the northern missions that they come to Loreto where they could be protected. They did as he suggested, but the Indians from all the missions held a conference and resolved to go in a body to plead for the return of their padres. Each group of Indians carried its mission's cross on their shoulders and, with tears in their eyes, they begged the fathers to return or they would all remain at Loreto to be near them. The padres were so overcome by the devotion of their followers that they returned with them to their missions, and none of them was molested.

After the rebellion was crushed, a presidio was built at San José del Cabo to house 30 soldiers, and each of the other southern missions received an armed force of 10 soldiers.

Once the presidio was built at San José del Cabo, the Manila galleons, which had been diverted from the area by the rebellion, again anchored in the bay sheltered by the Cape of San Lucas to pick up water and supplies before sailing to the mainland. As relative stability returned, the missions continued to expand. Each mission father was responsible for increasing his church's influence beyond its immediate confines, and satellite chapels were set up far beyond each mission's lands.

With expansion came the inevitable spread of diseases, such as the scourge of syphilis, to which the Indians had no immunity. In 1722, the wild crops were largely destroyed by a plague of locusts, and the Indians who survived had nothing to eat but the insects. An epidemic of ulcers, due to their inadequate diet, killed many of them. German Padre Everardo Helén at the new mission at Guadalupe was just one of many who worked around the clock to save those who did not die quickly from dysentery.

When Father Helén had taken over the mission the year before, he had insisted that the Indians cease their pagan ways by giving him their paintings and figures, and their capes woven of human hair. They had objected strongly, but some of the animosity towards him departed when he worked so unselfishly to save their lives during the famine.

Despite the best efforts of the padres, Indians died by the thousands from many causes. So heavy were their losses that seven missions had to be abandoned in the 18th century while three others barely survived until the Jesuits were expelled by the Spanish Government from their missions.

Epidemics of smallpox, dysentery and the ravages of syphilis by 1750 had reduced the original 40-50,000 Indians to 5-7,000. Seventeen years later only one Indian was still alive in the entire Uchitie tribe.

The southern Indians, who had more direct contact with civilization, suffered the most. The missions at Todos Santos and San José del Cabo were closed, and their remaining converts were transferred to Santiago de los Coras while their padres were reassigned to missions farther north.

Despite their successes in the New World, the Society of Jesus lost favor in the courts of Portugal, Spain and France. They had long criticized what they called corruption in high places. They were expelled from Portugal in 1759 after denouncing licentiousness among the country's nobles. In France, they openly denounced Louis XV as immoral, citing his relationship with his mistress Madame de Pompadour, and demanding her dismissal. Their charges were backed by action when a Jesuit priest refused to give Madame de Pompadour absolution for her sins until she ceased her relationship with the king. She joined forces with the Duke of Choiseul, the king's prime minister and, in 1764, they convinced the king that the Society should be banned in France. Only the Spanish Crown continued its loyalty to the Society, but Charles III of Spain became infuriated when forged letters – one supposedly written to a member of the Company of Jesus – declared there was proof of the illegitimacy of the Spanish king. France's Prime Minister Choiseul evidently had a hand in circulating these forged letters in conjunction with Prime Minister Aranda of Spain. The Spanish king demanded that the Pope suppress the Society of Jesus, but he refused. The king, acting on his own, expelled the Society from all Spanish lands, including those in the New World.

Don José de Gálvez was designated by the Crown to see that the Jesuits were expelled from their missions in Mexico and Baja California. He came to the peninsula as a Royal Visitor to see that the king's orders were carried out. The missions ranged from San José in the south to Santa María in the north. The padres were desolated by the news, as were most of their converted Indians. They were arrested like criminals and taken first to Loreto. There were 16 Jesuits – 15 priests and a lay brother. Six were of Spanish origin, two were from mainland Mexico, and eight were Germans. An equal number had died in the service of the Society of Jesus and their remains were buried on the peninsula.

A solemn High Mass was celebrated February 3, 1768, at the church in Loreto, with the picture of the Virgin of Loreto draped in black, as was done on Good Friday. At 9 p.m. they were embraced by the new Governor Gaspar de Portolá and they boarded a ship for San Blas on the mainland. All the people of Loreto stood on the shore to see their departure, many with tears in their eyes, as the Jesuits embarked for an uncertain future.

Don José de Gálvez, designated by the Crown to supervise the expulsion of the Jesuits, had arranged for members of the Franciscan missionary college in Mexico City to take over Baja California's missions. The Franciscans made a wise choice in selecting Padre Junípero Serra as president of the California missions. He had accomplished small miracles in Mexico's central plateau by establishing good relationships with the Chichimecas and the Otomíes, whose fierce independence had thwarted the work of less able men.

He and Portolá were charged by the Spanish Government under His Highness Charles III with the exploration of Alta California, to establish missions, with the aim of resisting the encroachment of the Russians and converting the Indians along the Pacific coast. They were singularly successful, despite the efforts of the Dominicans in Spain who kept pleading with the king to be granted equal rights to participate in the development of missions in Baja and Alta California.

Serra tried to explain that the decline of the Indian population – now less than 5,000 throughout the peninsula – plus the increasing aridity of the land, and the lack of suitable mission sites (where ranching could make them self-sufficient), made such a move unrealistic. Instead, he proposed that the Dominicans be assigned responsibility for Baja California's missions, while the Franciscans retained full authority for those in Alta California.

The Spanish viceroy in Mexico City approved Serra's plan, but due to the untimely death of Padre Juan Pedro de Uriarte, the Order's procurator in Madrid, it wasn't until 1773 that a new president, Padre Vicente Mora, was assigned to take over the Baja missions. Soon after his arrival, Father Mora explored the Pacific Coast northward. In a large valley named Viñaraco by the Indians, he later established a mission, called Nuestra Señora del Rosario Viñaraco.

Governor Portolá and Serra were both born on the Mediterranean island of Majorca. Serra had an excellent record as a teacher and he became an outstanding missionary on the mainland. A good administrator, Serra was unhappy when military rule was placed over him, but he worked closely with Governor Portolá to explore Alta California. Eventually he founded a new chain of military presidios and missions along the Pacific coast.

Governor Portolá was charged with responsibility to outfit an expedition for exploring the far north-from the bay at what is now San Diego and beyond. So little was known about the land between the northernmost mission at Santa María and San Diego that ships were sent to the bay while two forces were dispatched by land.

The packet *San Carlos* was first to leave from La Paz on January 7, 1769, with soldiers and supplies. The *San Antonio* left a month later, but arrived at the bay 17 days before the *San Carlos*. The latter had been blown off course, and made slight progress due to constant head winds. Its faulty charts also posed a problem because San Diego's bay was shown as lying a hundred miles farther north than the actual location. As a result, the *San Carlos* eventually anchored in a bay at what is now San Pedro, southwest of Los Angeles. She actually went as far as present-day Point Conception, some 45 miles northwest of Santa Barbara, before turning back. The ship arrived at the bay 110 days after setting out from La Paz.

Captain Fernando de Rivera y Moncada was assigned to lead the first overland expedition. He had an excellent background, having served on the peninsula for 20 years, and he had participated in expeditions with Fernando Consag and Wenceslao Linck. He had already explored parts of the northern end of the peninsula and had been to the Colorado River's delta region on the gulf side. They departed from a place called Velicatá – 30 miles southeast of El Rosario – on Good Friday, 1769, more than two months after the packet *San Carlos* left La Paz. Captain Rivera took Father Juan Crespi along instead of the ailing Father Serra. He had a pack train with 180 mules and 500 domestic animals for the

The San Carlos *left La Paz for Alta California in 1769 with a farewell gun salute and flags flying. It took 110 days to reach San Diego. During the long voyage all but two of the crew died of scurvy.*

350-mile trip to the bay at San Diego. The barren country-side quickly led to disillusionment. In the words of Father Crespi, "The land is sterile, arid, lacking in grass and water, and abounding in stones and thorns." En route, most of the Christian Indians either died or deserted, but the remainder of the party arrived at their destination in mid-May.

The second land expedition was formed by Portolá and Serra and left Velicatá May 15 after Velicatá was selected for the San Fernando Mission. Supplies were picked up at mission settlements along the route, leaving some of the villages in dire straits. Portolá wrote in his diary that, "In consideration of the great deserts into which I was going, and of the Russian hunger with which I foresaw we were going to contend, I was obliged to seize everything I saw as I passed through these poor missions, leaving them, to my keen regret, scantily provided for." Portolá's party still ran out of food, and many Indians died as they tried to live off the land's game and fish.

Portolá's party reached present-day San Diego on July 1. At the start he had 219 men, but only half were still with him at the end of their journey. A quarter of the Indians perished during the land party's traverse of the northern peninsula.

The condition of the men in the first overland expedition, and those who came by ship, was not much better, and Portolá realized that his expeditionary force needed help to survive. He dispatched the *San Antonio* to San Blas on the Mexican mainland to report their dire straits, and ordered it to return with much-needed supplies. The ship had started out with 28 sailors. For its return trip to San Blas only eight sailors were available. When the *San Antonio* reached San Blas only two sailors were still alive.

Portolá continued his journey overland to Monterey in the northern part of Alta California as he had been ordered. He set off with a company of men whom he described as "skeletons who had been spared by scurvy, hunger and thirst."

Father Serra remained temporarily behind and July 16, 1769, he raised a cross at a site overlooking the bay to establish Alta California's first mission in what is now the United States. He sang High Mass and preached to the few survivors of the land and sea expeditions. The mission was dedicated to St. Didacus of Alcala, a Franciscan friar who had been elevated to sainthood in 1588. While the High Mass was sung Indians watched suspiciously, eagerly accepting gifts of beads and clothing afterwards, but refusing to trust these strange, bearded men. Their resentment was due, in large part, to fear, because the Spaniards had arrived from the south in what the Indians called "floating houses" or had ridden animals that they had never seen before.

In the days and months following the establishment of the mission, the Indians at first refused to take part in mission activities. Soon their fear gave way to insolence, and they tried to steal anything they could get their hands on. Their thievery was resisted by the soldiers, and frequent armed clashes were inevitable. It was not an auspicious beginning for the Franciscans in their first endeavor to colonize the Indians of Alta California.

Under the Dominicans, nine more missions were added to the chain that extended from Baja's tip to the border of Alta California. The last mission was established at Guadalupe del Norte in 1834. But the missions declined rapidly because of diseases introduced by the Spaniards. The padres proved more efficient at saving Indian souls than they did in preserving their lives. Syphilis was a deadly killer, destroying men and women, and also killing most babies, who contracted the disease from their mothers at birth. By 1822, the number of Indians had declined so much that 17 missions were without priests because there was no need for them.

As the missions were reduced in Baja California, others grew and prospered in Alta California under the guidance of Father Serra. El Camino Real, or the King's Highway, tied the missions together from Baja California's tip to the northern part of Alta California. It was not a road in the modern sense, merely a winding dirt path filled with ruts and obstructions permitting passage only by horse, mule, or high-wheeled vehicles.

When Mexico revolted from Spain, an independent republic was created in 1821. Three years later, the Mexican Constitution declared Baja California a separate federal territory with a governor appointed by the President of Mexico and a territorial legislature elected by the people of Baja.

Governor Manuel Micheltorena in 1843 ordered that all mission lands be given to the Indians. By then, there were few survivors to take ownership. The peninsula was further denuded of people by the California gold rush that attracted hundreds of Indians and Mexicans from Baja and the mainland. Many of them never returned to their homeland. So desolate were the once-thriving missions that only six Dominican priests still served the remaining missions.

President Benito Juárez changed the Mexican Constitution in 1857 so that all church properties had to be sold, except for the churches themselves. Catholic authority was further reduced when President Plutarco Elías Calles closed all churches in the 20th century. This order was later rescinded by a more conservative administration, and the people of Mexico were again given freedom to worship at the churches of their choice, although complete separation of church and state was established.

The Mexican-American War of 1846-48 left a different kind of legacy, and to this day many Mexicans speak with bitterness of the actions of Americans who invaded their country with limited provocation. That the rights of a sovereign nation were violated by the United States is now accepted by most historians.

To Mexicans, the Military Academy cadets who fought to the last teenagers in the defense of the fortress of Chapultepec on top of a hill in Mexico City is an enduring chapter of courage in their long history as a nation. While the Mexican people revere their memory, the United States Marines also immortalize the event in the Marine Hymn with its "halls of Montezuma."

Baja California became a vital part in that war because the Mexicans were suspicious of the large investments made by Americans in their farmlands and mines. The United States Marines and a regiment of New York Volunteers fought against native Californians and Yaqui Indians on the peninsula. Baja California was actually occupied and Lieutenant Gould Buffum headed the army of occupation at La Paz in 1847. Through the failure of the American president, James K. Polk, to properly instruct the American peace delegation meeting at Guadalupe Hidalgo, Baja was returned to Mexico under terms of the treaty. Initially, Polk insisted that the treaty grant Baja California, as well as Alta California and the territory of New Mexico, to the United States. American negotiator Nicholas Trist was given instructions that the United States must have New Mexico and Alta California and "Baja California provided the Mexicans did not hold out too firmly." The courier carrying these instructions died at Vera Cruz of fever enroute to Guadalupe Hidalgo and his dispatch case was rifled by the Mexicans. In the final negotiations between Trist and President Antonio López de Santa Ana, the Mexican president was handed a note that revealed the contents of the courier's dispatches from Washington. He realized that if he stood firm in his insistence that Baja California should remain part of his country the Americans would agree and sign the treaty. Nicholas Trist was unaware of his president's latest instructions because the dispatches were never delivered to him. Anxious to conclude the agreement, Trist agreed that Baja California should remain part of Mexico.

In Baja today there are only a few hundred Indians remaining of the 40,000 to 50,000 who inhabited the peninsula when the Spaniards first arrived. Their descendants live in the northern mountains and in the desert near the Colorado river. In the mountains, there are approximately 50 Kiliwas alive today who are descendents of the original natives. The Paipáis, descendants of those who lived around the Santa Catarina Mission, have a reservation near the Colorado River's delta where the Mexican Government has granted them 160,000 acres. Only a few dozen Típais are alive today, and they live closer to the United States border. A few Cocopahs live in the desert between the mountains and the delta region.

There are many reminders of man's inability to cope with the merciless sun and the interior's limited water resources. Crumbling adobe homes and barns can be found throughout the peninsula, providing stark evidence that Baja can be an unforgiving land for those who are unprepared to withstand its harsh realities. Much of the interior desert areas remain the same as the Jesuit padres and Spanish soldiers first found them. Then, as now, survival was easier along the coast.

From 1697, when the first mission was established by the Jesuits, through the period when the Franciscans ran the missions following the expulsion of the Jesuits, until the Dominicans' rule over them ended in 1840, 30 missions were established in Baja. Of these the San Fernando Mission was the only one founded by the Franciscans before they moved northward to establish a new chain of missions in Alta California, now the United States. Only two churches at San Ignacio and San Javier remain much as they were in those days. Remains of four others are in various stages of preservation. Two others have been almost completely rebuilt, like the church at Loreto; 15 others are in ruins and there is no trace of another seven missions. Aside from the few churches that remain, the padres have left little physical evidence of their long presence on the peninsula.

The padres will be long remembered, however, for their heroic efforts to colonize Baja California – without enriching themselves. Their efforts to transform this land of cactus deserts, mountains, and pitiless sun into a paradise for Indians willing to seek salvation from a Christian God they never fully understood is an enduring memorial to man's inherent good intentions.

Tijuana

There are two main roads from the United States border to Baja's interior. Highway 1 leaves from Tijuana, while Highway 5 starts at Mexicali. But there is an additional port of entry at Otay Mesa, just east of Tijuana's International Airport, and south of California's State Route 117. Unlike the two main ports of entry that are open at all hours, this one is only open from 6 a.m. to 10 p.m. It is designed to relieve the horrendous congestion at the San Ysidro/Tijuana crossing, particularly on weekends and holidays.

The Tecate border crossing is rarely busy, but it is open only from 6 a.m. to midnight. Within those hours it is a sensible alternative to the crossing at Tijuana/Ysidro. There is still another entry at Algodones from Yuma, Arizona. It is not as well known or as well traveled and is open from 6 a.m. to 8 p.m.

The principal border cities of Tijuana and Mexicali are also linked by Mexico's Highway 2.

HISTORY

Long before Juan Rodríguez Cabrillo explored what is now San Diego Bay in 1542, Indians settled where the Tijuana River meets the Pacific Ocean. They called their village Ti-Wan, meaning "by the sea."

It was not until July 1, 1769 that another Spanish exploring party arrived at the site. Captain Gaspar de Portolá and Father Junípero Serra spent a short time there before heading north. At what is now San Diego, some of their party remained behind to establish a mission.

San Diego Bay was charted more fully three years later by Don Tobar y Tomares who renamed the Indian village Ranchería de la Punta. In his diary, he further identified the spot as near a river that runs in the spring.

The rancho's name was changed again in 1820 by José María de Echeandía who had received a Spanish land grant in the northwestern part of Baja California. He called it Rancho Tío Juan or Uncle John Rancho.

The Mexican flag was raised over the area in 1822 when Mexico achieved its independence from Spain. After Santiago Arguello received title to the Uncle John Rancho in 1829 he established a large sheep and cattle ranch. The few Indians who still lived on their ancestral lands worked for him. A rich grassland, ideal for cattle and sheep, permitted the new owner years later to develop it as the sixth largest rancho in the area. So prosperous did the area become that ranchers formed a pueblo called Tía Juana on the site of the original Indian village of Ti-Wan. It is possible that this name – Aunt Jane in English – is derived from the name supposedly given to the owner of a small inn whose charm and home-cooked meals earned her a wide reputation on both sides of the border.

The American town across the river originally was named Tía Juana, and it grew at an even faster pace. By 1876, Tía Juana had a general store and a post office located in the old ranch building owned by Don Andrés Ybarra. A school was built seven years later, and students from both countries attended it during the week, returning with their parents on Sundays for religious services that later were highlighted by the playing of an organ.

The San Ysidro Rancho, on land now inside the United States, once belonged to the Ybarra family, and it was sub-let by Arguello. It was later considered public domain land following the Mexican-American War that ended February 2, 1848 and it was homesteaded by Don Lino Opez.

To preclude future controversy, the border between the United States and Baja was delineated by the treaty. "To avoid all difficulty in tracing on the land the limits that separate Upper and Lower California, it is agreed that the limits should consist of a straight line drawn from the middle of the Gila River, at the point where it meets the Colorado, to a point on the Pacific Coast, one marine league distant to the south of the most southerly point of the port of San Diego, according to the drawing of this port which the second pilot of the Spanish Armada, D. Juan de Pantoia, made in 1782."

A marble monument was set in place July 16, 1851, as International Monument Number 1. When the area was resurveyed in 1883, a second marker of white stone was placed in the bed of the Tijuana River at the point where it crosses the American border.

In their early years, both villages benefited from the rich valleys on both sides of the border where agricultural products grew profusely. Fruit orchards were common in this frost-free area, and railroads vied with one another to serve the communities. At one time, San Diego had a railroad line as far as Ensenada. It was known as the Peninsula Railroad of Baja California.

Upper California did not begin to grow until the late 19th century when Easterners arrived in droves to homestead land. Along the border, both villages expanded with the influx of new settlers.

North of the border, the International House gave an air of luxury with its 53 bedrooms and a grand ballroom. Beneath the ballroom's crystal chandeliers, Mexican and American dancers enjoyed a setting that their parents had never known. After a race track was established, an unwelcome throng of gamblers descended upon the American Tijuana much to the dismay of its long-time residents. The Mexican

Tijuana strove to compete by establishing a bull ring and numerous saloons that, for a time, gained an unwelcome notoriety.

Both Tijuanas suffered economically when promoters established a town called Lemon with a new sports arena and a dance hall. In an atmosphere of "anything goes," Lemon became the border's most notorious sin spot. With vast sums of money to be made, the leaders of Mexico's Tijuana established the Agua Caliente Hot Springs health resort. The ever-capricious fun crowd swarmed to the new spa to enjoy its mud baths, and Lemon soon declined.

On February 27, 1891, it began to rain heavily along the border, and the rain continued for five days and five nights. The Tijuana River's banks overflowed and flooded the Mexican side, inundating hundreds of homes that had been built along the river. The destruction on the American side was equally bad, and many residents tied themselves to trees to escape the rampaging waters as they watched their homes and businesses disintegrate and head towards the sea.

After the waters receded, the job of rebuilding began and soon saloons, racetracks and the bullring were back in operation. Americans returned to Mexican Tijuana in even greater numbers after the new bridge was built across the river in December, 1891. For Americans coming to Mexican Tijuana for the first time it was a sight they never forgot. Brothels and saloons lined the street. Tijuana had grown by now to a village of a thousand people, many of whom lived off the tourist dollars that flooded their community, particularly on weekends.

During this period, Porfirio Díaz was in his second term as president of Mexico. He had served first from 1877 to 1880 and, after a lapse of four years, had returned in 1884. A virtual dictator, he ruled with an iron hand. But many Mexicans rebelled against his harsh regime. One of them, Francisco Madero, recruited an army on the mainland to overthrow him.

On the peninsula, however, a rebel force under Ricardo Flores Magon, first captured Mexicali in January, 1911, then Tecate in March, before he marched to Tijuana. Magon's army attacked the border city on May 8. Caryl Welch, a soldier of fortune, led the rebel soldiers against 39 Mexican regular army men who had remained loyal to their government. Before the battle, most residents fled to the United States, and the unequal contest soon ended in victory for Magon's men, who immediately went on a looting spree. A red flag was raised over Tijuana with the inscription Tierra y Libertad (Land and Liberty) and Magon prepared to attack Ensenada.

President Díaz sent federal troops to the northern part of the peninsula and forwarded a letter of protest to President William Howard Taft in Washington, along with an odd request. To the United States President he said, "I write you to instruct your people not to come on our battle field. Every time we have a battle your people run excursion trains to the border. This causes embarrassment and interferes with the discipline of our troops as your girls make cat-calls to my men. Your people are buying the loot of Tijuana from Madero's rebels and they are saying it is priced too high. There are many other things we could complain of but if these rules are observed we can fight out this war in peace." At length Madero's army defeated the Mexican president's soldiers on the mainland, and Díaz was forced to resign.

In Tijuana, Caryl Welch deserted his rebel forces when federal troops approached the village and he crossed the border with loot that he had personally confiscated in Tijuana. A United States Marine Corps deserter, Jack Mosby took command of Magon's army. While Americans swarmed the heights of the hills on their side of the border, Mosby hijacked a San Diego and Arizona train and headed east with his army to meet the advancing federal troops. At sight of the Mexican soldiers and their Yaqui Indian recruits, Mosby had a change of heart and he and his men fled across the Tijuana bridge to the safety of the American side. There, his men were arrested by United States troups, and Mosby was shot trying to escape. Magon later moved his headquarters to Los Angeles, and allied himself with the radical Industrial Workers of the World, or Wobblies, who often used terror tactics in trying to form one large industrial union in the United States. Mexican federal troops captured Tijuana without a fight on June 22, 1911, and it wasn't long before business in the village's sin spots was as brisk as ever.

Mexican Tijuana went into decline in the following years, particularly when the city of San Diego's exposition in 1915-1916 proved more exciting to tourists and took away much of its business. But the banning of boxing and horse racing in upper California gave Tijuana a resurgence, especially after a gambling casino known as Tijuana Fair was completed by Antonio Elousa on July 15, 1915. Gambling in many forms was now available to visiting Americans – including bullfights, cock fights, and boxing matches. A race track was opened January 1, 1916 by James Cofforth, and Elousa built a $100,000 casino called the Monte Carlo between the border and Cofforth's race track.

Wealthy Americans invested in Tijuana's gambling and racing, but these sports went into decline when American military men were forbidden to enter Mexico in uniform after the US entered World War I. Later, passports were required for all US citizens. Much of the tension was caused by strong anti-American feelings expressed by many Mexican citizens who openly espoused the German cause. With loss of the American trade, Tijuana's tourist attractions all but closed down.

The racetrack reopened January 16, 1920, after prohibition of alcoholic beverages became law in the United States with passage of the Volstead Act and approval of the 18th Amendment to the Constitution. Thirsty Americans looked to their favorite bootlegger to supply them, or came across the Mexican border where there was no prohibition. Ministers and priests denounced the road from San Diego to the border as the road to hell, but tourists flocked to Tijuana in greater numbers than ever. The main street was filled with an ever-increasing number of saloons to satisfy the thirsts of Americans, while dancing halls, gambling casinos and moving picture barns catered to other whims.

A reporter for *The New York Times* wrote that Tijuana's main street resembled a western cowtown in the 1880s. "The air reeks of dust, warm humanity, toilet perfume and stale tobacco," he said. "The street vibrates with the laughter and chatter of abnormal good spirits, and the noise of the occasional fracas, the whirl of the roulette wheels, the tap-tap-tap of hammers where new joy palaces are being shot up overnight to accommodate the business of the prohibition boomtown, and above all, the continuous jingle of jazz."

Sinful pursuits were big business, and they ranged from games of chance played in elegant casinos to the lowly shell game played on the sidewalks. And, behind sleazy bedroom doors, lustier male appetites were satisfied by hundreds of young girls.

The Mexican Congress in 1920 renamed Tijuana. It was called Ciudad Zaragoza in honor of the general who defeated French forces at Puebla in 1862. The name was changed back to Tijuana in 1929 by popular demand. Nine years earlier, American Tijuana's name had been permanently changed to San Ysidro, the name of an early ranch in the area.

A group of San Diego doctors exploited the therapeutic values of the waters at Agua Caliente in 1889, building a two-storey sanitarium. By 1900, the sanitarium was all but shut down. It was not until 1926 that the property was turned into a casino whose sparkling chandeliers and rose-brocaded walls brought the tourists back in droves to see the Casino de Agua Caliente. Gold leaf covered the ceilings of the Salon de Oro, and tourists ate off gold plates. Soon a hotel was built with inner patios that welcomed the elite of many nations while mariachi bands played for their enjoyment through its magnificent corridors. It became world famous as a luxurious spot whose warm waters supposedly cured numerous ills. Movie stars and international gangsters like Al Capone mingled with the less affluent to admire the Italian tile floors and the sculptured fountains that dispensed the spa's famous water. Rita Hayworth, who later achieved fame as a movie star, and her father once were featured as flamenco dancers at Agua Caliente along with other international celebrities.

Avenida Revolución in downtown Tijuana acquired the dubious title of being the world's longest bar as saloons ranged side-by-side with gambling joints. Perhaps the most famous was the Tivoli because it catered to a variety of tastes. Bar girls, many imported from the United States, danced and drank with the tourists, and were available for more intimate entertainment in adjoining rooming houses. A small red mill wheel, turning on the roof of the Moulin Rouge, provided a beacon for those seeking unadulterated sex. Inside, young girls of a variety of races paraded before the eager eyes of the Moulin Rouge's patrons in a garish setting of gilded mirrors and red carpets.

The depression that began in 1929 in the United States soon had an impact on Tijuana and the number of tourists dwindled each year during the 1930s. Mexico's President Lázaro Cárdenas almost dealt Tijuana's sin spots a death blow when he outlawed gambling on July 20, 1935. Many of the places were converted to schools, and businesses like the Moulin Rouge and Agua Caliente were closed by presidential order. Tijuana again reverted to a more sedate Mexican city.

World War II revived Tijuana as tourists flocked again to the city, although it never attained the wide-open status of former years. Peninsula cities had been granted status as free trade zones in 1933 and now with civilian goods in short supply north of the border, tourists thronged to Tijuana's shops. Jai Alai became a popular sport, and the Caliente Race Track reopened under stricter government supervision for horse and dog racing.

After the war, American financial interests declined as well-to-do Mexicans invested in businesses and factories in the city. However, American firms continued to establish manufacturing assembly plants in Tijuana because of its cheaper labor costs.

TIJUANA TODAY

In recent years, Tijuana has changed dramatically. Its population has grown to more than a million people as Mexicans have left the interior for the border city. It is now Mexico's fourth largest city, and the fastest growing city in North America. No longer does Tijuana cater exclusively to young male tastes. It welcomes American families with new shopping malls, fine restaurants and excellent tourist accommodations. As a result, more than 50 million people cross the border at Tijuana each year from the United States, making it the world's busiest border crossing. On weekends and holidays, American tourists and others have learned to their regret that two- to three-hour waits to come back across the border are common.

Tijuana is now a city with a diversified economy that is not necessarily geared to tourists, although their trade is still important to the city's economy. In the old riverbed, once occupied by thousands of Tijuana's poor squatters in sordid shacks, there are new shopping malls, industrial complexes and business places that are as modern as any in the world. In its own right, Tijuana has become an important commercial center.

Casa De La Cultura

The Casa de la Cultura, at Paseo de los Héroes and Avenida Independencia, was formerly a school house but is now a multi-arts center with a 1,000-seat theater. It is unique in its interpretation and presentation of Mexico's past... and its present. Open daily, the installations include a Space Theater, a Museum and a Performing Arts Theater. It is less than a mile from the border, and only five minutes from Avenida Revolu-

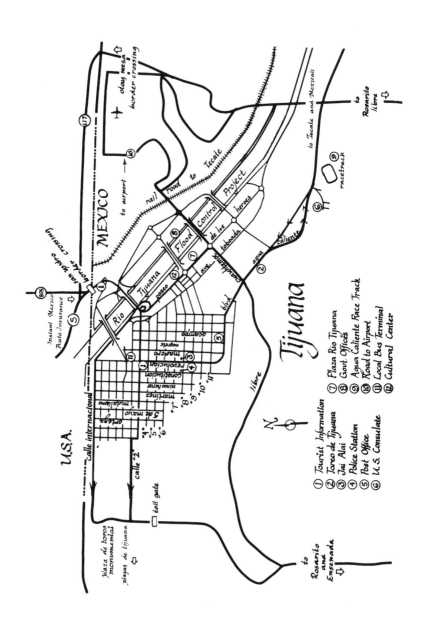

Tijuana

① Tourist Information
② Toreo de Tijuana
③ Jai Alai
④ Police Station
⑤ Post Office
⑥ U.S. Consulate
⑦ Plaza Rio Tijuana
⑧ Govt. Offices
⑨ Agua Caliente Race Track
⑩ Road to Airport
⑪ Local Bus Terminal
⑫ Cultural Center

ción in downtown Tijuana. The center revolves around two themes. The first deals with Mexico's "National Unity" and depicts events and characters in the nation's history. The second theme is "National Diversity," showing the many traditional life styles as expressed in Mexican food, clothes, dances and other traditions.

The sphere-like shape of the "Space Theater" has a capacity for 300 people. Inside, visitors are enveloped by a 180-degree screen, with a multi-channel sound system, that gives you the sensation of being part of the show. "People of the Sun" is shown daily, giving visitors the sights, sounds and sensations of Mexico's most beautiful sites such as Cancun, Copper Canyon and the Mayan and Aztec Pyramids. Tijuana's Cultural Center has one of only 25 theaters of this type in the world, and it has at least three films plus audiovisual and multimedia shows on the solar system and other space themes.

For the performing arts the 1,000-seat theater is fully equipped to produce all kinds of shows throughout the year. The Ballet Folklorico performs every Sunday. At other times Mexico City's Philharmonic Orchestra performs, along with such diverse groups as the Ballet of Cuba or the Dance Troupe of Senegal.

Outdoors in the summer the famous Papantla Flyers from the state of Veracruz do a 1,500-year-old ritual dance on top of a 100-foot pole. And there are outdoor dance and musical affairs that take place in a family atmosphere.

Mexican regional cuisine is not only varied but sophisticated, ranging from the succulent seafood dishes of Veracruz to the subtle dishes of Puebla and Yucatán. There's a restaurant at the center where visitors can savor Mexico's traditional foods and beverages, and a quaint shopping arcade that offers the finest in various arts and crafts from different regions of Mexico.The diversity and quality of Mexican textiles, as exhibited here, demonstrate Mexico's rich tradition in weaving and costume design.

In the past, the Cultural Center has included art works by such world renowned painters as Rivera, Orozco and Siqueiros.

The twin towers of the Nuestra Señora de Guadalupe Cathedral rise majestically above the old downtown district at Calle 2 and Avenida Constitución. The cathedral is a classic example of Mexican church architecture.

The Parque Teniente Vicente Guerrero at Calle 3 and Avenida F is a pleasant place to relax and enjoy oneself. It's named in honor of Lieutenant Guerrero, one of those who successfully quelled the 1911 revolution. The "Héroes of 1911 Monument" here is dedicated to the defenders of Tijuana.

In the Chapultepec Hills, south of the Tijuana Country Club, is a beautiful modern building called "Parroquia del Espíritu Santo" or Church of the Holy Spirit. From its site there is an impressive view of the whole valley.

Bullfighting

For those who enjoy bullfighting, Tijuana has two rings: the "El Toro" two miles east of downtown Tijuana on Boulevard Agua Caliente, (66) 86-1510; or the more prestigious "Plaza Monumental" or "Bullring by the Sea," six miles from downtown by way of Highway 1/D – (66) 80-1808. Tijuana attracts top matadors and fights alternate between the two sites on Sundays at 4 p.m., usually starting in May with two fights. There is normally one fight in June, and then weekly events from July through September. Ticket prices start at $15 with more expensive seats priced according to the amount of shade provided by the ring's circular walls.

Rodeos

From May through September Charreadas, or Mexican rodeos, are held each Sunday afternoon, alternating among four charro grounds in the Tijuana area. Call (66) 81-3401.

Dog Racing

Dog racing has long been popular in Tijuana at the Agua Caliente Racetracks, three miles east of downtown, off Boulevard Agua Caliente. Greyhounds run every Wednesday through Monday at 7:45 p.m., and on Monday and Wednesday at 2 p.m. General admission is free, while reserved seats are $1.

Horse Racing

The old Caliente Racetrack was destroyed by fire in 1971, but it has been rebuilt. There are horse races at Agua Caliente with a 12-race card every Saturday and Sunday. Post time is at noon with admission of $1 for the grandstand, $2 for the clubhouse and $5 for the "Turf Club." There are group plans for both races that include admission, meals, seating, taxes and gratuity, with a race named in a group's honor, and free parking for those who travel by bus.

For those who do not wish to make the eight-minute drive across the border, the Caliente Express Bus leaves from San Diego's Amtrak Station, or you can catch a taxi at the border.

At Caliente there are three "Foreign Book" locations where you can wager on the world's top thoroughbreds racing at the continent's most prestigious tracks such as Aqueduct, Belmont, Pimlico, Saratoga, and Hollywood Park. They are located just as you enter Caliente, with two others inside.

Off-track betting is also available downtown in Tijuana at 4th and Revolución, downtown Mexicali at 116 Melgar Street, and in Ensenada in the Salon de los Cristales, PRO-NAF Building, Avenida López Matéos and Floresta Street.

Golf

For golf fans, the Club Social y Deportivo Campestre, or Tijuana Country Club, is three miles east of downtown via Boulevard Agua Caliente. Call (66) 81-7855 or 81-7863. It is semi-private, with an 18-hole, par-72 course that is 6,200 yards in length. The club is open daily with a weekday fee of $40 and $45 on weekends.

Jai Alai

Jai Alai is a game that no one should miss, played on a court with a basket-like device that acts as a net or catch-all for the ball. It is played at the Frontón Palacio on Avenida Revolución at Calle 7, or you can telephone (66) 85-1612. This fast-moving court game has to be seen to be appreciated. Games are played Friday through Wednesday at 8 p.m., with tickets priced from $2.50 to $5, and parimutuel betting is permitted. It is similar to handball or racketball and it's probably the fastest sport in the world. Balls have been clocked at speeds in excess of 160 miles per hour. Jai Alai originated in the Basque province of northern Spain about 200 years ago. Originally it was played off church walls. The game begins with one individual serving the ball with his basket-like device against the front wall, ricocheting it back to his opponent. He, in turn, fields the ball and sends it against the wall until one misses, or a point is scored. (Points are scored when one player throws the ball out of bounds, lets it bounce twice, or fails to return it.) The winning team, regardless of whether the game is played by singles or doubles, is the one that scores the first seven points. From the first cracking of the ball against the front wall, there is non-stop action until the game is won.

Restaurants

Eating in Tijuana is a unique experience, whether you like "High Mexican" food like mamacita used to make, or Guaymas shrimp, lobster, steak, chicken and game birds. There is a restaurant suitable to your appetite and pocketbook. In the Central District there is **Bol Corona** at Avenida Revolución 520, noted for its burritos and seafood. **Pedrins** on the same street and across from the Frontón Palacio, and **La Costa** around the corner, both feature seafood. **Reno Steak House** at Calle 9 and Hidalgo, just west of Revolución, features continental cuisine, steaks and seafood. **Victor's** on Calle 4 between Revolución and Constitución specializes in Mexican cuisine.

In the Río Tijuana District, Spanish and international cuisine is served at **Alcazar del Río** on Paseo de los Héroes 56-A. A variety of types of meals are served at **Rivoli** in the Hotel Lucerna at Paseo de los Héroes and Avenida Rodríguez. Mexican food, steaks and seafood are featured at the **Guadalajara Grill** at Diego Rivera 19, while a varied menu is offered at **La Calandria** in the Plaza Río Tijuana shopping center. In the Agua Caliente District, **Boccaccio's** near the Tijuana Country Club on Boulevard Agua Caliente 2500 serves continental food. **La Escondida de Tijuana**, on Calle Santa Monica 1, specializes in seafood, steaks and international dishes. **Place de la Concorde,** in the Hotel Fiesta Americana on Boulevard Agua Caliente, a quarter-mile east of Avenida Rodríguez, specializes in French food.

Hotels

There are no campgrounds and trailer parks suitable for tourists in Tijuana, but its hotel and motel accommodations range from adequate to magnificent. Among the best are the following. **Best Western Plaza de Oro,** downtown at Calle 2 and Avenida Martinez, with single rooms starting at $45 and double rooms from $50 − call toll-free (800) 528-1234.

Hotel El Conquistador opposite the Tijuana Country Club at Boulevard Agua Caliente 700 has single rooms for $65 with double rooms at the same price. Its lobby is decorated with Mayan and Aztec replicas; (800) 326-8995. The 23-storey **Hotel Fiesta Americana Tijuana,** with single and double rooms at up to $145, is located at Boulevard Agua Caliente No 4500, a quarter-mile east of Avenida Rodríguez and adjacent to the Tijuana Country Club. Their toll-free number is (800) 343-7811. The **Hotel Lucerna** at Paseo de los Héroes and Avenida Rodríguez, in the new Río Tijuana development, has single rooms for $60-$70 and doubles for up to $70; (66) 34-2000. **Hotel Palacio Azteca** on Highway 1, two blocks south of Boulevard Agua Caliente, rents single rooms for $55 and doubles for $60; (66) 81-8100. **Hotel Paraiso-Radisson**, adjacent to the Tijuana Country Club on Boulevard Agua Caliente No 1, has single rooms priced at $72 and doubles at up to $80. You can call toll-free at (800) 333-3333.

After-dark entertainment runs the gamut from sleazy bars with hostesses that are best avoided to night clubs such as El **Reno,** Avenida Revolución at Calle 8; **The Fiesta Room,** in the Motel La Sierra on Highway 1, just south of Boulevard Aqua Caliente; **Ti Juana Tilly's** in the Frontón Palacio on Avenida Revolución at Calle 7; the **Marko Disco** on Highway 1 at Tijuana's southern end. **Flamingo's** is also on Highway 1, two miles south of Boulevard Agua Caliente.

Shopping

Tijuana is a duty-free port and, with the depressed value of the peso, discriminating shoppers can find bargains compared to US prices on perfumes, jewelry, art objects, cosmetics and textiles. Some of the best merchandise is made in Mexico, but care should be exercised when buying pottery, ceramics, musical instruments, silver, leather goods, and a host of other things. Quality varies from the cheapest to exquisitely-crafted items of exceptional value.

Many of the best shops are on Avenida Revolución, along with those that sell shoddy goods, where bargaining – not permitted in large shops and department stores – is not only permitted but expected.

In Zona Río, Tijuana's equivalent to Mexico City's Zona Rosa, colorful ethnic restaurants coexist with elegant dining places and sophisticated shops. Tijuana's new shopping centers, including the Plaza Patria in the racetrack area, are ideal for visitors. Plaza Patria is an enclosed shopping mall with rooftop parking and marble halls. It primarily represents the shoe manufacturers of Leon.

Summer weekends it's always a holiday on Avenida Revolución when folk dancers cavort in brilliant costumes to the rousing strains of Mexican music.

Mexicali To San Felipe Or Tecate

History

Mexicali was settled by ex-miners in the late 1890s when their claims in the mountains southeast of Ensenada failed to produce sufficient gold to make them profitable. The community grew slowly – unlike Tijuana, its chief competitor for tourist dollars 123 miles to the west.

By 1902, agricultural products were being produced after the Imperial Canal in the United States brought water to the rich soil of farms on both sides of the border.

During the Mexican Revolution, Mexicali was occupied by American fortune hunters led by Colonel Esteban Cantú who took control of the town in 1915 from the hands of its citizens. Cantú, who ruled until 1920, moved the capital from Ensenada to Mexicali. American tourists poured into the area when gambling, prostitution and drugs were legalized.

The railroad from Tijuana through Tecate and Mexicali to Tucson, Arizona, was completed in 1915. This was an important link for all three villages, and as they started to develop their natural resources, the railroad provided a more efficient way to get them to market.

During the 1920s Mexicali, like Tijuana, was a hot-bed of vice and lawlessness, particularly after prohibition became law in the United States. Authorities in Mexico City finally outlawed gambling in 1935 and Mexicali began to grow as agriculture and industry expanded.

For many years most of the fertile Mexicali Valley was owned by the Colorado River Land Company, an American company that raised cotton. Prior to 1919, the company brought in thousands of Chinese immigrants to work the cotton fields. After that year, the Mexican Government restricted the flow of Chinese workers, but today there is a large Chinese population in the city. The Mexican government forced the American company to sell its land holdings in the mid-1930s, and the land was bought by Mexican farmers who converted it into a series of *ejidos* or collective farms.

Mexicali Today

Now Mexicali is the capital of Baja California Norte, a modern city with more than 750,000 residents across the US border from Calexico. Despite its proximity, Mexicali's prosperity and financial well-being is not determined by the tourist trade. Water is the key to Mexicali's success, plus the silt that has been deposited for centuries in its valley, making this the hub of a rich agricultural region. Mexico no longer relies on the vagaries of the Colorado River, whose flow across the border has been restricted for years by dams upstream in the United States. The Mexican Government built Morelos Dam on the Colorado River south of the border to harness its waters and to irrigate an area larger than the Imperial Valley on the American side.

Wheat is the major agricultural product, but other grains and vegetables are grown, plus citrus fruits that thrive in the hot summers and mild winters. Industry has expanded in the last few decades, and there is a thriving electronics business in Mexicali as well as a truck assembly plant.

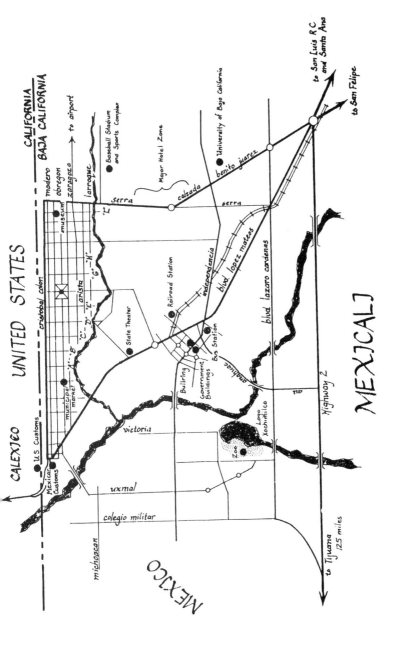

The new Centro Civico-Comercial de Mexicali, under development along Calzada López Matéos in the city's southern part, has become the center for the city's social and political life.

Three wide boulevards – Calzadas López Matéos, Justo Sierra and Benito Juárez – control the traffic through Mexicali, but traffic circles or *glorietas* can create problems for drivers unfamiliar with the city (bearing right when entering and then following the flow of traffic counterclockwise). These traffic circles on the main boulevards often have magnificent monuments that are a sight to behold. Many Americans, crossing the border just to shop, wisely leave their cars on the American side and walk across the border. Most of the good stores are within a few blocks of the border at Calexico. Mexican pottery, wrought iron works, silver and leather goods are usually good buys, but beware of shoddy material and workmanship.

Cultural Attractions

Those who want to visit the city's many cultural attractions can use public transportation (bus fare all over Baja California is extremely inexpensive) or drive their own cars. Parking is only a problem in the business district. The city park or "Bosque de la Ciudad," is at Avenida Ocotlán and Calle Alvarado in southwest Mexicali. It has a zoo, a museum of natural history with a picnic area and a playground for children, and it is open every day. For information call (65) 55-2833. The Galeria de la Ciudad at 1209 Avenida Alvaro Obregón between Calles D and E is open Monday through Friday to exhibit the works of Mexican painters, sculptors and photographers. It was formerly the state governor's residence. For information call (65) 53-5044. The Museo Regional Universidad de Baja California at Avenida Reforma and Calle L contains exhibits in paleontology, archeology, ethnography, landscape photography and Baja's missions; (65) 54-1972. The museum is closed on Monday. The cathedral or Temple of Nuestra Señora de Guadalupe is located at

Calle Morelas 192. Mexicali's industrial park is of little interest to most visitors, but it is located at Avenida Brasil and Boulevard de los Americas between Calzada Justo Sierra and the airport. Owned by American and foreign interests, these plants have become an important part of the area's economy. A mile and a half south of the American border is the State Theater at Calzada López Matéos where plays, musicals and dance exhibitions are performed. For information call (65) 54-0757.

Bullfights

Bullfights are held twice a month from October through May at the Plaza de Toros Calafia at Calle Calafia in the Centro Civico-Commercial. Call (65) 57-0681.

Rodeos

Mexican rodeos, or charreadas, are popular and an average of one a month is held through the winter season, usually on Sunday or major Mexican holidays. They are held at either the Charro grounds on Highway 2, west of Mexicali, or the one that is 3.7 miles east of Calzada Justo Sierra on Calle Compuertras.

Golf

For those interested in more prosaic entertainment, there is the Club Deportivo Campestre de Mexicali, A.C., west of Highway 5 on the city's southern outskirts where one can play golf. It's an 18-hole, semi-private course with a par 72 and totaling 6,629 yards. The course is open daily and all the amenities usually associated with such places are available. For further information call (65) 61-7130 or 61-7170.

Restaurants

Diners will find a variety of good restaurants such as **Casa Carmina,** 1080 Avenida Reforma, offering a varied menu. **El Acueducto** in Hotel Lucerna at Calzada Benito Juárez and Independencia offers the same but specializes in seafood. **Los Búfalos,** 1616 Benito Juárez, has ranch-style cuisine, while a number of Chinese restaurants (Mexicali has a large Chinese population) serve good food, including the **Palacio Imperial** at Calzada Benito Juárez and Lázaro Cárdenas; **El Dragon** at Boulevard Benito Juárez; **El Nuevo Pekin,** Calzada Justo Sierra; and **El Palacio Mandar** at Calle de la Republica and Prolongación Alfarareros in the Centro Civico and Commercial Center.

For real Mexican food, lovely Spanish music, and an authentic atmosphere try **La Casita de Patzcuaro** on Avenida López Matéos 648.

Hotels

There are three major hotels, ranging in price from $60 single to $75 for double occupancy. **Del Norte** is at Avenida Madero and Calle Melgar. The **Holiday Inn** is located at Boulevard Benito Juárez and Calle Transito del Estado (they have a toll-free number – (800) 238-8000). **Lucerna** is at Benito Juárez 2151; (65) 66-1000. Each hotel has a variety of entertainment and/or places to dance.

The best motels are **Azteca de Oro** at Calle de la Industria 60; **Canchanille,** Calzada Justo Sierra 1495; **Cosmos,** Calzada Justo Sierra 1493; and **La Siesta** at Calzado Justo Sierra 899. They also offer a wide range of luxurious living, dining and some entertainment opportunities. In general, motels with room accommodations only are cheaper but clean and well-kept. Prices start at $30.

Tourists swarm to Mexicali's palm-lined boulevards in the winter because its climate is like that of the American Southwest. Summer days can be hot, however, with temperatures reaching 120 degrees Fahrenheit.

THE ROUTE SOUTH TO THE GULF

Many Americans use Mexicali as a gateway to reach San Felipe and the Gulf of California, or to continue east on Highway 2 to the mainland state of Sonora. It is about an hour's drive or 41 miles to San Luis R.C. (Rio Colorado), which is 23 miles north of Yuma, Arizona. This route, and its connection with Highway 15, provides the fastest and most direct route between California and Mexico's interior. A word of caution: from San Luis to the junction with 15 it is a barren desert.

Prehistory & Ecology of the Gulf of California

The area from Mexicali south to the Gulf of California and San Felipe has a long history of exciting events, and much of it retains its pristine grandeur largely unadulterated by mankind's presence.

The Jesuit explorer Father Kino called the large river that emptied into the Gulf of California the Colorado – Spanish for red – when he first saw it in 1701. Since then, the flow of the Colorado has been drastically reduced by dams. The river still runs heavy with silt, however, and it still retains its dull-red color.

Underlying the entire area along the border between the United States and Mexico is a continuation of the San Andreas fault that begins in northern California on the American side and runs for 700 miles into Mexico. It is a visible cleft in many places, revealing the pulverization of rocks that for millions of years have been grinding together as segments of the earth's crust have slipped.

MAR DE CALIFORNIAS

SENO DE CALIFORNIAS
Y su Costa Oriental
nuevamente descubierta, y registrada
Desde el Cabo de las Virgines
hasta su Termino
que es
EL RIO COLORADO
Por el
P. Fernando Consag
de la Comp. de Iesus
Missionero
de Californias
1746

PIMERIA

SONORA

PARTE SEPTEN.ᴸ DE CALIFORNIAS

NACION

COCHIMI

MAR
DEL SUR

Sierra de S. Juan Gualberto
Los 3 Reyes
Rio Colorado
S. Ignacio
Marismas
Pantano
S. Phelipe de IHS
Buenaventura
Aguaje o S. Firmin
Aguaje o S. Isabel
La Visitacion
S. Estanislao
Aguaje
Ju.y S. Pablo
CANAL DE BALLENAS
I. del Angel de Guarda
Las Animas
Baia de los Angeles
Pagaju
S. Raphael
S. Gabriel
Aguaje
S. Miguel
Aguaje
S. Juan
S. Bernabé
La Trinidad
S. Carlos
C. de las Virgines
Agueda
Miss. de N.P.
S. Ignacio
Frontera del Norte
Virgines
año de 1746
S. Clara
Esta Costa esta delineada...
Caboreo
Tepoca
I. del Pedro
I. de S. Estevan
ISLAS DE SALSIPUEDES
I. de S. Lorenzo
S. Augustin
Baya de S. Juan Bautista
Rio de Sonora
Megros
Antigua
P. de Guaimas
R. Hiaqui
I. de la Tortuga
C. de S. Marcos

ESCALA
Leguas Españolas
Leguas Francesas

Petrus M.ᵃ Nascimben Soc. Iesu delineavit

Baja is believed to have split away from the Mexican mainland by one such cataclysm of nature about 20 million years ago, when long-extinct volcanoes erupted, the earth split into a huge fracture, and the Pacific Ocean's waters rushed in to form the Gulf of California, or the Sea of Cortez as many Mexicans prefer to call it. Since that time geologists believe the whole area has moved as much as 250 miles to the northwest.

Volcanic activity continues today, and earthquakes are common to this area. Tips of volcanoes can be seen as barren islands of solid rock in the gulf. Many of them have never been explored, and some are only 50 miles from the United States border.

The Gulf of California once extended farther inland. The Salton Sea, 279 feet below sea level, once was part of the gulf. The Colorado River starts 1,400 miles away in springs and snow-fed streams of the Rocky Mountains and, after carving out the Grand Canyon, drains 265,000 square miles of the western region. Over the last 7 million years, sediment has built up to form the present delta, and effectively landlocks the Salton Sea. This sediment may be three miles thick, having been deposited on top of the former ocean floor over millions of years.

Since Baja broke from the mainland, the Colorado River has been depositing organic material and minerals into the Gulf of California. Dams now restrict silt deposits but soluble nitrates, phosphates and organic matter continue to flow into the gulf and to provide food for its plankton – tiny plant and animal life nourished by these materials and by the action of the sun. In turn, many of the Gulf of California's sea-dwelling animals live off the plankton, from one-celled organisms to whales. Each whale eats up to eight tons of plankton a day.

Jesuit priest Fernando Consag ascended the Gulf of California in 1746 to Montague Island at the mouth of the Colorado River. He made this map to prove once and for all that Baja was a peninsula and not an island.

In effect, all living creatures in the gulf either directly or indirectly live off the plankton.

In February and March, plankton reaches its peak production and the normally blue waters of the gulf change to a brilliant green or, if the rains have been heavy in the north, sediment changes the color to brown.

Where there are fish in abundance, birds thrive because most of them live off the fish population. Man reaps an added benefit by using bird droppings, or guano, as a high-nitrogen fertilizer.

Crustaceans provide another vital link in the food chain here. In addition to the usual varieties, there are odd-ball types like opossum shrimp that carry their babies in belly pouches. At times, along the shores of rocky islands, they are so numerous that the water turns a greenish hue to a depth of 10 feet. These shrimp make excellent eating and they are low in fat – less than 10 percent, with 75 percent protein.

Whales and porpoises have long inhabited the gulf. Porpoises often reach 18 feet in length. The whale population includes most known varieties. The killer whale has a triangular dorsal fin that extends 10 feet from its body. There is a large white spot on the side of its black head. It can attain a length of 30 feet. Not necessarily a threat to man, the killer whale is so-called because it attacks other sea mammals. False killer whales look similar except that they are all black with no white markings. The pilot whale has adapted well to captivity because it is friendly to humans. It has a bulging forehead, with a sickle-shaped pectoral fin, and reaches 20 feet at maturity. The bottle-nosed dolphin is the great show-off in the gulf as elsewhere, leaping in and out of the water with his entire 12-foot length often rising above the surface. The 80-ton finback whale is a huge mammal, second in size to the 100-ton blue whale. Whales congregate in the gulf because they live on plankton, and the gulf is a living pasture for such mammals. Finbacks, who remain in the middle of the gulf, are seldom seen, and the same is true of sperm whales.

Sharks and rays abound in the gulf. Some of the rays have poisonous spines at the tips of their tails. Their sting can be painful, and sometimes life-threatening to those with weak hearts. In addition, there are numerous eels and squids.

For millions of years vast numbers of fish have migrated from the tropics. As a result, there are more than 650 varieties of fish in the upper reaches of the gulf where the Colorado River flows into it. About half of these types are considered edible game fish. The Pacific jewfish, sometimes exceeding 1,000 pounds, is found almost everywhere. It is a member of the bass family. The Pacific striped marlin poses the greatest challenge to anglers and reaches a weight of 250 pounds.

In the more northerly reaches of the gulf on the peninsula side, Mexican anglers seek the giant totuava – the largest croaker in the northern hemisphere, weighing up to 300 pounds. Non-residents can't fish for totuava, although they can buy them in legitimate markets.

In spring, huge numbers of yellowtail, bonito and skipjack seek out concentrations of sardines, herring, and other small fish in the middle of the gulf. Concentrations are so heavy the water looks as if it were covered by a silver blanket. The sea boils with activity as the smaller fish leap into the air to escape their predators, who come from the depths to feast on this bounty. Overhead, birds go into a frenzy as they, too, join in the feast. Sharks slash at everything in sight until the surface of the water turns red with blood and tens of thousands of small fish succumb to the voracious appetites of their natural enemies. Huge manta rays, jewfish and black seabass rise from the depths and the slaughter is sickening to behold. So uncontrolled is their madness that some species eat their own kind. Bottlenose dolphins ram sharks, leaping high out of the water in sheer excitement. On the fringes, anglers eagerly try their luck, and large fish become easy prey for them.

The Gulf of California is spotted with barren islands. The Isla Tiburon, where Seri Indians once practiced cannibalism, is just one of many such islands that are noteworthy mainly for their huge population of birds. The Indians were moved to the mainland in 1956 after two Mexican fishermen disappeared on the island. The Seris have now almost died out, but girls and unattached women still paint their cheeks and noses with colored stripes as in the old days.

Francisco de Ulloa reached the head of the gulf in 1539. He described a phenomenon that has intrigued people for centuries. "We perceived the sea to run with so great a rage into the land, and with a fury it returned back again with the ebb." He speculated that some great river might be the cause of this tidal bore.

His assumption was only partly correct. Tidal bores are fairly common, but in the Colorado River delta area they reach an intensity that is unusual. In the narrow upper part of the gulf tides can reach 30 feet, sending a wall of water up the river. Before the Colorado River's flow was restricted by dams on the upper reaches, this wall of water met the swift-moving current of the river and reversed its flow dramatically. The river's level suddenly rose 10 feet in five minutes or less and swept almost everything in its path as it rushed inland, inundating the delta's flatlands with a terrifying noise. Those in contact with the raging torrent quickly lost their lives, unless they could reach high ground in a hurry. Mexicans call the tidal bore "el burro" or ungovernable beast. James Ohio Pattie, a trapper with a load of pelts he hoped to sell to a Spanish settlement on the lower Colorado, was caught in 1826 by such a bore. His campsite was flooded, and he lost most of his pelts, but he escaped with his life. Eighty-six people lost their lives in 1922 when their small steamer was caught in a bore and capsized.

The northern coast of the gulf is desert and twice daily these huge tides move across the land and inundate it. Then the trapped water evaporates due to the intense heat and the hot desert winds. The land here appears white because of the salt deposits that glitter brightly during daylight hours when the sun causes temperatures to rise as high as 125 degrees Fahrenheit. It is an awesome land whose surface is constantly in motion through the effects of wind and sea. Shifting sands alternately uncover and bury everything in their path while dust devils whirl masses of dirt skyward in a macabre exhibition of nature at its most playful – and dangerous.

In the 19th century, flat-bottomed steamers and barges carried cargo on the Colorado River from La Bomba, where one can still see pilings of the old wharf, to such remote places as the US Army fort at Yuma. They were put out of business when the railroad was completed to Yuma in 1877. Today, due to the damming of the river, it is impossible for anything but the smallest boat to cruise the Colorado.

The Desert Of The Chinamen

In the 19th and 20th centuries, thousands of Chinese were brought to the American West to work as laborers, particularly on the intercontinental railroads. A group of Cantonese came to Mazatlán on Mexico's mainland in 1900. Work there proved impossible to find so they walked to Guaymas, a distance of 500 miles to the northwest. Three died on this trek, but the remainder boarded a small steamer and crossed the gulf to San Felipe on the peninsula side. This small village also had no work for them, but they heard there was plenty of work at Mexicali 127 miles to the north. The Mexicans were building irrigation canals there, so the Chinese pooled their money and paid $100 in gold to a man who claimed that he could take them because he knew the waterholes in this desert country. Forty-three Chinese men went with José Escobedo in August, 1902, a time when desert temperatures ranged up to 125 degrees Fahrenheit. Prior to their departure they filled whisky bottles and old cans with water, stringing them over their shoulders. No party of people ever started out to cross a desert so ill prepared. Their black clothes absorbed the heat and soon became a torment. Many Chinese wore no hats, and they were barefoot. Their bare feet on the hot sand and gravel soon became blistered and then infected.

Their guide had told them there was a waterhole at Pozo Salado about 30 miles from their starting point at San Felipe. The next waterhole, he said, was another 30 miles beyond at Tres Pozos.

The first Chinese died of the heat during the first 20 miles, but the rest hurried on. They never found the first waterhole. To many, it was soon evident that their guide had lied, but they had no choice but to press on to the second waterhole. The desert soon became strewn with the bodies of the Chinese who collapsed and died. Only nine remained alive when they reached the site where the second waterhole was supposed to be. This waterhole wasn't found either, and two more men died. Finally, only Escobedo and six Chinese men reached the Río Hardy more dead than alive after nine more days under the blistering sun. The wasteland they crossed is now named El Desierto de los Chinos – the Desert of the Chinamen.

Today, it is only 119 miles to San Felipe from Mexicali over a good road. For the first 25 miles the road crosses rich farmland. Then comes the Cerro Prieto Geothermal Zone where mud flats bubble, and the stench of sulphur fumes hangs heavy over the hot springs that are known locally as Laguna de los Volcanes, or Volcano Lake. Fumaroles screech during eruptions, and thick mud pools are formed that are yellow, white or orange. Many Mexicans believe that the hot mud has curative powers, but of more value is the harnessing of the steam geysers to produce electric power. It is hoped that these steam-powered generators eventually will supply power for all of Baja's northeastern corner. The underground water's high sulphur content, however, similar to places in the Imperial Valley on the American side, has long frustrated plant engineers because of the corrosive effect of the sulphur on metal pipes. Ways are being found on both sides of the border to overcome this problem. Here, one of the world's largest geothermal electric generating plants takes boiling water from deep in the earth's surface and uses it to provide a pollution-free energy source.

At the Río Hardy, one of the Colorado River's delta channels, hunters and sports fishermen come each year to try their luck. Many have rustic cabins that they use for weeks at a time. Off to the west, travelers can see the barren slopes of the Sierra de los Cocopah – named for one of the original Indian tribes.

The Indian settlement of El Mayor is near the end of this mountain range and it is occupied by the Cocopah Indians. There are only a few survivors of this tribe who once occupied parts of Baja California long before white men settled in the south. Few of their primitive ways remain, although they still farm as they did hundreds of years ago, and their huts are still made of reed and thatch. Most younger members of the tribe have departed for Mexicali, or they work in fishing camps along the Río Hardy. Today, El Mayor is inhabited mostly by older Indians. Some still gather piñon nuts in the mountains like their aboriginal ancestors, making the long trek across the deserts and mountains of northeastern Baja. One of the original trails is still used over the Sierra de los Cocopah, across Baja's largest dry lake, the Laguna Salada, and into the high mountains of the interior, where the piñon trees grow. In ancient times, their ancestors also walked the 70 miles from El Mayor to San Felipe, across one of the worst deserts on the peninsula, to gather clams. The desert today, driven by modern vehicles, can be forbidding. In those days on foot the trip must have been murderous.

In traveling south on Highway 5, desert is encountered 40 miles south of Mexicali. Today's travelers cross vast mud flats, with sand dunes farther on, until the tidal salt flats of the gulf appear shimmering brightly in the desolate wasteland on both sides of the road. Salt deposits are created by huge tides that race inland over the flatlands twice each day. The sun's intense heat, plus the desert winds, evaporate most of the water soon after the tides recede, leaving behind a dazzling white rime of salt. Land in this area is in a perpetual state of change, due to the actions of tide and wind. Winds can be worse than the tides, whipping through the flatlands between the sea and the mountains with a scouring action, and increasing in velocity like air in a wind tunnel whose velocity increases as it reaches its narrowest point. Wind-whipped sand only stops its forward motion when it comes against an immovable object such as a mass of stone. When that happens the sand piles up, creating a dune, until further wind actions change the shape again. Dust devils dance in a seemingly mad dervish ritual that can be deadly to one caught in them.

Storms in the northern part of the Gulf of California are infrequent, but they can strike with tropical suddenness. All low areas should be avoided when storm clouds appear on the horizon. A dry arroyo can become a raging torrent of water as it races down its course seeking a path to the gulf. The soil is so hard, after baking for centuries in the relentless heat, that very little water can seep into the ground. The humus that otherwise would soak up heavy rainfall like a sponge is almost completely lacking.

Mirages in these desert areas create weird images of water or foliage to torment minds almost overwhelmed by the oppressive heat. An unwary traveler, who walks the desert floor in the heat of the day without sufficient head covering and full water bottles does so at his own risk. Mirages may temporarily help a person to escape from reality, but disillusionment follows with frightening suddenness.

Ninety-two miles south of Mexicali, Highway 5 meets Highway 3 from Ensenada at Crucero La Trinidad. This is a lonely spot, wind-swept and desolate. From here the road continues straight ahead for another 32 miles until it reaches San Felipe on a crescent-shaped bay.

FROM MEXICALI TO TECATE

For travelers not wishing to drive into Baja's interior from the east, with its rugged terrain beyond Puertecitos, Highway 2 will take them 89 miles from Mexicali to Tecate, a relaxed city on the US border that is surrounded by mountains and rich agricultural valleys.

Cañon De Guadalupe

There's a side trip about 23 miles from Mexicali, en route to Tecate, that you might want to consider. Close to the center of the northern part of the peninsula there is a beautiful canyon that few visitors to Baja ever see. Cañon de Guadalupe is a palm oasis in the heart of the Sierra de Juárez. It can be reached from Highway 2 by taking a dirt road along the edge of the Laguna Salada and driving about 36 miles. This road is graded but it is rough on passenger cars and is very poorly marked. I tried to find the canyon and failed to locate the turn-off despite following my map's precise details. Others who have seen it say that the canyon remains green because a year-round water supply flows to it from the mountain peaks above. In the lower part of the canyon, hot mineral springs well up between the rocks. A walk along the stream bed is a delightful experience, with two tall peaks standing sentinel above. The highest peak rises to 4,500 feet. Early explorers named the lesser peak the Virgin of Guadalupe, thus giving the canyon its name.

From the east, the dreaded Laguna Salada or Salt Lake starts at one end of this idyllic setting. Long ago this salt lake, now covering 500 square miles, was a part of the Gulf of California, but it has been dry for years. Now it serves as a roadbed for trucks that bring spring water to Mexicali from nearby wells.

Palm trees shade the canyon, their roots deep in the ground to absorb the precious moisture. There are two types of palm trees, and both are fan palms. The California fan palm towers to a height of 60 feet while the blue fan palm reaches only 40 feet. The latter – its fronds have a bluish tinge – grows naturally here. Blue fan palms have been widely transplanted to other parts of the world where climate and soil are suitable. In all, there are more than 1,100 palm trees in the canyon. The California palm also grows across the border in Alta California, but they are not as common as they once were. Their habit of folding their dried fronds around their trunks to form a skirt gives them a messy look and, at times, when vandals set them on fire, they are dangerous to nearby dwellings because they burn like torches.

Birds flit happily from tree to tree in Guadalupe canyon, and their cheerful songs brighten the atmosphere. There are no large animals, but numerous small ones live off the bounty that water provides for all living things. There are the usual lizards and snakes. The red racer is not poisonous but, when alarmed, this snake will vibrate its tail so fast that it sounds like a rattlesnake. It is a feisty animal that, if cornered, will lash out with its fangs at anyone who approaches too close. It has been known to climb a tree to escape if no other way seems possible.

A stream cascades down a rocky slope that ends in a wide, shallow pool. A large willow tree shades the spot, sharing honors with a huge cottonwood whose limbs branch over the pool. Palms complete the pool's encirclement while ocotillo and cholla cacti compete for nourishment farther up the canyon on the steep cliff above the former "Pool of the Virgin." Cacti maintain a tenuous hold on life in each spot of earth wedged within the rocks.

In 1967 Hurricane Katrina flooded the canyon, uprooting its trees, and filling the Pool of the Virgin with sand. Someday the cascading water may dig itself a new pool at the foot of the falls and bugs will return to skitter across its mirrored surface. This pool was formerly set in a large rocky bowl that was constantly replenished by a slender waterfall dropping 20 feet from the rocks above. Its once deep, blue waters are no more. The thin ribbon of water that falls sinks immediately into the sand, and then flows down through a channel to its old outlet, ending in a shallow pond farther down the canyon.

TECATE

Back on Highway 2, you soon reach Tecate. It was founded in 1831 by Don Juan Bandini, who was of Peruvian origin. Two years later, the Mexican government gave him an extensive concession of land to develop around his original settlement. It was named Tecate – possibly derived from the English words "to cut." This area was once known as weed valley. Bandini and his heirs continued to live at Tecate despite raids by marauding Indians, who frequently made their existence almost impossible. Although only 34 miles from Tijuana, it never acquired the stigma of most border cities because it is somewhat isolated from major population centers on the American side of the border. A typical Mexican community, Tecate's population exceeds 46,000 people. With its tree-shaded plaza around which the life of this pleasant community revolves, the city has warm summers and cool winters, with few extremes of temperature. Basically a farming community dependent on cultivation of grain crops, thousands of grapevines and millions of olive trees, it lies at the junction of Highway 2 and Highway 3. Highway 3 connects this growing community to the Pacific side of the peninsula at El Sauzal just above Ensenada. This 66-mile stretch of Highway is heavily traveled by produce trucks from the large farms south of Mexicali.

Hotels

Tecate has modest accommodations priced from $50 per room, such as **La Hacienda,** at the extension of Avenida Juárez 861; the motel **El Dorado** at Avenida Benito Juárez and Esteban Cantú 1100 – (665) 4-1333; and **El Refugio** at Avenida Hidalgo and Aldrete.

Restaurants

Places to eat include **Restaurant 70** at Avenida Benito Juárez and Calle Esteban Cantú for Chinese food; **El Passetto,** at Callejon Libertad 200 for Italian food; Mexican food at **El Gourmet,** Avenida Hidalgo 289; **La Carreta** at Avenida Juárez 270; and **La Hacienda** at Extension Avenida Juárez 861.

Other Attractions

There is an arts and craft center on the highway to Ensenada in front of López Matéos Park. Summer dances and serenades are held at the park on an outdoor dance floor. Also on this road is a drag-racing track at the airport.

The **Rancho Las Juntas** is an authentic-looking street of old Mexico or the early American West. It accommodates individuals and small conventions in country cabins or kitchen apartments. The Rancho is a former movie set and families or groups of five or more can use the street to shoot their own Western movie. **Los Búfalos Restaurant,** named for its real buffalo herd, offers unusual private or group dining. Additional information can be obtained by calling Tijuana 85-0501 or 02. The **Rancho Santa Veronica** is a country estate famous for its bull-breeding. For the tourist seeking the unusual, it can be a delightful experience. You can watch a baby bull being caped – or take over the cape yourself – and enjoy a picnic or barbecue while staying at the ranch's new hotel.

After leaving Tecate you can take Highway 2 to Tijuana, and shortly thereafter pass the world-renowned resort spa, **Rancho La Puerta.** It can house 100 guests but provides a strictly vegetarian diet. In a lovely setting with tennis courts, pools and indoor and outdoor gymnasiums, it was established in 1940.

The rest of the trip passes through a prosperous farming area, then through La Mesa, a fast-growing industrial region. Four miles from Tijuana, Highway 2 passes the Agua Caliente Racetrack, and on the hills to the south there is a pleasant residential neighborhood. This highway is in good condition, but rather narrow in places. Traffic in Tijuana and La Mesa is heavy and if this part of Highway 2 can be avoided, it should be. There's an alternate route with a divided road along a seven-mile stretch east of La Mesa. Better still would be to cross the border into the United States at Tecate – the gates are open daily from 6 a.m. to midnight – because tourists seldom use it.

HIGHWAY 3 TO EL SAUZAL

If you choose to drive to Ensenada and points south, Highway 3 from Tecate to El Sauzal takes about an hour and a half for the 66 miles through scrub-covered mountains and small upland valleys. Sharp curves and steep grades on this route require caution.

About half way to El Sauzal is a tiny rural village called El Testerazo where local craftsmen produce fine carvings from cottonwood for sale in a house alongside the road.

At Sordo Muda you encounter the vineyards of several wineries (the Domecq Winery is in an impressive new building), but none are open to the public.

Forty-eight miles along the highway from Tecate is Guadalupe. This farming area was settled by Russian immigrants in 1906 when 350 people arrived after fleeing the wrath of the Russian Czar. President Porfirio Díaz permitted them to settle in this remote valley and, through their hard work and thrift, they prospered. After the Mexican Revolution most of these families emigrated to the United States, and only a few remain today. Few of them are pure Russian; the others have intermarried with the Mexican people. In some homes, the Russian language is still spoken, but all the children speak

Spanish as their primary language. On feast days, Russian girls still wear the traditional blouses of their native land, and most former Russians retain their own religion.

Guadalupe is also the site of the **Nuestra Señora de Guadalupe mission**, the last of the California missions, built in 1834.

At El Sauzal, this highway meets Highway 1, where you can drive 60 miles north to Tijuana, or six miles south to Ensenada.

San Felipe

San Felipe, where the waters of the 70-mile-wide gulf meet the desert sands, is a study in contrasts. Now grown to a community of 12,000 people, San Felipe has changed from the once-sleepy village of post-World-War-II days to a popular resort. From here, the traveler has access to the northern part of the gulf. The sandy shores of the bay curve to the southeast for 12 miles to Punta Estrella, ending in a rocky point that provides some protection for small boats in the bay. However, tides that reach a height of 22 feet can quickly beach boats that are not securely anchored. From the shores of the bay, the coastal plain slopes gently upward to the foot-hills of the Sierra San Pedro Mártir, with Baja's highest peak, the 10,126-foot Picacho del Diablo, rising majestically into the bright blue sky. These mountains, with the Sierra de Juárez below the US border and the Sierra de la Giganta (Mountains of the Giantess) along the southern coast, form the peninsula's backbone. During winter months the northern ranges receive heavy rain, and snow occasionally falls on their peaks.

The Sierra de San Pedro Mártir appears from San Felipe as a vertical wall of granite, rising from desert sands that stretch to the waters of the gulf. For thousands of years, the spring runoff from the mountain range's snow-capped peaks, plus occasional torrents of rain from tropical storms, have gouged out huge sections of the mountains' eastern face and sent rocks tumbling into ravines below.

The San Pedro Mártir, and the Juárez Mountains farther north, have long served as formidable barriers to travelers between east and west Baja. Experienced mountain climbers use rough trails, but these trails are not for amateurs. Ranchers use older trails that date back to the aboriginal days to take their cattle to meadows in the high mountains where grass is plentiful during the spring and summer months. A few passes can be negotiated by high-clearance vehicles, but even these roads should be avoided except by those familiar with mountain driving conditions.

Cottonwoods and willows grow in the creek beds of these mountains, while scrub oaks and pines cling to their slopes. The Parry piñon has edible nuts that grow in egg-shaped cones. These pines grow only in northern Baja and in certain mountains across the border in the United States. Kiliwa and Paipái Indians gathered these nuts for centuries, as did members of the Cocopah tribe along the Colorado River Delta, and they became a staple part of their diets. A few Indians still live in these mountains where once they were numerous, until diseases brought by the early white men decimated their ranks.

Piñon nuts can be stored for later use, so they were a vital part of the diets of these early Indian tribes. The cones are picked in early fall, then placed briefly in a fire to loosen the resins that hold the nuts in the cones. In the early days, once the nuts were removed from the cones they were ground into a meal on rock depressions chipped out of flat-topped granite boulders.

Highway 3, from Ensenada to its eastern junction with Highway 5 on the gulf side, crosses much of this area. It is now a paved highway extending diagonally across the northern part of the peninsula for 128 miles. Through the San Matías Pass, piñon trees are so thick that their pungent aroma fills the air. Alpine meadows are numerous, and grass and clover thrive in this cooler climate. Birds are numerous, most of them unlike desert birds, and more akin to those in northern climates. Wildcats and mountain lions once were numerous, but excessive hunting of these predators has reduced their number. Mountain sheep also have been largely eliminated by hunting. Those that remain cling to mountain peaks whose remoteness gives them some protection.

Streams in this area have brightly-colored trout. It was once believed that the missionaries brought them from Spain, but this is unlikely because of the difficulty of keeping trout alive over the vast distance from Europe with the primitive conservation facilities available in those years. These may be a form of rainbow trout that migrated from the Pacific Ocean in the ages past when Baja California's streams flowed constantly year around. Today, such a fish migration would be impossible because most brooks and rivers disappear once torrential rains run off. These trout average eight inches in length, or about the same size as the rainbow trout that are planted in Alta California's streams and reservoirs. Some trout, however, are known to reach a length of two feet.

At the higher elevations of these mountains, thunderstorms are common during the summer months, and snow flurries are not unusual in early fall. Lupines provide a lovely carpet of blue for mountain meadows once the rains start to fall. Penstemon cover other areas with clusters of dark red blossoms. At these higher elevations, there are several varieties of pine trees, including the piñons, along with cottonwoods, sycamores, junipers and the inevitable live oaks.

Although Picacho del Diablo is the highest mountain in this area – actually Baja California's highest peak – there is another peak that rises to 9,170 feet. On top, there is an observatory that was built by the University of Mexico. It is staffed by Mexican astronomers who periodically invite astronomers from other countries to participate in their work. The observatory was built on the rocky eastern rim of the San Pedro Mártir mountains. Access to it from the San Felipe side is by a dirt road that winds tortuously through the mountains for more than 100 miles. This site was selected because Baja is one of the three most cloud-free areas in the world. The other two are in Chile and Africa.

To construct the observatory, the University of Mexico built a 75-mile road through the mountains from the Pacific side of the peninsula to carry building materials and equipment for the laboratory. It is a rough road, and unpaved, so it should not be attempted in a passenger car. A mile short of the observatory, there is a barrier across the road to prevent anyone from going higher. This is to prevent dust from contaminating the air. The telescope must be operated in an atmosphere free of dirt, smog contamination, and light pollution. The latter has posed a problem for Mount Palomar in the mountains of eastern San Diego county in the United States. As cities have grown on both sides of the border, light pollution at night causes increasing concern for the future. The Mexican observatory takes on an added importance because light pollution there is not expected to be a problem for the foreseeable future. At the top, San Felipe seems only a short distance away to the east by air. The straight-line distance actually is only a few miles.

San Felipe was first used in the late 18th century as a base to supply the northern Dominican missions, but a permanent settlement was not established until much later. In the 1920's, roads were built to provide access to neighboring communities, and San Felipe started to grow with permanent residents.

A hurricane virtually destroyed the settlement in 1967, but it has been rebuilt and is now a thriving community due to its popularity as a fishing resort. There are also areas set aside for campers. Off-road vehicles and dune buggies are permitted to explore certain inland areas.

Huge catches of shrimp and totuava are taken off San Felipe by Mexican fishermen. The totuava is a giant member of the weakfish family, and some of them weigh 300 pounds. They are excellent game fish for those permitted to catch them, and they are good commercial catches. Decking a large totuava requires more brawn than skill, even with heavy tackle.

Despite protection offered by the rocky point that screens San Felipe from northern winds, chubascos from the east and south can cause heavy damage. They form in the gulf of Tehuantepec far to the southeast, opposite the narrowest part of the Mexican mainland on the Pacific side, and sweep northward.

Hotels

San Felipe has good to excellent accommodations. Perhaps the best is the **Hotel Las Misiónes,** which has a restaurant and bar, with singles and doubles at $75. It is south of town at Misión de Loreto 148. In California, you can call (800) 336-5454, or (619)422-6900.

Other places include: the **Motel El Capitán** on Avenida Mar de Cortés 298 at the corner of Manzanillo, a modest motel charging $40 per person single and up to $45 double. For reservations call (706) 577-1303. The **Hotel Riviera** rests on a bluff a half-mile south of the center of town and overlooks the Gulf of California. Its rooms rent for $27 single and $27 double; call (706) 577-1186. **Hotel La Trucha Vagabonda** is new and is situated two miles from the center of town; most rooms have a view of the gulf. Its rooms are $35-$50. Call (657) 7-1333. **Hotel Villa del Mar** is on an elevated piece of land overlooking the Gulf of California with a rate of $27 single and $33 double; (706) 577-1333.

Restaurants

Good Mexican food is available at the restaurant **Las Misiónes,** a mile and a half south of town center in the **Mar del Sol RV Park** on Avenida Misión de Loreto, facing the gulf. Only dinners are served and they range up to $15 every day but Monday. **El Nido Steakhouse**, a quarter-mile south of town center, has a ranch atmosphere with prices up to $13.

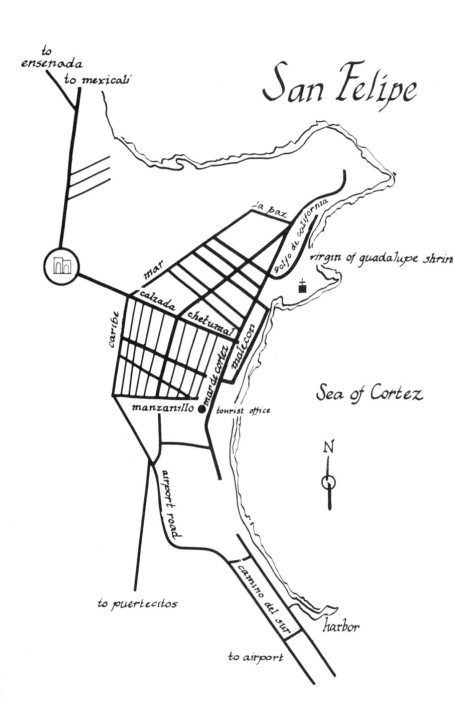

RV Parks

San Felipe is well equipped with trailer parks. Playa Bonita is a mile north of town on Avenida Mar de Cortés in a picturesque area with a beach and a backdrop of rocky cliffs. There are 35 RV or tent sites with full service costing up to $18. Their phone number is (657) 7-1215. **Ruben's Trailer Park** is much the same in location and amenities but with 48 hookups. They accept no reservations, but for information call (657) 7-1091. The **Campo San Felipe Trailer Park** is on the beachfront in San Felipe at the Avenida Mar de Cortés, with fees up to $16 for two people, and $1.50 for each extra person; (657) 7-1012. **La Jolla Trailer Park** is in a residential area, a half-mile west of town center at Avenida Manzanillo and Mar Bermejo. Its 55 sites have canopies. There is a $13 fee for two persons, with $2 for each additional person; (657) 7-1222. The **Playa de Laura Trailer Park** is also in town on Avenida Mar de Cortés with 45 RV or tent sites. The fee ranges up to $15 per person, and $2 for each additional person. Reservations are not required. The **Club de Pesco Trailer Park** is a mile south of Avenida Mar de Cortés. It is a large, landscaped park on the shore of the gulf with 30 RV or tent sites. The fee is $16 for two people, and $2 for each additional person. In addition to the usual services it has a boat launch and a storage area. No reservations. Mail address is P.O. Box 130, Calexico CA 92231.

Adjacent to Castel San Felipe is the **Mar del Sol RV Park**, a mile south of town on Misión del Loreto. There are good but unshaded beach sites for 85 RVs and 30 tents. There's a restaurant available here and groceries may be purchased. The fee ranges up to $21 for two people, $2 for each additional person, although children under 12 are free. The hotel's facilities are available to campers. You can reserve space by calling (800) 336-5454, or (619) 422-6900. On Punta Estrella, 10 miles southeast of town via the paved road, is the **Faro Beach Trailer Park.** It overlooks the Gulf of California on a terraced slope, offering 150 RV or tent sites, with access to the beach and tennis courts. There's a $17 fee per site. Their mailing address is Apartado Postal 107, San Felipe, Baja California, Mexico.

DRIVING SOUTH FROM SAN FELIPE

Before leaving San Felipe to drive south, travelers should stock up on necessary supplies because it is the last reliable place to do so for many miles. A paved portion of Highway 5 continues beyond San Felipe for part of the way along the coast to Puertecitos, but the unpaved section must be driven with care. Beyond Puertecitos, the rough road gets worse, crossing arroyos or rocky washes that are dangerous during the season when heavy rains can change dry creek beds into foam-flecked torrents. When water cascades off the mountains to the West, and races towards the gulf, these low areas can be death traps. The road is not only narrow, but some of its bed has been carved out of solid volcanic rock. Most of the coast from here is composed of salt flats with sand or clay. Farther south, there are scores of lovely beaches that are difficult to reach. But it is well worth the effort to seek out their almost invisible access tracks through the chaparral wilderness.

Those intending to travel the route beyond Puertecitos should do so with high-clearance vehicles well supplied for emergencies that may befall either the vehicles or their occupants. The rewards are great for those prepared to take the risks. After a rain, the wildflowers spring into bloom, covering the dunes with a riot of color, and parts of the countryside turn into a fairyland of indescribable beauty.

The dirt road eventually reaches the Bahía San Luis Gonzaga. There it turns inland, passing the site of the former Calamajué mission, before connecting with paved Highway 1 in the peninsula's center – at the abandoned El Crucero rancho some 50 miles from the Bahía San Luis Gonzaga.

Ensenada & Beyond

In late 1973, La Carretera Transpeninsular Benito Juárez –
the Benito Juárez Transpeninsular Highway (or Highway 1)
– was completed from a point near Tijuana to the peninsula's
tip at Cabo San Lucas. Construction began at each end, and
road crews met near Rancho Santa Inés to complete the highway named for one of Mexico's most revered heroes. He was
president from 1857 to 1872. President Luis Echeverría Al-
varez officially dedicated the new highway December 1,
1973, in ceremonies held at the 28th parallel near Guerrero
Negro. He told the distinguished gathering that the highway
was built to further the economic development of Baja California, and to traverse the peninsula with a modern road to
replace the rutted, dirt road that few had dared to travel in
modern vehicles.

After the new road was opened, the territory below the 28th
parallel became the new state of Baja California Sur, with its
capital at La Paz. At first, many of the tourist accommodations were primitive, but the Mexican Government financed
modern hotels, trailer parks and facilities for recreational vehicles.

FROM TIJUANA TO ENSENADA

After you leave Tijuana, there are two roads to Ensenada.
The divided peninsular highway – Highway 1/D – charges a

fee (approximately $7 for the trip to Ensenada in a passenger car, or up to $19 for a vehicle with a trailer), but there is no toll on old Mexico Highway 1. The divided toll road travels along fog-shrouded beaches. Homes line much of the shore, and many are perched high on cliffs over-looking the pounding surf where the Pacific Ocean ends its long journey from Asia. Rolling crests of waves pound against jagged rocks and promontories, sending cascades of white spray into the air, particularly at high tides. **Rosarito Beach Hotel,** on the beach of the same name, was built during the period when gambling was legal in Baja. Ornate in style, the hotel has long had an appreciative clientele. It was built in 1926 literally on the water's edge and its original 12 rooms have been expanded again and again. The dining rooms and the bars look much the same as in the old days, and they are incredible reminders of what artisans used to create. The lounge can seat up to 800 people. There are miles of beaches to walk just outside your door, and a beautiful blue ocean in which to swim, or you can use the Olympic-size pool. The accommodations are still as quaint as ever, despite refurbishing to make them more elegant. But the vacation suites are new and truly beautiful. There's a shopping center across from the hotel's entrance where they sell a wide variety of duty-free imported items. Many Hollywood stars of the past and present have visited the hotel and it is still used for movie and television locations. One of the best features of the hotel are the prices – $60 or $70 for a single or double room. New ocean suites are priced at up to $145. For reservations call toll free (800) 343-8582.

The **Quinta del Mar Resort Hotel** is in the center of Rosarito on Boulevard Benito Juárez, with a tower and a two-storey motel building. Singles are priced at up to $45, with doubles up to $50. Suites are also available, plus houses, condos and townhouses with kitchens. For reservations call toll free (800) 228-7003.

Two miles south of town on Boulevard Benito Juárez is the two-storey brick **Motel Quinta Chico** with single and double rooms at $38. Call (661) 2-1300 or 2-1644.

There are more modestly-priced places and they provide good service in clean surroundings. These include: **Rene's, The Hotel Baja del Sol, Hotel Don Luis,** and **Motel Colonial.**

There are a number of excellent eating places in Rosarito but perhaps the best is **El Nido Steakhouse** at Boulevard Benito Juárez 67. It has a ranch atmosphere and the seafood and steaks are especially good. They are open from 8 a.m. to midnight and their dinners range up to $16. For reservations call (661) 2-1431.

About 15 miles south of Rosarito, on either the toll road 1/D (Cantamar exit) or Highway 1, lies **Puerto Nuevo,** a fast-growing community with over 20 restaurants specializing in lobster.

Another eight miles farther is an exit for **La Fonda** and **La Misión** with their varied and exciting attractions, including the "Plaza Del Mar Archaeological Gardens." This is a resort complex unlike any other. It is situated on a vast expanse of oceanfront with half of the grounds devoted to archaeological gardens, featuring a climbable pyramid and numerous reproductions of Mexico's most famous stone monuments. There's a special museum for the display of artifacts and handcrafts. Accommodations are first-rate, and so is the food, including Mexican and international dishes. At La Misión, there is the **Best Western Plaza del Mar** right on the seashore with single and double rates up to $50. Call (800) 621-0852.

After another seven miles of driving you reach the exit for Jatay and Bajamar. **Villas by the Sea** at Bajamar is at an especially lovely setting that was developed for travelers. It can be reached by following the road to Misión Todos Santos from the toll road. There's an 18-hole golf course with a club-house, restaurant and bar. The villas have one to four bed-rooms, most with woodburning fireplaces, and they include linens, dishes, bottled water and fully-equipped kitchens. They offer daily maid service and 24-hour security. There are daily, weekly and monthly rates, with special mid-week rates. Groups and seminars are particularly welcome. The daily rate for two on a weekend is $60, or $50 at mid-week. For further information call (800) 522-1516 in California, or nationally (800) 2252786.

RV and/or tent sites are plentiful along this route. Twelve miles south of Rosarito off Highway 1/D (the San Antonio exit), is **KOA Rosarito** with 50 RV or tent sites offering hookups at grassy spots on a bluff overlooking the ocean, with a restaurant and bar nearby. The fee is $18 for two persons and $1 for each additional person. Write for reservations to Apartado Postal 2082, Tijuana, Baja California, Mexico, or call (66) 86-1412. On a beach facing the Pacific Ocean 27 miles north of Ensenada off Highway 1/D, there are 134 RV sites with hookups at **Outdoor Resorts of Baja California**. The fee is $26 to $33 for four people, with a charge of $3 for each additional person. Their mailing address is Apartado Postal 1492, La Salina, Baja California, Mexico. Reservations may be made from California at (800) 982-2252 or elsewhere in the United States at (800) 356-2252.

Eight miles north of Ensenada on Highway 1/D the **San Miguel Village** on Bahía de Todos Santos, has 45 RV and 55 tent sites with hookups. It is just south of the toll gate. Reservations should be made at Apartado Postal 55, El Sauzal, Baja California, Mexico. A mile south of Ensenada, near the intersection of Boulevard Lázaro Cárdenas and Calle Delante, is a fenced area near the bay for 85 RV or tent sites with hookups. The fee is $10 for four persons. Their mailing address is Apartado Postal 55, El Sauzal, Baja California, Mexico, or call (619) 286-4289 in San Diego.

Farther along, Highway 1/D crosses a bridge over a large bay, giving the motorist a sensation of floating in space high above the blue Pacific. Beyond El Sauzal, the highway clings precariously to the coastal mountains, seemingly almost dipping into the ocean at times.

ENSENADA

Ensenada is 67 1/2 miles from Tijuana. It was discovered by Juan Rodríguez Cabrillo in 1542 during his voyage of discovery along the Pacific Coast of North America. Sebastián Vizcaíno arrived in 1602. He was so impressed by the beauty of the protected bay that he called it the Bahía de Todos Santos, or the Bay of All Saints. Later, fur traders and whaling ships used the harbor. Today this magnificent bay provides a harbor with modern dock facilities that has made Ensenada Baja California's leading seaport.

Ensenada, with a population of 230,000 people, lies on a gently sloping plain half-surrounded by scrub-covered hills. Fog is common, but sunsets are often spectacularly beautiful.

The city's eastern outskirts are in the foothills of the Sierra de Juárez. Punta San Miguel extends to the north while Punta Banda juts out into the bay from the south. In-between there is an opening or window to the sea that permits cool breezes to flow from the ocean most of the time.

The Ensenada waterfront is a beehive of activity. The development of the Mexicali Valley on the peninsula's eastern side as an important agricultural area created the need for a major seaport on the Pacific Ocean. Ensenada was selected in the mid-30's because it is so ideally situated. Mexico Highway 3 was built to connect the two cities by joining Highway 1 six miles north of Ensenada at El Sauzal.

El Sauzal is a fish-canning community that was established by General Abelardo L. Rodríguez, a former governor of the northern territory, who later was President of Mexico from 1932 to 1934. His ranch was used to experiment with various agricultural products, including olives, in an attempt to improve their strains.

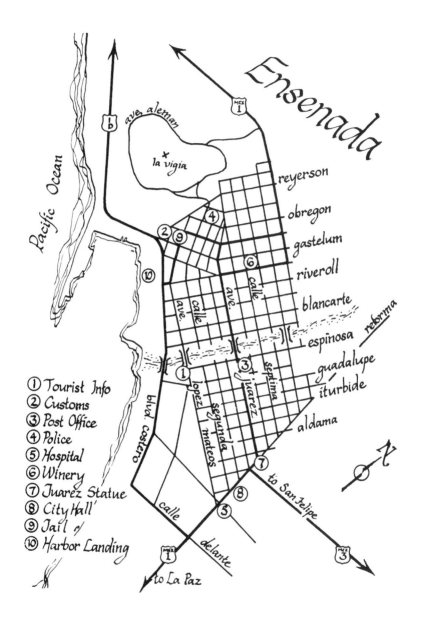

Ensenada

Pacific Ocean

ave. aleman

× la vigia

reyerson
obregon
gastelum
riveroll
blancarte
espinosa   reforma
guadalupe
iturbide
aldama

calle
calle ave.
calle ave.
septima
j. juarez
lopez mateos
segunda
blvd. costero
calle
delante

to San Felipe
to La Paz

① Tourist Info
② Customs
③ Post Office
④ Police
⑤ Hospital
⑥ Winery
⑦ Juarez Statue
⑧ City Hall'
⑨ Jail
⑩ Harbor Landing

Many of the older frame houses in the center of Ensenada were built originally in Canada for early colonists, dismantled, and then transported to Ensenada by sailing ships.

To the west of the city lie the Islas de Todos Santos. Robert Louis Stevenson is thought to have been inspired by them when he wrote *Treasure Island*. In the 1880's he owned a home north of the city in the village of San Miguel, where he wrote his famous book.

Stevenson is not the only famous author who resided in the area. Charles Nordhoff, who co-authored *Mutiny on the Bounty* with James Norman Hall, lived near the city in his ancestral home at Punta Banda.

On the outskirts of Ensenada, a part of the old **Riviera del Pacifico Hotel** is still in use as a community center. This ornate Spanish-Moorish structure was called the Riviera of the Pacific Coast when it opened on Halloween Night in 1930 as a hotel and gambling casino. Heavyweight Boxing Champion Jack Dempsey was one of the casino's original owners. It cost $2 million to build, an enormous sum for the time. On opening night, Xavier Cugat's orchestra played, while Bing Crosby sang, and the famous dance team of Veloz and Yolanda entertained throngs of guests. The grand ballroom in its heyday had a vaulted ceiling with a magnificent wrought-iron chandelier. In a nearby chapel, the walls are covered with murals that once provided a picturesque background for the marriages of many Hollywood movie stars.

The Depression in the 1930s sharply reduced the number of free-spending Americans coming to Ensenada and the rest of the northern peninsula. For a time, cruise ships had plied the coast from San Diego but they soon had to cease operations. The road from Ensenada in those days was bad, so few motorists ventured beyond Tijuana.

President Lázaro Cárdenas's banning of gambling in 1935 caused a further reduction in tourism. Through the years since then the Riviera Pacifico tried to make a comeback as a hotel, but it finally had to close and its hotel rooms were demolished.

Ensenada has had a phenomenal growth from its 1955 population of approximately 15,000. Now the peninsula's third largest city, its growth continues. During the summer months its duty-free shops, excellent sportfishing and proximity to Southern California make Ensenada a main center for tourists, wbo seldom go further south. The protected harbor and modern dock facilities make it Baja's leading seaport, and the bay is usually jammed with yachts of all descriptions, from the cheapest to the world's most elegant. Ensenada has a slower pace than Tijuana in everything, which adds to its charm.

The **Bodegas de Santo Tomás Winery**, at Avenida Miramar and Calle 7, offers daily tours at 11 a.m., 1 p.m. and 3 p.m. for a charge of $1.50 per person. Some of its wines are superb. **The Chapultepec Hills**, reached by way of Avenida Aleman, gives a magnificent view of the bay and city from this lovely residential area. **Nuestra Señora de Guadalupe** at Calle 6 and Avenida Floresta is one of the city's most prominent churches. It was built in the Spanish colonial style with twin towers.

Ensenada is a shopper's paradise because sellers are low-key and enjoy watching you browse. Also, prices are somewhat lower than in Tijuana. This is a duty-free port so import items are good buys, and there are the usual Mexican crafts.

Hotels

Ensenada's accommodations are designed for varied income levels. The **Casa del Sol Motel**, just south of town center, at Avenida López Matéos 1001, has single rooms for $52 and doubles for $57-$70. Call (800) 528-1234. **Las Rosas Hotel and Spa** is on Highway 1, four miles north of Ensenada, situated on a bluff with a spectacular view of the ocean. Its rooms are $90-$132 single and the same for double occupancy. For reservations call (667) 4-4320. **El Cid Motor Hotel** at Avenida López Matéos 993 on Ensenada Bay is truly luxurious. Each room is specially decorated to represent a principal city of Mexico. It has complete banquet and convention facilities designed to reflect an old Mediterranean atmosphere. The single rate starts at $68 for Sunday through Thursday, going up to $82 on Friday and Saturday. The double rate is $100 on weekends and $62 to $86 for the rest of the week. Call (667) 8-2401. The **Corona Hotel** is across the street from the Riviera del Pacifico Convention Center. A four-storey hotel with a magnificent view of the bay and the city, the Corona charges $72 double and the single rate is $67.

Nico Saad's **San Nicholas Resort Hotel** is in the heart of Ensenada, a block from the beach, in a 25-acre setting including a "roller derby" track! It has 130 luxurious rooms on Avenida Adolfo López Matéos and Guadalupe. The phone number is (667) 6-1901/1902.

Hotel La Pinta Ensenada at Esquina Floresta y Bucaneros, (call 800-336-5454 from the United States) is housed in a charming colonial building. It is part of the Hotel Presidente chain and offers a travel pass for four nights in a double room, eight American breakfasts with tax included for two people at $132. The **Travelodge** is at Avenida Biancarte 130. Call (706) 678-1601 or from the United States (800) 255-3050. The single rate starts at $46 while double rooms are $60 to $78.

Some of the smaller motels are excellent, including the **Cortés Motor Hotel** on Avenida López Matéos 1089 at Avenida Castillo with singles and doubles from $60 to $66. Reservations may be made through Best Western reservations. Call (800) 528-1234 or (667) 8-2307.

The **Villa Marina** is between Boulevard Costero and López Matéos downtown with a new restaurant on the top floor overlooking the city and the bay. Its rates vary according to the day of the week. Singles start at $50 on weekdays and rise to $66 on weekends. Doubles are $10 more.

Another relatively inexpensive hotel is **Hotel Misión de Santa Isabel**, Avenida López Matéos between Biancarte and Alvarado; (667) 8-3616.

The Estero Beach Resort Hotel, with beachfront accommodations, is eight miles south of Ensenada on a paved side road from Highway 1. From March 1 through November 30, single and double rooms cost $60-$95, while from December 1 through February 28 the rates drop to $42-$72. Suites are $109-$185. There's a private beach with a boat ramp, boat rentals, tennis courts, horseback riding and excellent fishing. Reservations can be made by mail to Apartado Postal 86, Ensenada, Baja California, Mexico, or by calling (667) 6-6225 or toll free (800) 762-2494.

There's an adjoining trailer park offering 75 RV sites with hookups. They charge $15 for two people, and $2 for each additional person.

Restaurants

There are a number of fine eating places in Ensenada but by far the best are the **El Rey Sol Restaurant, Enrique's Restaurant**, and **La Cueva de los Tigres**. El Rey Sol is a half-mile from the center of town on Avenida López Matéos at Avenida Biancarte. It specializes in French and Mexican food at reasonable prices (dinners $10-$24) and is open from 7:30 a.m. until 11 p.m. It is literally world famous. Call (667) 8-1733. Enrique's is on Highway 1/D, a mile and a half north of the city, and it specializes in Mexican and seafood dishes. Enrique's shrimp has to be eaten to be believed! Dinners range from $4.50 to $17.50 and they are open from 8 a.m to 11:30 p.m. Call (667) 8-2461. La Cueva de los Tigres is two and a half miles south of Ensenada. You take Highway 1 and then a half-mile-long gravel road to this beachfront restaurant that specializes in seafood, steaks and Mexican food.

Dinners range from $8 to $27. It opens daily but later than the others at 11 a.m. and closes at midnight. Call (667) 8-2653.

Nightlife

Ensenada does not have a rollicking nightlife like Tijuana but it has its attractions. **Hussong's** famous bar on Avenida Ruiz near López Matéos, is not for everyone, with its rough, old-fashioned interior, but most people stop by to join the boisterous crowd for at least a drink. There's dancing and live entertainment of a more sedate nature at several hotels, including the **Bahía**, **El Cid**, **La Pinta** and **San Nicholas** – all on or near Avenida López Matéos.

Fishing

Ensenada is best known for its sportfishing, and is often called the "Yellowtail capital of the world." Hooking one of these scrappy fish is an experience no angler should miss. They are most plentiful from April to November, along with barracuda, bonito and albacore. Bottom-feeding fish are plentiful the year around. The piers off Boulevard Lázaro Cárdenas offer places where you can obtain a mandatory license and charter a boat.

Rates are determined by the boat's size and the number of people. Surf fishing is also good along the beaches and rocky shoreline north and south of the city.

Beaches

Most beaches on the south side of the city and at Estero Beach are lovely for long walks, particularly at night, or for swimming. North of the city, surfers congregate on the rocky beach near San Miguel Village. Skin diving, particularly around Punta Banda, is ideal throughout the year.

La Bufadora

There's an interesting spot a few miles beyond the environs of Ensenada along Highway 1 where a natural blow hole at Punta Banda forces water to rise 100 feet through a rock crevice. A sign on the highway reading "La Bufadora" marks the turnoff. This is a lovely drive around the bay until you reach the parking site identified by a small tourist stand. A short walk behind the retaining wall in the rear brings you to the place where the blowhole explodes with spray every few minutes. It is especially exciting at high tide. There are picnic facilities, and an area for skin diving.

LAGUNA HANSON

One of the most rewarding side trips in Baja is to Laguna Hanson (Lake Hanson) in the high plateau country of the Sierra de Juárez. It can be reached from La Rumorosa on Highway 2, mid-way between Tecate and Mexicali, over a rough dirt road that should be traveled only with high-clearance vehicles. A far better way to reach this lovely spot is by way of Highway 3 from Ensenada over a paved road to Ojos Negros and then by a graded road for 29 miles that is accessible to passenger cars during the dry season. This road passes a number of prosperous ranches before it enters brush-covered hills. It climbs steadily up the mountains, although there are no steep grades.

At higher elevations, forests of ponderosa pines appear, and there is a cluster of wooden buildings around a large sawmill. The route then swings to the north at this point and enters the boundary of Parque Nacional Constitución de 1857. Laguna Hanson is four miles beyond. It's a small lake, surrounded by tall pines, whose waters are crystal clear. There are good primitive campsites and, if you like solitude, this place is ideal because few tourists ever come here. Park regulations permit camping, and there may be a small fee. Hunting is prohibited, however, as is use of motorcycles in the park.

HIGHWAY 3 TO SAN FELIPE

Those who are not interested in taking the side route to Laguna Hanson, preferring instead to go on to San Felipe on the gulf side, should remain on Highway 3 after Ojos Negros and continue on to the east side of the peninsula. The highway is wider through this area as it climbs through semi-arid foothills until it reaches a plateau called the Llano Colorado and descends along the edge of the Valle de Trinidad. This agricultural area is filled with vegetable fields and orchards that are soon left behind as Highway 3 follows a canyon to San Matías Pass. From there it drops to the floor of the arid San Felipe Valley. The view from here is magnificent, showing the Sierra San Pedro Mártir topped by its highest peak, the Picacho del Diablo, which is 10,154 feet tall.

There are only two places on this route where one can buy necessities, including auto parts and gasoline. **Ejido Héroes de la Independencia** on the Llano Colorado has a small settlement with two small stores and two cafes, plus a Pemex gasoline station that sells some auto parts. It's about 57 1/2 miles from Ensenada. A dirt road leads to the ruins of the **Santa Catarina Mission** that was founded in 1797. The next place to purchase supplies is 18 miles down the road at **Valle de la Trinidad**, rapidly growing from what was a tiny village a few years ago to a town of more than 12,000 people, with stores, cafes, a bank, a school, a tire repair shop and gasoline station. The latter has a mechanic available (a rarity in Baja California's interior).

Almost 11 miles beyond Valle de la Trinidad a good dirt road connects the main highway with **Mike's Sky Rancho,** 22 miles to the south. It can also be reached by way of Highway 1 at Colonet, but that road is too rough to be driven by passenger cars. From a knoll, the Rancho overlooks Arroyo San Rafael, a wooded valley surrounded by steep, brush-covered mountains, where hunters find deer, rabbit, quail and dove, with a small stream through it that occasionally yields trout. There are motel-type accommodations, with family-style meals and a swimming pool. Campsites are available, with guided trips into the surrounding mountains to the east. There's a 5,000-foot graded airstrip six miles north of the ranch for those who have their own airplanes. Reservations are advised. Write Post Office Box 1948, Imperial Beach CA 92032; (619) 428-5290.

Nine and a half miles farther east on Highway 3 there's a turn off to San Felipe via a sandy road that should not be attempted by the average traveler, who would be better advised to stay on the main highway. The sandy road leads through a wash to the pass of the Sierra San Pedro Mártir. Climbers start their ascent of **Picacho del Diablo** from Cañon El Diablo, 20 miles south of the junction. It is a difficult climb, and should not be attempted except by experienced climbers, preferably with a local guide who knows the area. This is a desolate, primitive area and it is NOT for the uninitiated.

About seven miles further along Highway 3 a new road intersects the main route – Villa del Sol – and provides a better access to this area and to San Felipe beyond.

Highway 3 intersects Highway 5 at Crucero La Trinidad about 32 miles north of San Felipe, after a trip that totals some 123 miles from Ensenada.

For those with limited time and resources, the route from Tijuana, Ensenada, San Felipe, Mexicali and back to Tecate or Tijuana is an ideal weekend jaunt. It involves only one night's lodging, at San Felipe, with good places to eat in-between and truly captivating countryside along the way.

HIGHWAY 1 SOUTH TO SAN QUINTIN

The main Highway 1 to all points south on the peninsula extends from Ensenada through a number of small villages.

There are two camp sites eight miles west of Maneadero at Punta Banda on the shores of Bahía de Todos Santos that can be reached on BCN 23. The **La Jolla Beach Camp** has hookups for 120 RV's and 180 tent sites. It is exceptionally well equipped, with a beach, boat launch, and tennis court. Some groceries can be purchased at the store. The fee is $6.50 for two people, and $2 for each additional person. No reservations are required. Their mailing address for further information is Punta Banda, Apartado Postal 953, Ensenada, Baja California, Mexico. The **Villarino Camp** has much the same accommodations with higher fees of $12 per couple, and $4 for each additional person. Reservations are advised. Write Apartado Postal 842, Ensenada, Baja California 22800, Mexico. Or call (667) 6-4246.

Once Maneadero is passed, the road begins to climb into the coastal mountains. There are ample warnings against speeding, but they are largely superfluous: most cars barely crawl as the road winds upward in tight switchbacks.

At the crest of this range the green vineyards of the **Santo Tomás Valley** provide a welcome respite to the barren countryside. There is only one place to camp, **El Palomar Trailer Park** on the north side of Santo Tomás. They have hookups for 50 RV sites and a large area for tents. There's a restaurant and bar, a place to purchase fuel, and a curio shop. The fee is $11 for two people, and $2 for each extra person. They can be contacted by writing Apartado Postal 595, Ensenada, Baja California, Mexico. **El Palomar Motel** is next to the Pemex gas station and curio shop. It has only five rooms, although they do have showers and double beds. Call (667) 7-0650.

The Santo Tomás Valley is 34 miles south of Ensenada. Today, rows of grapevines, taken from the best of European and California rootstock, provide some of the best wines in Mexico. The narrow valley nestles between high mountains, extending eastward for more than 12 miles before ending in a marshy delta to the west on the Pacific coast.

One can almost believe the old tale that Spanish priests found the valley's soil so rich that, when one of the padres left his walking stick in the ground by mistake, within days it sprouted leaves.

Dominican priests founded a mission there when the Indians proved peaceful and they called it Santo Tomás de Aquino – Saint Thomas of Aquinas – who was revered by the Dominicans. The valley was renamed the Valle de Santo Tomás.

The valley proved ideal for raising grapes to make mission wines for Mass. Early Spanish colonists at first were forbidden by the Crown to cultivate grapes and olives, in order to protect industries in Spain. Jesuit priests, and later the Franciscans and Dominicans, each insisted that wine was needed for communion, and that there was no way to get wine from Spain to Baja's interior missions. At Santo Tomás, the Dominicans secretly brought cuttings from Spain and planted them, then began production using an ancient Dominican wine-making process. Eventually, the government gave permission, if the missions agreed to provide wine for the Spanish aristocrats as well as for Mass.

In nearby Ensenada there are two of Mexico's finest wineries. The Bodegas de Santo Tomás came first and, much later, the Spanish firm of Casa Domecq was established in the city. These wineries also use grapes grown in the Guadalupe Valley.

The first grapevine cuttings were brought to the mission at San Javier in the southern part of the peninsula by Jesuit priests in 1687. Soon the practice spread up the peninsula and into Alta California. Both Californias proved to have excellent growing conditions for wine grapes similar to those grown in regions of Spain.

The Santo Tomás Valley proved particularly good because days are hot and nights are cool due to coastal fogs. The soil is perfect because it is made up of decomposed granite and therefore highly porous. In 1800, there were 5,000 grapevines in Santo Tomás, irrigated by nearby springs through stone aqueducts. But by 1840, when mission properties were taken over by the Mexican Government, the Santo Tomás vineyards were abandoned. Two Spaniards. who had emigrated to upper California in 1883, reclaimed them and founded the Bodegas de Santo Tomás Winery five years later. In 1906, Russian immigrants brought their own cuttings and established extensive vineyards. Twenty years later, General Rodríguez acquired the Santo Tomás Winery.

Highway 1 crosses a level plateau south of Santo Tomás and Rancho Costeño spreads for miles on the left side of the road in a vast agricultural valley where *vaqueros* round up cattle in swirls of dust devils. The scene is reminiscent of the American West a hundred years ago. There are thousands of acres of rich farmland under cultivation, and they seem to extend to the east almost endlessly. Such large ranches are uncommon because of the perennial shortage of water, but Baja's ranchers are the most self-reliant in the world, performing miracles of desert reclamation while others shake their heads in disbelief. Like America's early pioneers, they have learned to do most things themselves. Here and there are fields of red chili peppers that add a bright touch to an otherwise drab countryside.

In the past, dry farmers have often tried and failed in Baja. They did not take into account the fact that the peninsula lies at approximately the same latitudes as the Saharan, Arabian, Kalahari and Atacama deserts. There are parts of Baja that get rain only in traces for years at a time. Only the lower end of the peninsula gets tropical summer storms typical of those that reach the Mexican mainland. In effect, both ends of the peninsula receive most of the moisture, while the middle section – particularly the Vizcaíno Desert – goes almost rainless. These areas are dry because the mountains in the peninsula's center cause the prevailing westerly winds to rise and, after cooling at night, moisture condenses and falls on the western slopes. Meanwhile, the gulf-side mountains, with their granite peaks rising over 10,000 feet, provide a barrier that effectively keeps moisture from falling on the eastern side, where the slopes descend abruptly to the waters of the Gulf of California.

Mountain meadows are rich with plant growth because they receive moisture from summer and early fall storms out of the Pacific Ocean. Blue lupines and red penstemons provide a carpet of color while manzanita with its red branches and gray-green leaves rise above white and purple sage. At lower elevations, the mountains have large groves of pine trees, cottonwood, aspen, live oak and junipers. Higher up, forests thin out and only the hardy Jeffrey Pines subsist in the colder temperatures. On Picacho del Diablo the peak is solid rock with little or no vegetation.

About 52 1/2 miles south of Ensenada, Highway 1 passes through **San Vicente**. This busy farming center has a growing population in excess of 8,000. It includes gas stations, automobile repair places, cafes and stores. There is only one motel, **El Camino**, which has 10 rooms, only four of them with bathrooms.

The next place for goods and services is **Colonet**, another 13 miles along Highway 1. Farmers and ranchers in the area use it for their own supplies. There are two side routes with adequate dirt roads to the coast from here but facilities at San Antonio del Sur and Cabo Colonet are limited, and often downright primitive. The fishing at both places is excellent.

South of Colonet you catch occasional glimpses of the Sierra San Pedro Mártir across cultivated fields to the east, including the highest peak, Picacho del Diablo. The southern end of these mountains is still largely a virgin wilderness, almost untouched by the hands of men since the days of the early

Spanish explorers. There are a few rough trails across these mountains, but they should be used only by experienced mountain climbers. Some of the people who live here belong seemingly to another age, living off the land as their ancestors did hundreds of years ago.

The people who live on the old **Meling Ranch** are an exception. Harry and Ella Johnson came from Texas in 1889 and founded a ranch 150 miles below the border. In 1910, they bought Rancho San José, 2,000 feet up on the western slope of Picacho del Diablo. They learned to become self-sufficient, growing their own food, raising cattle for meat and making butter and cheese. Despite several years of severe drought that drove most other European and American settlers from Baja California, the Johnsons survived. They were helped, in part, by Harry's success in mining gold from the mountains. He recovered a quarter of a million dollars in gold from gravel river beds. He succeeded where others failed because he built an eight-mile-long aqueduct to bring water to his mining claims. It was a hard but satisfying life, and the young daughters worked cattle with the men. One of the daughters, Alberta, died in the 1970's at the age of 93. She was a dominant personality and worked as a cowboy, hunter, cook and housekeeper.

When the Mexican Revolution took place in 1911 their employees were forced to quit the gold mine at Socorro, so Harry Johnson left for San Diego. After he departed, bandits raided Rancho San José, burned the buildings and slaughtered the cattle. Alberta's brother rounded up loyal *vaqueros* and went after the bandits. They killed every one of them.

Alberta later married Salve Meling, a British-born son of Norwegian parents who had settled in Ensenada. They acquired the 60,000-acre Rancho San José from the Johnson family in 1919, and it became known as the Meling Ranch. For most of their lives they lived in almost total isolation from the rest of the world. When the transpeninsular highway was completed December 1, 1973, she was one of the first to drive to the tip on her 90th birthday.

The Meling's hospitality to travelers from all over the world became legendary. Guests became so numerous by 1944 that the Meling children insisted that Rancho San José become a guest ranch. Salve was horrified. "Charge my guests for coming to visit? Never!"

The children persisted, knowing that the family no longer could treat their numerous visitors as non-paying guests. Alberta and Salve reluctantly bowed to economic necessity and daughter Aida Meling Barre took over management of the guest ranch, while son Philip continued to operate it as a cattle ranch. The long drought between 1949 and 1963 was so severe that Meling cattle were reduced from 3,000 to 150. The remainder had to be taken to high mountain meadows to save them.

There is a private airfield near the Meling Ranch at San Antonio del Mar, about 60 miles south of Ensenada. The ranch is not as primitive as it used to be, but it does not have all the modern conveniences that tourists have come to expect. Guests use kerosene lanterns in their rooms. But the main buildings have electricity from the ranch's own generating plant.

The Meling Ranch can be reached by automobile if you turn off Highway 1 eight miles south of Colonet, then take a 31-mile road that is graded most of the way. It can be driven by a passenger car in dry weather. This is a winding road for the first six miles until San Telmo is reached. This small village lies in a beautiful bowl-shaped valley. Beyond San Telmo the road climbs into the foothills. Seventeen miles from Highway 1, another road branches off to Mike's Sky Rancho while the road to the Meling Ranch continues straight ahead through low hills. The Meling Ranch lies in a deep valley while the road continues on to the National Observatory located on a 9,000-foot plateau across from Picacho del Diablo. Adjacent to the observatory are forests of pine and fir, with mountain meadows and freshwater streams. From the grounds of the observatory there is a breathtaking view of Picacho del Diablo with the desert far below and the Gulf of California in the distance.

The Meling Ranch has 10,000 acres and offers excellent accommodations, with family-style meals, a swimming pool, horseback riding, and pack trips into Sierra San Pedro Mártir National Park. For information and reservations, write Apartado Postal 1326, Ensenada, Baja California, Mexico. There is a graded 3,500-foot airstrip just east of the ranch.

Highway 1 widens somewhat – never enough to make it truly safe – as it crosses a level plateau dotted with occasional farms south of Colonet. It dips steeply into Camalú before emerging on a flat coastal plain. But the beauty of the surroundings lies to the east as you near **Colonia General Vicente Guerrero**, where you see a view of the San Pedro Mártir with the ocean ahead of you. The most distinctive local features are the volcanic cones of the Bahía de San Quintín that lie straight ahead. This is a busy agricultural center with a full range of needed facilities for the average traveler – a hospital, gasoline station, stores and cafés.

Colonia Guerrero has two parks about a mile south off Highway 1. **Meson de Don Pepe RV Park** has 40 RV and 20 tent sites with good hookups and a restaurant. The fee is $7 for two people, with $1 for each additional person. Tents can be rented for $2.50. Their mailing address is Apartado Postal 7, Colonia Guerrero, Baja California, Mexico. The **Posada Don Diego** is beyond this park on an unpaved road, but it's a good spot with 100 RV or tent sites. The fee here is $19 for two people, and $1.50 for each additional person. Their mailing address is Apartado Postal 126, Colonia Guerrero, Baja California, Mexico. Call 01152 (666) 6-2181.

San Quintín is 14 1/2 miles from Colonia Guerrero with the Valle de San Quintín ending at a U-shaped bay. The bay separates cultivated fields from a row of volcanic cones on a long peninsula thrusting south, almost meeting a smaller projection from the mainland. Between the two is the passage to the inner bay.

Jacob P. Lease, who settled in Alta California in 1833, and Santiago Vizosco of Mexico, in March, 1863 obtained from the Government of Mexico a land concession that extended from the Gulf of California to the Pacific Ocean between the 26th and 31st parallels of latitude. In effect, the land reached from a point 100 miles south of the American border in the vicinity of Colonet to well below the middle of the peninsula. The concession included all islands, ports, bays, harbors and fisheries from the Gulf to the Pacific side. It amounted to 50,000 square miles of land, or 12 million acres. The agreement was signed in New York City on November, 1865, and was sealed by the payment of only 100,000 American dollars. President Juárez of Mexico formally ratified the contract in the City of Chihuaha the following August.

The corporation that was formed to administer the land hired J. Ross Browne, former U.S. treasury agent for the West Coast. This noted author and traveler engaged competent men from science and industry to explore the country. In January, 1867, the proprietors were incorporated in New York as the Lower California Colonization Land Company. But, like so many undertakings before it, this one failed to earn money for its backers – despite the small investment.

Although Baja remained a part of Mexico, Americans continued to move there to establish cattle ranches and farms, while exploring for precious metals. A San Franciscan raised cattle on the Vizcaíno Desert near the 28th parallel, and he made several drives of a thousand cattle each north to his native city. These drives over rugged and forbidding terrain often took several months.

An Englishman set up an enterprise to collect lichen called roccella that grows on trees from the Vizcaíno Desert south to the Magdalena Bay. In combination with indigo, roccella was valuable for dyeing silk and woolen fabrics red or violet. Hundreds of Mexican workers gathered the moss, until the Germans developed coal tar dyes that proved more effective. The lichens still adorn the trees, but they have no use today.

President Porfírio Diaz further opened up the peninsula to foreign investors in the last 20 years of the 19th century. American business interests took advantage of the liberal agreements and the Hartford Company of Connecticut was just one of many that invested. They reportedly paid $5 million out of a total commitment of $16 million to develop land now known as Baja California Norte from the 28th parallel to the present U. S. border. Among their ambitious plans was a railroad from San Diego to San Quintín – 200 miles south of the border – to connect with ports at San Quintín and Ensenada. It was thought that these ports would ship thousands of tons of wheat that the company hoped to grow. The years of drought that followed soon doomed the project to failure. The Americans sold out to an English firm for $7 million. So convinced were officials of the English firm that the project would be successful that the men brought their families. Flour mills were built, connected by a railway with a small English steam engine, and dozens of English-style homes were built at San Quintín. Countless acres were sown in wheat, but the rains failed to arrive when they were needed, and the English firm had to admit defeat. Most of the colonists either returned to England, or tried their luck as miners or cattlemen. Today there are numerous descendants of these settlers throughout the peninsula and English surnames are common.

San Quintín South to Cataviña

SAN QUINTIN

In the late afternoon at San Quintín gulls soar gracefully above the bay, dipping and wheeling as the sun goes down, with their raucous calls filling the air. This is an angler's paradise, but few fishermen are ever here to take advantage of it. In the past, black brant, a type of goose, lured hunters from all over the United States and Mexico, but this is no longer true.

In a wind-swept cemetery near town many of the original English settlers are buried. Here lie the remains of scores of English people who ended their dreams in a foreign land. These early pioneers, like the Spanish and other foreigners to the peninsula in the early years of colonization, were a hardy breed who struggled to survive in a difficult environment. Their descendents are still tough because nine tenths of Baja California's land is as empty as when Spanish explorers first saw it. Actually, many of Baja's interior villages have fewer people than they did a hundred years ago. Even today much of the interior is as virgin as it was before white men arrived. Ranches are widely scattered and ranchers raise cattle and staple crops. Basically, these people live off the land, enjoying an existence that is uncomplicated by modern conveniences.

During the early years only the most daring attempted traveling over the peninsula's dirt roads. Those who made the 850-mile trip from La Paz to Ensenada found it an excruciating experience. Men rode horseback while women traveled in *carretas* whose screeching wooden axles could be heard for miles. Despite their almost desperate existence, these early settlers learned to love their adopted country with its lonely grandeur and hint of mystery.

Hotels

An old grist mill with some of its original machinery, is now part of San Quintín's **Old Mill Motel.** For years Al Vela and his wife Dorothy, the owners, ran a gourmet restaurant that was famous throughout Baja. Vela learned to cook at the Waldorf Astoria Hotel in New York. San Quintín has changed much in recent years, and now has a population of 22,000. The Old Mill (Molino Viejo) Motel is on the eastern shore of San Quintín Bay, four miles west of Highway 1. It's on a dirt road which is rough but passable with care. Single rooms range up to $32, and doubles to $40. Extra persons in rooms cost $9 each, and some double rooms have kitchenettes. One unusual feature is provided by the motel. Its guest's cars are provided with mechanical services. There's a nearby 2,000-foot airstrip. The mailing address is Apartado Postal 90, Valle de San Quintín, Baja California, Mexico. Call (619) 428-2779 in San Ysidro for reservations.

There are several other motels/hotels including the best, **Hotel La Pinta** – two and a half miles west of Highway 1 on the paved road that takes you to outer San Quintín Bay. This is a modern, beach-front hotel with modern prices of $60 for a single or $66 for a double room. Each extra person is charged $11, with a maximum of four people to a room. Their mailing address is Apartado Postal 168, Valle de San Quintín, Baja California, 22930, Mexico. Their toll-free number is (800) 336-5454. **Motel Chávez** on Highway 1, one and a half miles north of the military camp, is a family-style hotel with modest prices of up to $29 for a single or double, but there are no

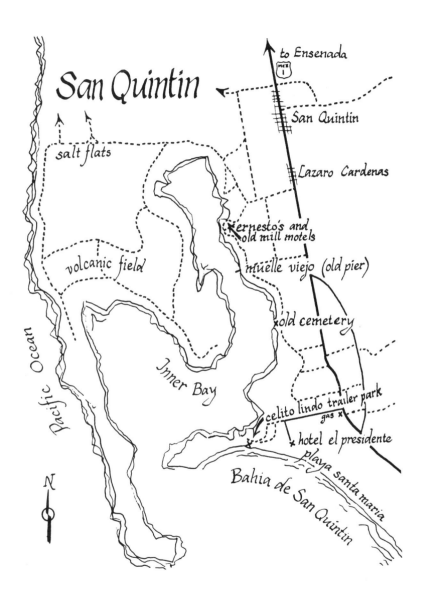

San Quintin

to Ensenada

MEX 1

San Quintin

Lazaro Cardenas

salt flats

Ernesto's and old mill motels

muelle viejo (old pier)

volcanic field

old cemetery

Inner Bay

celito lindo trailer park
gas ×

hotel el presidente

Pacific Ocean

playa santa maria

Bahia de San Quintin

N

dining facilities. Mailing address is Apartado Postal 32, Valle de San Quintín, Baja California 22930, Mexico. Call (666) 5-2005. En route to the **Hotel La Pinta** on the eastern shore of the outer bay and three miles west of Highway 1, is the **Cielito Lindo Motel,** whose single rate is $36, with doubles up to $43. There is a graded 2,800-foot airstrip 200 yards east of the hotel. Hotel employees are alerted when a pilot buzzes the hotel, indicating a pickup is needed. Their mailing address is Santa Maria #7, Valle de San Quintín, Baja California, Mexico. A trailer park here charges $6.

There are two other modest, smaller motels. **Ernesto's** has 10 rooms – two with kitchens – and there is a nearby restaurant. It's located three miles off the highway along a dirt road to the shore of the bay. The **Old Pier Motel** also has 10 rooms, plus a restaurant in the same area.

San Quintín also has a campground, **Honey's RV,** nine miles to the south off Highway 1 on a dirt road. It has an open area with access to the beach and 27 RV or tent sites with hookups. The charge is $5.45 per vehicle.

HIGHWAY 1 SOUTH OF SAN QUINTIN

South of San Quintín, Highway 1 narrows to 19 1/2 feet and there are no shoulders on the sides. There is an abrupt drop of three feet from the road's crown to the ground. This is an arid region of white sand dunes merging into coastal hills until a high plateau is reached north of El Rosario. From the plateau the road dips into a wide valley, in the center of which is the small agricultural community of **El Rosario**. This town once was considered the last outpost before entering the wilds of Baja.

Although cacti are numerous all over Baja, the peninsula's reputation as the world's largest cactus garden becomes more apparent from here on. Some 80 of Baja's 110 varieties grow nowhere else on earth.

After El Rosario, the highway turns inland, and travels down the middle of the peninsula en route to Cataviña. This is a rock-strewn land intermixed with clumps of cacti. The true ruggedness of the peninsula's interior is apparent as the road traverses a seemingly endless number of hills. There are mesas or isolated hills with steeply-eroded sides and level tops, and sharply-etched arroyos or ravines that were carved by floods centuries ago. A step off the road warrants caution because each shrub seems to be armed with thorns that pierce the flesh at a touch and can cause excruciating pain.

Desert Plants & Animals

Many of the desert's trees are strange, often with grotesque forms. The cirio looks like an upside-down green carrot, whose trunk sprouts branchlets the size of a pencil on its tapered stalk. It is just one of many trees that grow only in Baja. Its name means wax candle, which it resembles. These trees now appear in vast numbers, and seem to grow in an absent-minded manner. Some are 50 feet tall, while others curve to make an arch, or grow every which-way. Some people call the cirio the boojum because an early botanist, seeing the tree for the first time, thought it resembled the legendary plant that supposedly grows on deserted islands. Lewis Carroll wrote about boojums in his book "Hunting of the Snark."

Some parts of Baja's deserts get almost no rain, and cirios grow best where rain is infrequent. This particular area is ideal for cirios because it gets only an inch or two of rain every few years. Few desert plants can survive with such a lack of moisture, but the cirio's spongy trunk stores water whenever it is available. During drought periods, the leaves fall off and even its slender branches wither. Although it may appear to be dead, a sudden rain will cause the cirio to spring to life with new leaves and tassels of cream-colored flowers.

Another outlandish specimen is the elephant tree – leafless during dry periods and with branches tapering outward in a contorted fashion. Its elephantine branches and brittle twigs led to its name. Once the rains start to fall it springs to life with lovely pink flowers that cover its branches, similiar to the flowers of peach trees. Like the cirio, the elephant tree's swollen body and weird trunk-like limbs store water to survive the dry spells.

Thousands of cardón cacti, looking like the Arizona saguaro but a strain of their own, litter the interior's landscape. Each starts as a massive trunk that branches in all directions. Those cardón that have died leave only their ribs standing. These iron-hard slats are supple and widely used throughout the interior country as building materials, or for barbecuing meats because the wood burns down to glowing coals.

The ground throughout this area is often covered by groups of agaves growing amongst large boulders. Many are so-called century plants, though they do not take a century to blossom. Once they bloom, after years of growth, the plants die. All agaves store water and food in their fleshy leaves and stems. Some resemble artichokes, and the heart of this plant can be cooked underground in a fire pit of hot stones. It makes a nourishing vegetable. Throughout the centuries, agaves have saved many a desperate traveler dying of thirst. Its leaves can be squeezed to get a sweet-tasting water. The sap of the mescal agave is used to make a fiery liquor. Another agave produces a near-tasteless fruit, but it tints urine blood red. This is harmless, but many a non-native has had a joke played on him by Mexicans.

One must always be careful walking in the countryside because there are all kinds of snakes and other creeping things that can be dangerous, including varieties of rattlesnakes. Scorpions are common, some reaching a length of six inches. They have changed little in the past 400 million years, having originally come from the sea and adapted to life on land. They shed their external skeletons periodically as they grow in size. A scorpion can easily be identified by the curved stinger at the tip of its tail. The stinger can be arched over its back with a downward motion to stab its barb into a victim and inject venom. Some are black or reddish brown, but others are sand-colored. Scorpions capture small bugs in pincers that look like the miniature claws of a lobster. They hide by day and operate at night. Fortunately, a scorpion will only sting a human being if it feels trapped. Seriously ill people, or children, feel the effects of the scorpion's venom the most, and their sting can be fatal for some people. In Baja many more people die of scorpion stings than from rattlesnake bites. Scorpions should always be treated with respect.

There are 18 varieties of rattlesnakes in Baja. Most people see them after they hear the familiar warning rattle, but the Santa Catalina rattler gives no such warning because it has no rattles. When surprised, it will wave its tongue and vibrate its tail but no sound is emitted. Although rattlesnakes may not see a person, they can strike with accuracy by sensing the body's heat several feet away. The red diamondback is the most dangerous. A full bite by this six-foot rattler can be deadly.

Kangaroo rats are so named because they have long hind legs and move by hopping. They are unique because of their ability to survive without drinking water. The kangaroo rat gets moisture from the plants it eats, and by eating only at night when evaporation is less. By day, it sleeps in underground burrows.

Desert toads spend most of their life underground in an almost deathlike state. They appear when it rains, returning to their burrows during dry periods.

The Sonoran Desert that covers much of the southwestern United States and northwestern Mexico, has created a climate where certain types of animal and plant life have adapted to survive. On the western side of the peninsula there are two deserts. They extend from El Rosario, 200 miles below the US border, to Cabo San Lucas at the peninsula's tip. In the Magdalena Plain the Mexican Government has tapped underground water to make farming possible. North of this plain is the Vizcaíno Desert that extends inland to the mountains. It is an awesome wilderness. Moisture and fog along the Pacific Coast provide some sustenance for growing things, but rainfall is scarce. As a result, only plants and animals that can live on limited amounts of moisture from condensation are able to survive. Surprisingly, their number is quite large. There are few large animals, however, and the most common belong to the rodent family. For the most part plants and animals in the center of the peninsula have had to adapt to their surroundings to survive. Most animal activity, for example, is at night to avoid high daytime temperatures. Buzzards usually are the only animals seen during the day. They are often visible hovering almost motionless in the sky as they search for dead animals on the ground.

The hierba de flecha, or sapium biloculare as it is known botanically, is not seen much anymore. Residents have always called it the arrow tree, and desert dwellers have long been aware of its dangerous properties. The early Indians advised the padres that if one slept beneath an arrow tree he would awaken with painful eyes. At first the Jesuit fathers refused to believe stories about the tree, particularly when cases were cited that some individuals were actually blinded after sleeping or resting under such a tree, It has long been known that the hierba de flecha does have a poisonous juice that affects the eyes, although it is not as dangerous as was once reported. Indians tipped their arrows with the sap, and they also used it to stun fish. If the wood is burned, the smoke can be profoundly irritating to the eyes.

Another shrub, a form of poison ivy known as the hiedra maligna, can cause skin irritations. It grows in arroyos or along the banks of dry streambeds.

Side Trip To Onyx Mine

For years onyx was mined at El Mármol (Spanish for marble), until the development of plastics eliminated most of its market. The Egyptians used onyx to make funeral urns and various pots and tubs, as did the Romans. There are many

Italian churches today with ornamental pillars of onyx, although this stone comes from mines in Algeria and not from Baja. The Aztecs also used the stone for a variety of purposes.

Gold prospectors found onyx deposits in Baja in the late 19th century. Today, the mine at El Mármol is owned by the Southwest Onyx and Marble Company. The area lies in the center of an arid mesa reached by taking a graded dirt road off Highway 1 two miles southeast of San Agustín. The road should not be attempted by passenger cars except in dry weather. After a half-mile the road meets the old peninsula route with a wooden corral on the right, and a gravel quarry. Look for a windmill after driving about a mile, then another corral, and turn right. The rest of the road travels through relatively open country. There is little available water except from the springs where the onyx is formed, but this is undrinkable. One can still see large blocks of onyx in delicate shades of pearl white, light green and rose. The veins of rose-red in some of the stones are particularly beautiful. Here, the onyx is so close to the surface that it can easily be cut by hand. When it was first mined, the onyx was taken by trucks 50 miles over rutted dirt roads to the Pacific coast, where it was shipped to San Diego. Later, it was trucked north.

In 1934, Kenneth Brown ran the quarry after succeeding his father. He and his wife lived at El Mármol for 25 years, with occasional visits to San Diego. Having little communication with the outside world, the Browns made their home as beautiful as possible under the circumstances. Despite the vast wasteland that surrounded their home, Mrs. Brown maintained a beautiful garden.

The mine was located only a few miles from their home. It was in a canyon that today is accessible only by horses or burros. At the bottom of the canyon a carbonated spring deposits a lime crust that eventually becomes onyx through a chemical process. Lime is soluble in water, and it becomes more soluble if it is acidified by carbon dioxide. As the lime-impregnated water reaches the surface, the water evaporates and limestone, marble or onyx is formed – depending upon the type of crystals that are created. For onyx to form, the carbonation must be slowly released and the water heavily carbonated. The springs at El Mármol have produced onyx for thousands of years, and some of the colors are spectacularly beautiful. Colors are determined by impurities in the solution. If there is the right amount of iron and manganese present, brown and mahogany colors predominate. Delicate greens are caused by organic materials.

Some of the springs resemble those in Yellowstone Park except that here they are much smaller. Unlike the springs at Yellowstone that emit steam, those at El Mármol release gas and the water is cold. For generations the natives have called the place "El Volcan." This is a fitting name because the gas comes from deep in the earth in an area long known for volcanic activity.

Near the springs, an arroyo displays alternating bands of soft limestone and onyx. Unlike hard marble, limestone is soft. In contrast, onyx is harder than either one. Therefore, it takes a high polish, resists staining, and until the age of plastics it was widely used for desk sets and art works. Through the years, onyx has also been used for mantels, table tops, and ornaments.

All that remains today of El Mármol are a dozen or so dilapidated frame structures, plus a one-room school house and a jail made of onyx. These buildings are unpolished, rough and dull in appearance.

Valley Of Ancient Fossils

Fifty miles west of El Mármol, near where a road was constructed to transport onyx to the coast, there is a small valley whose floor is strewn with fossils of an ancient time. At first, the fossils look like huge snail shells several feet in diameter. They are not snails but ammonites – a form of cephalopod that was especially abundant during the Mesozoic era when dinosaurs were most numerous. This period started 280 mil-

lion years ago, and probably ended 65 million years before
the present. Here in Baja, when the sea left this land, the
ammonites were stranded. The former ocean bottom then
turned into a desert and the shells of the ammonites became
fossilized. Unlike the more familiar land and sea shells,
these strange creatures are related to the squid and octopus.
They had a head seemingly wrapped in tentacles whose body
protruded from a curved shell that resembles the horn of a
ram. The name ammonite is derived from the Egyptian god
Ammon, whose symbol was the ram. They used a form of jet
propulsion to move from one place to another. Ammonites
probably died out in Baja 50 to 100 million years ago.

A mammoth's skeleton has been found in the middle of the
peninsula. The huge creatures lived during the Ice Age that
began three million years ago, when ice covered much of the
northern hemisphere. Farther south there are fossilized
bones of bison, horses and camels. Near Punta Prieta, fossil
remnants have been found of a primitive horse called hyra-
cotherium. Unlike today's horses, this animal was about the
size of' a dog. Some horse and camel bones show charring so
they may have provided food for the aborigines.

At La Purisima farther south, fossils of oysters, scallops and
fragments of shark vertebrae give added proof that this area
once was covered by a sea.

In the opinion of most geologists, Baja broke away from the
mainland of Mexico about 20 million years ago. Before that
time, they believe the west coast of what is now Baja was hot
and humid, supporting a lush plant life far different from
today. Trees and plants that flourished under such conditions provided food for huge, duck-billed dinosaurs with massive hind legs and thick tails. Known today as hadrosaurs,
they could swim and had as many as a thousand teeth to
grind the aquatic plants and crustaceans that were their
principal foods. Near El Rosario, fossils of this 30-foot animal
have been dug from the badlands along the coast.
Hadrosaurs had an assortment of skull shapes. One had a
high-bridged nose, another's nose looked like a hatchet, a

third had a cockscomb, while still another animal had a nose shaped like a warrior's helmet with a swept-back projection from its head. Scientists disagree as to the utility of these crests. Some believe their long noses were used for snorkeling, or merely for improving their sense of smell to warn of possible predators.

There is evidence that there were other dinosaurs here – some 50 feet in length – who ate the flesh of smaller animals. Fossils also indicate that small mole-like mammals lived during this period as well.

HIGHWAY 1 TO CATAVIÑA

Traveling south on Highway 1 through the center of the peninsula one marvels at this unreal world of natural beauty with the distant mountains enveloped in a soft, blue haze.

Some of the international picture signs are intriguing, often bringing one's senses sharply back into focus. One of these signs warns speeders by using the familiar tortoise and hare story. The sign shows a happy tortoise sipping a cool drink under a palm tree while the impatient hare is carried away on a stretcher by ambulance attendants.

There are good accommodations at Cataviña. **La Pinta** hotel has 28 air conditioned rooms, 2 1/2 miles north of town, with an air-strip. It's a modern hotel with single rooms priced at $60 and doubles for $5 dollars more, with $11 for each extra person. Reservations can be made by mail to Apartado Postal 179, San Quintín, Baja California 22940, Mexico, or by calling (800) 336-5454. Adjacent to the hotel is the **Parque Natural Desierto Central de Baja California**, offering 48 RV or tent sites with hookups for $3.25 per site. A mile to the south, at a junction to a paved road, is the **Rancho Santa Inés**. Formerly an outdoor restaurant, it now offers dormitory accommodations with hot meals and refreshments. There's a paved air strip and a parking area for

planes. This is a favorite place for off-road vehicles and information is available to off-roaders from rancho personnel.

Beyond Cataviña the highway continues southeast through
a desolate, rock-strewn countryside. After climbing the
2,690-foot summit of Sierra Columbia, the road dips into
Laguna Chapala. This is a grassy dry lake bed where quail,
doves and rabbits abound during the rainy season. The road
stretches down a steep slope and across a valley studded
with cardón cacti and elephant and cirio trees. These exotic-
looking trees can be diverting, and drivers must keep their
eyes on the road rather than linger on the spectacular scenery.

As Highway 1 climbs into hilly country, only a few cirio and
elephant trees dot the landscape. There are steep dropoffs
and sharp curves in the road while flat-topped buttes are sil-
houetted on the horizon to the east. After crossing a sandy
plain, the road reaches a junction with the unpaved road to
Bahía San Luis Gonzaga and San Felipe far to the north.

The highway turns southwest and descends into the bleak
Vizcaíno Desert. This is one of the most desolate areas on the
peninsula, and only a few clumps of yuccas and salt bushes
break the monotony of miles of sand. The creeping devil or
caterpillar cactus thrives here and is aptly named, with
barbs that can inflict painful wounds. Each stalk may reach
10 feet, with a thickness of three feet, but it puts down roots
at intervals and seems to crawl over everything. Once the
older growth dies, the rest of the cactus feeds through new
roots that it has laid down so that each stalk becomes independent of those that have grown before. Eventually it turns
into a tangled mass that grows away from the original plant,
which in turn becomes dry and lifeless. The caterpillar cactus grows in such arid soil that it may gain only an inch of
length in a year's time. It has persistence, however, and
thrives under conditions that would overwhelm any other
plant – often growing for centuries. It has only one enemy:
man. Farmers are irrigating more and more acres in the

Magdalena Plain and plowing these cacti under to provide humus for the soil.

After Punta Prieta, the road winds through rolling hill country spotted with yucca validas, relatives of the Joshua tree, that make their first appearance in the valleys. Reaching a height of 25 feet, this tree yucca has rough bark, and gnarled branches that emerge from its upper trunk. They are members of the lilly family, and they thrive in the Vizcaíno Desert where they receive moisture from the western winds. They could not survive but for the attentions of night-flying yucca moths. The female moth collects pollen from the dill-scented flowers when they bloom in the spring. The flowers emerge in a cluster out of a clump of narrow leaves at the tip of each branch. The moth makes a ball of pollen that she deposits, along with her eggs, on the inside of a blossom. Half of the seeds produced by this process of pollination provide nourishment for the larvae when they are hatched. The seeds that are not eaten fall to the ground and root in the soil to continue the species.

Eight and a half miles north of Punta Prieta there is a junction on Highway 1 that leads to the Bahía de los Angeles. The road is paved and travels eastward toward barren mountains across a sandy plain dotted with typical central-desert vegetation. In the spring, wildflowers carpet the desert floor. After crossing for 10 miles, the road travels through a pass in the mountains, then descends to a dry lake. After 28 miles on this extension of Highway 1 there is a turnoff to a dirt road that goes to Mission San Borja, while Highway 1 drops quickly to the bay with a backdrop of mountains to the west and offshore islands jutting through the blue waters of the Bahía de los Angeles.

Mission San Borja

Father Jorge Retz at Santa Gertrudis had been hearing of a place the Indians called Adac that they said had water to irrigate farmland. On August 27, 1759, he founded a mission called San Francisco de Borja. It was named in honor of Señora María Borja, Duchess of Gandia. A former soldier, upon returning from service on the peninsula, he had taken employment with the duchess, and often told her of the privations suffered by the Jesuits in founding their missions. She was so moved by his revelations that she bequeathed a large sum of money upon her death in 1747 to found three missions. By 1767, with interest accumulating each year, the amount had grown to 70,000 Spanish pesos. Part of this money was used to start the new mission here and in appreciation the duchess was named as its benefactor. Wenseslao Linck was named padre, and this native of Bohemia soon had a thriving mission. In the mountains, he found places where 800 cattle could be supported on high meadows. Snow often fell on the mission during the winter months.

Padre Linck had to put down a rebellion by one tribe on the outskirts of his mission grounds. The men revolted because he would not permit Christianized Indian women to live with them, except as wives. The remote Mission San Borja is in a good state of preservation but the roads to it from either Rosarito or Highway 1 are only for high-clearance vehicles.

Bahía De Los Angeles

Padre Fernando Consag explored the Gulf of California in 1746 as far north as the Colorado River. His maps of the gulf were so accurate that they were used for years. This famous Jesuit explorer was responsible for the naming of Bahía de los Angeles, or the Bay of the Angels, and its large island offshore, Isla Angel de la Guarda or Guardian Angel Island. The strait between the shore and the island was called the Whale Channel or Canal de Ballenas. This area is still known for its California gray whales and turtles. Buccaneers used the excellent harbor in the upper gulf. In more recent years, it has been the haunt of smugglers, and most recently sport fishermen.

The Aguaje San Juan, or Spring of St. John, has provided water for thirsty travelers for centuries. It is close to the edge of the bay. Aborigines evidently used the waters because there are piles of clam and scallop shells nearby, as well as those of giant sea turtles. Scallops are still gathered here and shipped to markets in the north and to the Mexican mainland.

Missionaries marveled at the skill of the Indians when they speared turtles. They said it was done so expertly that the shell was pierced without killing the turtle. Some spears were equipped with pieces of leather to prevent their barbs from penetrating too deeply and seriously injuring the turtle. Indians with exceptional ability could throw their spears in such a way as to penetrate only two inches of shell where there are no blood vessels. In the days before refrigeration, it was important to keep the turtles alive until they were ready to be slaughtered for eating.

The catching of lobsters was unique. Natives waded into shallow water kelp beds, teasing the lobsters into action with their feet until their toes were siezed by a claw. The Indian then kicked the lobster out of the water so quickly that it lost its grip and sailed through the air just the right distance to land in the boat. Evidently the feet of these Indians were so toughened by going barefoot that a lobster's claws didn't hurt them.

Bahía de los Angeles is a natural harbor that is protected by the 45-mile length of Isla Angel de la Guarda, whose peaks rise up to 4,099 feet. A sandbar projects across the northern reaches of the bay, but it is submerged at high tide, while a headland on the south protects the bay from strong winds. In addition, islands form a barrier to shield the harbor. Anywhere else in the world such a magnificent harbor would have given birth to a large city. In Baja, water is the determining factor for growth, and the bay's one spring is completely inadequate to provide water for a large population. Despite its beauty, few tourists ever come to the Bahía de los Angeles because tourist facilities are limited.

The Gulf of California is only seven miles wide here – its narrowest section. Islands are numerous, numbering over 50, and ranging in size from Guardian Angel Island to rocky projections just above the surface of the water. Volcanic activity is common, and many smaller islands either change shape, disappear, or reappear each time there is an earthquake. These islands are all uninhabited, although Seri Indians once used Guardian Angel to hunt turtles and to fish the bay.

Inside the bay the current runs at five knots or higher which can pose problems for inexperienced sailors. Whales are common between the Baja shore and Guardian Angel Island. Finbacks are often 75 feet long, and weigh up to 80 tons. These baleen whales strain the sea water through comb-like whalebones in their jaws to obtain plankton as they move through the bay. Most finbacks remain outside the bay in the main channel, frequently traveling in pods of several dozen.

A phenomenal variety of fish inhabit the bay's depths that, in places, plunge to 3,000 feet. All but 10 percent of the known 586 varieties of fish that inhabit the gulf are found here in the Bahía de los Angeles. Yellowtail, roosterfish and dolphinfish inhabit the shallow waters in great numbers. Sharks prey upon them from the bay south to Cabo San Lucas. Most people shy away from shark meat, but there are many who insist that, when properly prepared, it is a tasty morsel. Throughout the Orient – particularly in China – shark is considered a delicacy. Some Chinese are convinced that eating shark meat will not only prolong their lives, but increase their sexual potency.

Southeast of Bahía de los Angeles, and south of Isla Angel de la Guarda, is a small island known as Raza. It is the only mass breeding and nesting ground for Heermann's gulls and elegant terns. These birds once numbered in the hundreds of thousands, but they faced extinction a few years ago.

Raza is part of a series of small islands. Each year in March the gulls would arrive first, breed, and then scratch nests in the soil. There were so many gulls in years past that they had to make nests two or three feet apart. By mid-March, nesting gulls appeared to cover the entire island. Then the terns arrived by the thousands, hovering over the nesting gulls, and trying to frighten them from their nests by their shrill cries and flapping wings. When this proved futile, the terns landed and scratched their own nests to lay their eggs between those of the gulls. By this time birds of both species were less than a foot apart. The gulls became maddened by the intrusion of the terns and they attacked, frightening many of the terns away and eating their eggs. The surface of the island became a madhouse of squalling birds as they fought for control of the island's surface. The terns put up a fierce fight, and some of them clung to their nests and refused to be frightened away. After reinforcements arrived, the battle momentarily turned in favor of the terns as dense flocks of similar birds joined to make war on the gulls.

In the past, those yearly battles helped control the huge numbers of terns and gulls. There were always enough of both that survived to perpetuate the species. This balance of nature changed drastically after hunters started to gather hundreds of thousands of eggs of both birds. They went first to the island to destroy all eggs in sight. In this way, they were assured that all eggs would be fresh when they returned a few days later. The birds still continued to survive in limited numbers despite these depredations because some eggs were hatched after the hunters left the island.

By the early 1960s, scores of hunters made more frequent visits to the island and nature's balance was almost irretrievably destroyed as the gulls and elegant terns were reduced to flocks of a few thousand. Royal terns survived this onslaught because they had other nesting grounds.

With extinction of the gulls and elegant terns a distinct possibility, conservationists became alarmed and urged the Mexican Government to take immediate action to save the birds. The government acted in 1964, and wardens now patrol the area during the mating season. As a result, the birds have shown a remarkable capacity to come back, although not as yet in the numbers of their former flocks.

The Colorado River, which has brought life to the gulf for millions of years, now is bringing unwanted pollution in the form of DDT This pesticide, largely banned in the United States, continues to drain into the delta. The problem with DDT is that it does not degrade quickly, maintaining its effectiveness in soil and water for years. One of its worst effects is to soften the egg shells of the gulf's birdlife through their diet of contaminated fish. Peregrine falcons have never been numerous, but one rarely sees them anymore. Ospreys and bald eagles have suffered the same effects. Pelicans are comparatively numerous, but their numbers are also being depleted.

RV Campgrounds

At Highway 1's junction with the road to the Bahía de los Angeles there is a camping ground with 40 sites for RVs or tent sites with hookups, and flush toilets, at **Parador Punta Prieta**. There are more extensive facilities at Bahía de los Angeles at **Guillermo's Trailer Park**, offering 40 sites with hookups plus a restaurant and bar. It is located on the beach, with a launching ramp for fishing trips. The fee is $5.50 for each site, and their mailing address is Fernando M. de Oca, No. 190-A, Fraccionamiento Buenaventura, Ensenada, Baja California, Mexico. **La Playa RV Park** is on the beach in town with 30 RV sites and a large area for tents, all with hookups. The fee is $5.50 per site. Their mailing address is Jimsair, 509 Ross Drive, Escondido CA 92025; or call (619) 298-4958. **Villa Vitta Motel** has 40 rooms priced between $36 and $60 for doubles or singles in the village of Bahía de los Angeles. Extra persons are $11 each. Mailing address is also Jimsair, 509 Ross Drive, Escondido CA 92025; or call (619) 298-4958.

Early Mining In The Area

A different breed of men came to the peninsula at the end of the 19th century. Greedy for the rich mineral deposits rumored to be mined with little effort, most of these men came to Baja to seek their fortunes and not to settle, like those who rushed west during the gold-rush days. Towns sprang up almost overnight around small deposits of gold, silver and turquoise, but few found riches. Some stayed to mine copper and iron, but most returned north of the border leaving ghost towns with crumbling adobes, holes in the ground, and ancient machinery rusting to the point of disintegration.

Water was the key factor to the success of any enterprise, just as it is today, and few of these men remained behind to live off the land by raising cattle or horses. Most who tried to become ranchers soon failed. Today there are wild horses and cattle descended from the small domestic herds left to fend for themselves after their owners gave up trying to farm this desert country.

Perhaps the most successful mine was established by a British company around 1890 and later sold to an American firm. It was located in the mountains 15 miles from the abandoned mission at San Borja and 12 miles south of Bahía de los Angeles. A tramway brought silver ore from the mine's head 3,500 feet above the plain down to a railroad at its foot. Then the tramway's buckets off-loaded the ore into waiting railroad cars that transported it to the mill at Las Flores. By 1910, two million dollars worth of silver had been extracted from the ground. And then the mine was abandoned.

Today Las Flores is a ghost town, and little remains but weathered buildings, the stone jail, rusted rail tracks, an old locomotive engine, and a cemetery with wooden crosses.

Through the years there have been rumors of ancient Indian mines whose entrances were boarded up by the greedy Spaniards. None has ever been found, despite innumerable treasure seekers.

Mines have been found with rich veins of free gold or quartz pockets with pure gold, but in the long run, these mines failed to be profitable. Even so, gold mining continued well into the 20th century.

Perhaps most mines were unprofitable because some miners skimmed the top-quality ore for themselves. One can still find "molinos de manos" where gold ore was secretly broken up and the free gold extracted. A "molino" is merely a rock hollow with a steel rod in its center. On top is a rock cap fitted so closely that few people ever notice that it is man-made, and that it has been chiseled out and polished to fit perfectly. A miner who purloined high-grade ore usually went off some distance into the desert away from the mine to a previously-prepared "molino de mano." Once its rock cap was lifted off, the miner used the hollow beneath it to grind the free gold loose from the quartz. The ore was then amalgamated with mercury and the pure gold removed.

GUERRERO NEGRO
& SCAMMON'S LAGOON

Inland, Highway 1 crosses a flat plain for miles as it approaches Guerrero Negro – 259 miles from San Quintín. At first the huge steel monument at the 28th parallel can be seen but dimly because of the coastal haze. Gradually it takes shape as the 135-foot "Monumento Aguila, " a modernistic version of Mexico's national eagle symbol, marking the division of the peninsula into two states.

Widely known as the breeding ground for the California gray whales at nearby Scammon's Lagoon, Guerrero Negro is also one of the world's largest salt-producing centers. It is a typical factory town surrounded by hundreds of salt-evaporation ponds along the coast.

Here on the west coast of Baja, a range of mountains extends 40 to 50 miles toward the Pacific Ocean. These mountains form a sickle-shaped headland where ocean currents from the south end in a huge eddy inside the Bahía de Sebastián Vizcaíno, named in memory of the Spanish explorer who first came here in 1602. For centuries ocean currents have gathered debris from the far Pacific and flung it ashore during high tides or storms. Even today the beaches are littered occasionally with glass globes used by fishermen in the Orient as floats for their nets. The action of sun and seawater often turns them a deep purple and the globes are prized by collectors. The surrounding desert sands are constantly in motion. Winds cover up debris in one area, only to expose it in others, seemingly at random. Oddly-shaped dunes form on the bay side and, when the winds are strong, shifting sands become airborne with an almost incredible scouring action that slashes at anything it touches.

Three lagoons open into the bay. Mañuela lies to the north, Guerrero Negro or Black Warrior Lagoon is in the center, and to the south is the very large Ojo de Liebre or Jack Rabbit Springs Lagoon – named for an old waterhole at the lagoon's eastern end. It is more commonly known as Scammon's Lagoon for the man who first found the breeding place of the California gray whales.

Inside the bay, wind and ocean currents have formed a huge basin that hides many an unknown ship after it has been wrecked by the vagaries of weather. The British ship *Black Warrior,* with millions of dollars in gold, lies somewhere in this area. The nearby city, and the center lagoon, are both named Guerrero Negro in memory of this ship.

Ojo de Liebre, or Scammon's Lagoon, plays host each year to the California gray whales after they travel 5,000 miles from the Bering Strait in February and March to bear their young in the protected waters here. When that happens the normally placid blue waters erupt as the whales put on a show of playful acrobatics. Woe betide anyone in a boat who comes between a mother and her baby. She will lash out in fury, and people have been killed when their boats were splintered and sunk. Once the young whales are reared, they all return up the Pacific coast to their home waters in the Bering Strait between the Pacific and Arctic Oceans.

For centuries gray whales – actually black in color but appearing a mottled gray once barnacles attach themselves to their hides – used the Baja lagoons unmolested by man. Scammon's Lagoon is one of several Baja lagoons that have been favored by the gray whales. The most southerly is at the Bahía Magdalena. One hundred and seventy five miles farther north is another: Bahía de Ballenas or Whales Bay. Here the 20-mile-long Laguna San Ignacio empties into the bay.

Scammon's Lagoon was ideal for the gray whales before whalers found the site and started to molest them. There are shoals here that enable mothers to lie in shallow water and give birth to their young. An infant can then raise itself to get sufficient air to breathe. Whales are mammals, not fish, so they must suck in large quantities of air before leaving the surface. But only gray whales seek shallow water for breathing. Other whales will often die in the shallows, suffocated by their own weight.

Prior to man's intrusion upon their breeding grounds, these 40- to 50-foot leviathans of the ocean frolicked in the lagoon without fear. It must have been an idyllic scene of huge nursing mothers, with spouts of vapor blowing high into the air like fountains as the whales exhaled moist air from their blowholes or nostrils, while the waters erupted occasionally as they hurled themselves out of the water in sheer exuberance – their barnacle-clad bodies slamming back with sounds like thunderclaps.

During their long journeys from the north, averaging 5 to 10 miles an hour, the gray whales evidently are able to communicate with one another, and they probably use coastal landmarks in addition to the sun and stars for navigating. In their haste to get to Baja's lagoons, the gray whales maintain so tight a schedule that they do not eat, living off their blubber to survive their exertions and the rigors of their long journey. They know they must reach the warmer waters or their babies will freeze if they are born in the frigid waters of the Arctic after ice begins to form.

Once calves are born, weighing more than a ton and 15 feet long at birth, they live on their mother's milk. Each calf feeds on a nipple under its mother's front fin through a slit in her side. To provide for her baby, a mother grazes continually, eating tons of plankton that she scoops from the surface down to a depth of 20 feet. Plankton are minute particles of live and dead plants, shrimp and other smaller forms of marine life. The mother must produce great quantities of milk every day because her baby puts on an average of 35 pounds per day following its birth.

In the mid-19th century, Charles M. Scammon was intrigued by reports from other whalers that there was a lagoon on the west coast of Baja California where whales gathered each year. Despite his best efforts, he sailed by the lagoon several times without spotting it. He was finally rewarded one day when one of his lookouts reported the sight of whale spouts on shore, seemingly coming out of the desert. Convinced that he had found the place, Scammon sent the smaller of his two ships and two whale boats to seek the entrance. The cutter and the whaleboats spent two days and nights before they were successful in locating the channel – almost impossible to find at low tide because it crossed a sandbar through a heavy swell. The cutter was dispatched into the lagoon first, finding that the channel was deep enough at high tide for Scammon's larger ship, which was sent in on the next high tide.

Scammon was astonished by the great number of whales at the extremities of the lagoon and he ordered whaling to get underway. He noted that during birthing, the bodies of the whales were so huddled together that it was difficult for whaleboats to pass through them. Two whales were quickly harpooned, but the others proved more elusive. When pressed, they turned on their attackers. So fierce were these attacks by what the seamen called "devil fish" that the sailors refused to continue against them. After some persuasion, Scammon got volunteers to try again. As these men approached the first whale, it turned to attack the boat, and the men jumped overboard.

In the following days, half of Scammon's men were injured as they tried to harpoon the whales. He tried anchoring his boats in shallower water by the edge of the channel, knowing that the whales could not pursue his boats there, and his men harpooned them in relative safety as the whales swam past in the deeper waters of the channel.

At dawn each day Scammon's whaleboats went out. Once a whale was spotted by one of the boats, a small flag was erected and they took off in hot pursuit. This flag indicated a prior claim to that particular whale; other boats honored it and did not follow. A whaleboat kept a short distance behind the whale and tried to drive it into the shoal waters of the lagoon. The hunt grew more exciting at times when the tormented whale tried to elude its pursuers. The race could go on for hours. If the whale had a cub, she was often at a disadvantage because she had to match her speed to the limitations of her offspring. Thus, she was easier to take.

Once a whaleboat reached a distance of 18 feet from a whale, a harpoon was dispatched and, after striking, the whale usually went into a frenzy, lashing with its tail. If a whaleboat failed to keep proper distance, it was smashed easily by the thrashing tail.

Once a harpoon was set properly, the boat's officer waited for an opportunity to shoot a bomb-lance that would explode and, if it reached a vital spot, would kill the whale. Oftentimes, several bomb lances were required to kill a whale. Perhaps the most dangerous aspect of whaling was the setting of a hand lance at close range to pierce the whale's heart.

Kelp beds became refuges for whales at first, but so relentless were the pursuers that they quickly learned these beds could become death traps if they lay in shallow water.

It was brutal and dangerous work for boat crews and many sailors were either killed or maimed for life. Even a mortally wounded whale could be dangerous, particularly if she had a calf with her, because she would unexpectedly turn ferociously upon her pursuers. At times boat crews had to rush for shallow water when an enraged whale, goaded beyond endurance, took after them.

After Scammon returned to his home port of San Francisco loaded with whale oil and whale bone following a few weeks at sea, the other whalers did their best to learn where he had killed so many whales in such a short time. Whalers normally took four to five years at sea before they could fill their holds. Scammon's crew members worked on shares so when he swore them to secrecy, they kept their mouths shut about where they had been.

When Scammon secretly departed again for the lagoon on the west coast of Baja, returning again in a few weeks with full holds, excitement mounted to a fever pitch. While other whalers searched in vain to learn the secret of this "whale paradise" discovered by Scammon, he made plans to increase the size of his fleet during the next season.

The following year other whalers decided to follow him, and a horde of ships set out in pursuit although he departed at night. The pursuing ships were so numerous that, despite doubling back and using other evasive maneuvers, he was never able to completely elude them. Due to the nature of the narrow entrance to the lagoon, he was successful again in getting his growing fleet of ships inside without being spotted.

Later, an alert lookout on one ship cruising back and forth off Cedros Island smelled the odor of whale blubber being cooked to separate the oil. The captain of the ship gave orders to follow the scent, and he was soon rewarded by another cry from a lookout who said the spars of ships could be seen as if they were sprouting from the desert. As before, the lagoon was hidden by surrounding low hills. Closer in, whale spouts were seen rising up to 15 feet, again seemingly coming out of the desert sands. Even with Scammon's ships located, it was some time before the entrance to the lagoon could be pin-pointed.

On his fourth voyage, Scammon's fleet found 40 ships outside the channel, and this time eight followed him into the lagoon. Now that Scammon's secret was out, the area swarmed with whalers and the slaughter of these magnificent mammals, once numbering as many as 25,000, sickened even the whalers. Scammon wrote later that between 1846, when whaling started in the lagoon, and 1874 10,000 gray whales were slaughtered for their oil and whalebone.

After the turn of the century, the whales all but vanished. For a period, there were none at all sighted along the Pacific Coast, and it was feared they had all been eliminated. Actually, the gray whales still were active but they had changed their migratory habits and the few hundred remaining had gone to new breeding grounds off the coast of Korea in its warmer lagoons.

Once they were located there were numerous reports of boats being attacked without warning by the gray whales. With a high intelligence that baffled many a whaler, the grays would disappear from an area frequented by whale boats, but continue their placid ways when fishing boats were around. Whalers tried to fool the whales by using small boats with only two people, including one with a harpoon in the bow. The whales were not tricked for long. They soon avoided all small boats.

The extensive use of petroleum products probably saved all whales from extinction, but world-wide concern forced nations to regulate the slaughter of whales in the world's oceans. International agreements were signed in 1937, and again in 1946, that forbid the killing of gray whales. Although still low in numbers compared to a hundred years ago, the grays have made a comeback, and some now return each year to Scammon's Lagoon to bear their young, while a few seek the isolation of the Laguna San Ignacio farther south. Today the Mexican Government carefully guards the area as a refuge for whales.

In January, February and early March California gray whales can be seen in Scammon's Lagoon. A dirt road that branches off Highway 1, 5 1/2 miles south of Guerrero Negro, leads to the best view sites. The turnoff is marked by a sign that says Parque Natural de Ballena Gris or Gray Whale Natural Park. The road is graded, but rough in spots, with some loose sand. Passenger cars can make the trip, but it is advisable to drive slowly over the worst parts of the road. There are side roads off the main dirt road but signs with a picture of a whale provide direction along with an arrow to point the way. These side roads should not be used because they are private and are owned by the salt company. After four miles, salt dredges can be seen as the road crosses a levee between evaporating ponds. Ten miles farther, there is a small shack that serves as park headquarters. Beyond the building the road forks, and the dirt road to the left leads to a beach where one can get the best view of the whales in the lagoon. Overnight camping is permitted, but there are no facilities for tourists. In daytime, whales often are at some distance from this watch site so binoculars are advised.

Inland from the coast, salt-evaporation ponds are laid out in dreary monotony, each consisting of a low dike enclosing an area several acres in size. Modern technology is used to extract pure salt from sea water. If dried only by the sun, the mixture would not be pure salt because solid ingredients such as calcium carbonate, magnesium and sulphates in sea water are soluble at different stages. There are five stations, and each is under the direction of a water master, so all unwanted ingredients are separated as the sea water moves from one station to the next through canals linking each settling pond. After six months, sodium chloride ends up in the

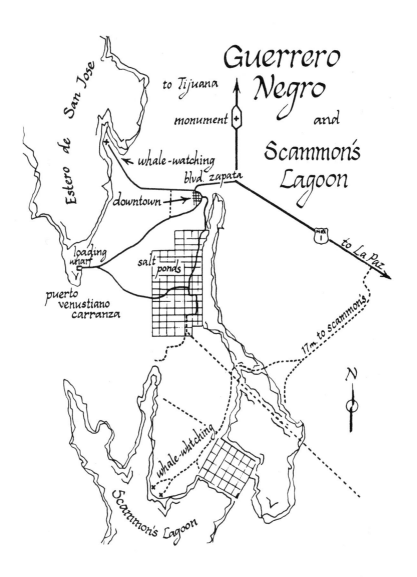

Guerrero Negro and Scammon's Lagoon

Estero de San Jose

to Tijuana

monument

whale-watching

blvd. zapata

downtown

loading wharf

salt ponds

puerto venustiano carranza

to La Paz

17m. to scammon's

N

whale-watching

Scammon's Lagoon

crystallizing basin and it is washed with heavy brine to remove any remaining impurities. This is one of the few spots in the world where salt can be produced so economically. It is then shipped to the United States, Canada and Japan.

Seals, along with the California gray whales, almost became extinct along Baja's Pacific coast because whalers and sealers during the 19th century systematically shot or clubbed them to death. Elephant and fur seals became so scarce by 1922 that the Mexican Government imposed a ban on future killings. One Pacific Coast island, Santa Guadalupe, was almost devastated by importations of goats to provide meat for whalers and sealers. The goats bred so fast that almost all of the island's plant life was destroyed, until little but weeds remained. Even worse was the destruction of plants used by birds for food and for places to nest. When cats were brought to the island by the sealers, the devastation of the bird population became almost total. The Mexican Government finally got rid of the goats, but the cats are as destructive as ever.

Fortunately a small herd of seals was found on Santa Guadalupe and they have formed the nucleus for a strong comeback up and down the coast. Both American and Mexican Governments now offer protection all along the Pacific coast, but their actions came almost too late to save the seals.

Hotels In Guerrero Negro

Other than fishing, and whale-watching in season, there isn't much to do in Guerrero Negro, and the accommodations reflect that fact. The **Dunas Motel,** located a mile west of Highway 1 on the road leading into town, charges $15 for a single, $18 for a double, with extra people at $2 each. Rooms have showers and they are neat and clean. Their mailing address is Boulevard Zapata y Division del Norte, Guerrero Negro, Baja California Sur, Mexico. In the same area is the **Hotel El Morro** whose rooms are $13 and $22 respectively for singles and doubles, with a $3 charge for each additional person. For reservations, write Apartado Postal 144, Guerrero Negro, Baja California Sur Mexico 23940, or call 01152 (685) 7-0414.

The **Hotel Pinta**, at the 28th parallel near the monument that divides the peninsula, is quite modern and this is reflected in their prices of $60 for a single room and $65 for a double. An extra person in a room is charged $11 with a maximum of four people. Pets are strictly forbidden. The nearby airstrip can be reached by unicom (radio) on 122.8. There is also a dining room and bar. Their mailing address is Guerrero Negro, Baja California Sur, Mexico 23940, or you can call toll-free at (800) 336-5454.

There is only one good place for RVs and tent sites, which is **Malarrimo Trailer Park.** It's located on Highway 1 near its junction with the town's main road, and there are 22 sites with hookups, charging $5.50 per vehicle. Their restaurant specializes in seafood and Mexican food, and there's a bar and a local museum. They are open from 11 a.m. to 11 p.m. with dinners priced up to $14.

Highway 1 turns inland from Guerrero Negro en route to San Ignacio and crosses the Vizcaíno Desert diagonally at the center of the peninsula. It rides on the crests of mountain ridges, some of which drop hundreds of feet almost vertically into deep canyons, Driving this route is an awesome experience. There are few places in the world to match its loneliness as one travels for three hours or more without seeing another human being. This can be an eerie feeling, as if you are the last human being on the face of the earth. There is usually not another automobile, an animal or even a bird in sight along this route. In a state covering 28,450 square miles, there are approximately 340,000 people, and 52% of them live in La Paz.

South to San Ignacio

SIDE TRIP TO MISSION

SANTA GERTRUDIS

Mission Santa Gertrudis is one of the best preserved of all the missions. Its belfry, rather than being placed on top of the church, is separate and some distance from it. Although it is a detour on the way to San Ignacio, and care should be exercised driving from Highway 1, it is well worth the trip.

Approximately 17 miles southeast of Guerrero Negro, Highway 18 leaves the main highway for El Arco about 26 miles down a paved road that normally is not well kept and often is severely potholed. For most of the distance the terrain is flat and uninteresting, but it changes to lush desert vegetation about six miles from the former gold-mining town of El Arco with its 200 inhabitants. South of town there's a landing field for airplanes, but the community has no tourist accommodations – although "Nova" or leaded gas is available in addition to some supplies.

From El Arco to the mission the road is rather wide and graded despite its dirt surface. This road begins where Highway 18's pavement ends, and a hard right turn puts you on it. Passenger cars should avoid it because of the frequent rough spots and high crown. The mission lies in a narrow arroyo approximately 23 miles from El Arco. You'll have to retrace your route to return to Highway 1.

Mission History

Explorations above the 28th parallel in the northern part of Baja had been limited after Loreto was founded in 1697, but Padre Fernando Consag and Military Commander Fernando Rivera y Moncada selected the first mission site 50 miles north of San Ignacio in 1752. It was named Santa Gertrudis, and its construction was placed in the charge of Andres Comanji Sestiaga, the blind Cochimí Indian who had helped to build several missions. Due to a shortage of adequate building materials, the original church was built of timbers with walls of mud and stones, and a red roof. Padre Jorge Retz, a German Jesuit, was sent to open the mission after learning the Cochimí language in San Ignacio. He soon had a mission with 1,500 baptized Indians and it prospered after the other missions contributed animals to get it started and put it on a self-sustaining basis.

A small spring was found nearby and a canal carved out of solid rock to bring water to the mission's grounds. Soon the fields were producing two crops a year. In contrast, the nearby mountains were covered only with scrub and small trees, and the desert surrounding the mission could support only cardón and other cacti.

The vineyards surrounding the mission proved fruitful, and a wine industry thrived for many years. Wooden casks were not available so containers were hewn out of stone to age the wine. These containers were sealed with wood covers and a gum taken from the pitahaya trees.

In 1918, the mission was turned over to Doña Luz Pico Romero, Viuda de Arias, who was given the keys to it by her mother-in-law, a part-Cochimí Indian. She supported her family of eight children after her husband died by selling the fruits and vegetables that were grown in the old mission's orchard. It is believed that the Romero part of her family dates back to Felipe Romero who was given a land grant at San Luis Gonzaga in 1768. The Pico family name may well descend from Pio Pico, the governor of Alta California.

Padre Fernando Consag explored farther north of Santa Gertrudis to seek other mission sites. His explorations in the upper part of the Gulf of California had convinced him that the area would not warrant further settlement. For several years, he found no suitable sites.

SAN IGNACIO

Twenty miles west of San Ignacio on Highway 1, a group of flat-topped cinder cones appear whose reddish-brown rocks indicate past volcanic activity. These rocks seem to have been tossed helter skelter by some prehistoric giant. It is more likely that they were spewed into the air from nearby volcanoes during eruptions hundreds of years ago.

To the north and south a few cattle ranches seem incongruous in this vast wasteland of low cactus-covered hills.

A paved road leads off to the right toward San Ignacio, an early mission settlement founded while the United States was still a British colony. This delightful oasis is halfway between the Pacific Ocean and the Gulf of California. The town is entered over a road that crosses a small dam in the bottom of a wide arroyo. Thousands of date palms, some planted in the 1730's, surround a fresh-water lake that, after the parched crossing from Guerrero Negro, looks particularly inviting. Thatched-roof dwellings and pastel-colored buildings are clustered around an old mission church that was erected by the Dominicans in 1786 to replace the earlier Jesuit church.

The Region's Early History

San Ignacio came into being after Padre Julián de Mayorga led a group of Christian Indians on an exploration trip northwest of Loreto in 1708. In a place that Indians called Comondú, Mayorga was pleased to find a well-watered valley surrounded by bluffs that had more land for farming than was usually found around other missions. Later, he founded a permanent mission here that he named San José de Comondú. Several rancherías were later joined together to form the pueblos of San Ignacio and San Juan. San José was selected as the site for the mission.

Two seminaries were built later: one for girls and the other for boys, along with a hospital. San Ignacio proved the ideal site for planting trees and grapevines and, through the years, abundant harvests were produced on a regular basis.

An American who visited Comondú in 1849 wrote of his trip to it through a barren region. "The earth, or rather the rocks, have been convulsed in a singular manner and piled fantastically one on another," wrote W. C. S. Smith. "Over such a country we picked a difficult way, depressed by the suffering of our poor horses and the utter desolation around us." After they reached a chasm, and saw Comandú below them about 200 feet, Smith described it as a beautiful little valley green as an emerald, while the sunlight glancing from the water "fairly made the very horses laugh."

The deep arroyo at San Ignacio had long been known as an ideal spot for a mission since early Jesuit explorers had told their superiors at Loreto about the plentiful water, the acres of sedge grass, and the fact it had long been occupied by many Indians. Padre Mayorgo, who had seen it for himself in 1708, ordered the founding of a pueblo first and a mission later.

The volcanoes to the north and southeast, during the period in ages past when they were active, had dispersed lava that flowed across the area in two main streams, but left a low area of the original surface in between. After draining from mountain springs, water eventually cut through the rock in this trough and eroded the soil beneath. Eventually, the San Ignacio arroyo became a vast delta of sediment that ultimately empties into the Pacific Ocean at Bahía de Ballenas. The land surrounding the arroyo is an area of mud-rock and sand dunes, with a great lagoon called Laguna San Ignacio. There is little annual rainfall, but the basin around San Ignacio is so large that it collects a great quantity of water. At times flash floods are a problem, but these are rare. Some of the earth that was washed out by periodic storms was deposited in the San Ignacio arroyo, making the soil there unusually rich.

Father Francisco María Piccolo, while stationed at Mulego, referred to it as the Valley of the Sedges or Kadakaaman. He first visited the site in 1716 and was so impressed by the well-watered arroyo that he returned several times in the next 10 years with Father Sebastián de Sistiaga, thereby winning the confidence of the Indians who lived there. Indians were taught the basic elements of Christianity, and Sistiago personally chose sites for corn and wheat that he taught the natives to sow and irrigate.

Father Juan Bautista Luyando was so enthralled by these reports after he arrived in Loreto that he decided to investigate the possibilty of establishing a permanent mission there dedicated to Saint Ignatius, or Ignacio, who had founded the Jesuit order. The mission was set up in 1728, although the church was not built until some time later. Influential friends, including the Queen of Spain, gave large sums of money. The queen supposedly contributed a million and a half pesos towards the cost of building the original church at San Ignacio.

In 1728, Easter services were held in the first church and 500 Indians gathered for the occasion. Padre Loyando was pleased to find upon his arrival that the Indians were advanced in their lessons because a young Indian named Francisco had come earlier from the mission at Mulegé to teach them how to become Christians.

The mission grew as more of the Cochimí Indians came to San Ignacio. Once these docile Indians saw what bounties the fruitful land could supply under the capable direction of Father Loyando, they came in even greater numbers.

The Jesuits introduced date palms to San Ignacio and even today the vast groves create a picture of incredible beauty as their fronds rustle gently in the breeze. They were first planted in the middle of the 18th century, and they now dominate the town and the surrounding countryside. Although the quality of the dates is poor by modern standards, for years they have given pleasure and sustenance to thousands of people.

The Jesuits learned early that San Ignacio's mission had to be protected from the ravages of floods that infrequently devastate the area. A wall of rock and earth was first built around the farming lands, but it was swept away in 1761 by a storm of unusual intensity. Another wall was built, stronger and higher than before. The Indians from six neighboring rancherías labored on it without respite for months. This too was destroyed by another massive flood. Again and again walls were built, some of mortar and rock, but each one was eventually swept away by rampaging floods.

Although the Cochimí Indians in the area were more tractable than any other tribes, they would only work hard if they were properly led. Father Baegert, who wrote extensively about Baja California's Indians, was most critical of all Indians. He wrote, "Gratitude towards benefactors, respect for superiors, reverence towards parents, friends or relatives, politeness with fellow man, are unknown to them, and words for these attributes are not in their dictionary." He insisted that laziness, lying and stealing were their three hereditary vices – their original sins. He claimed they never worked, never bothered about anything except when it was absolutely necessary to still the pangs of hunger. "To work today in order to gather the fruits of their labor a quarter or half a year later seems unbearable to them. Although I have many means to educate them, together with the seed of the Divine Word, which was preached to them many times, my labor has borne little fruit."

Father Baegert admitted reluctantly that some Indians were exceptions to his generalizations. He specifically mentioned infants who died young before they had a chance to sin. His opinion of them reached a new low when he said that the 14,000 or more California aborigines who were sent to heaven during the 70 years since the priests had arrived was reward enough for the efforts of the missionaries.

Fortunately for Baja California's future, there were other priests who believed in the Indians and their future prospects.

After Loyando's arrival at San Ignacio in 1728, he built chapels at nearby rancherías, despite opposition from Indian medicine men who resented the church's expanding influence.

Attacks by Indians were infrequent, but Father Loyando and Father Sebastián de Sistiaga from Mulegé once had to enlist the aid of 350 faithful Indians to put down a rebellion to the north of San Ignacio. They caught the rebels by surprise, arrested their leaders, and brought them back. Not one person was killed or injured. After the rebel leaders learned how much better the Christian Indians lived than they did in their primitive northern villages, they brought their families to San Ignacio.

Father Loyando's health broke down and he was forced to retire in 1832. He was replaced by Father Sebastián de Sistiaga from Mulegé.

During the reign of the Dominican Order in Baja, Mission President Juan Crisostomo Gómez experimented with live smallpox vaccine at San Ignacio. This dreaded disease was one of the worst Indian killers on the peninsula, and Gómez is credited with saving about 1,400 Indians with the vaccine who otherwise would have died in epidemics.

Other remedies of doubtful value were tried for various diseases, including the juice of the cardón cactus for ulcers, and the liquid drawn from a pot in which a horned toad had been cooked was used to treat a variety of sores,

MODERN SAN IGNACIO

Today San Ignacio is a quiet scene of pure delight for weary travelers. In addition to its 90,000 date palms, there are large groves of orange trees and numerous vineyards; all irrigated by stone-lined ditches.

At the plaza, ancient Indian laurel trees provide shade for some of the adobe buildings and stucco homes. While burros hitched to small carts doze in the afternoon heat, the plaza seems deserted. But quite likely eyes are peering at new arrivals from recessed doorways and shuttered windows. Any newcomer is a curiosity.

The massive stone church rests on one side of the plaza. It is still in use, like those other churches that have survived through the years. None of today's communicants are related to the aborigines for whom this church initially was designed. Influence of the early missionaries has declined among modern churchgoers. Those who attend these churches are descendents of people who came later from the mainland to colonize the peninsula.

Entrance to the church at San Ignacio is through carved doors that have been stained green. Seeing the ancient altar for the first time one has a feeling of antiquity and permanence. It is usually bathed in prisms of light created by the church's windows set in walls of lava blocks four feet thick.

There is a legend that some of the old padres are interred in front of the altar on top of a large treasure chest. If these graves are ever disturbed, according to the legend, Las Tres Virgenes volcanoes, "The Three Virgins," will erupt and destroy not only those who have desecrated the graves, but the whole of San Ignacio. In reality, if gold or treasure were buried under the old stone floor someone long ago would have dug it up without worrying about the consequences.

Most nights fog spreads across the arroyo, engulfing San Ignacio. Cool moist air from the Pacific Coast is spread inland by offshore winds in the evening, settling in low-lying areas. When this cool ocean air meets the superheated desert air, fog develops. At San Ignacio, the stark outline of the church's tower is the last to be engulfed.

The volcanoes lie to the north, and lava once flowed from them across this area, leaving a cleft in the terrain. This long-ago volcanic action created a vast catchment basin around San Ignacio. Therefore, the surrounding area has water the year around despite being surrounded by a desert so dry that it gets less than five inches of rain a year.

The remains of a giant dike still can be seen to the east of the village. "La muralla" is three miles long. It was built by mission Indians and is 12 feet high and 40 feet thick. It was used primarily to store water, but it also served to contain some of the flash floods that occasionally hit the area.

Where To Stay In San Ignacio

Accommodations are limited at San Ignacio to a hotel, a motel, and one trailer park. **Hotel La Pinta** is a mile west of Highway 1 on the paved highway that leads to the town's plaza. It's a lovely spot, nestled in a palm grove, and the rooms are air conditioned. Single rooms are priced at $60 and doubles three dollars more. Extra persons – a maximum of four – are charged $12 additional. The dining room is open all day, and there is a bar. For reservations write Apartado

Postal 37, San Ignacio, Baja California Sur 23943, Mexico, or call toll free (800) 336-5454. **La Posada Motel** is a half-mile southeast of the plaza on Calle Carranza 22. Its rates are $22 for a single room and $27 for a double with each extra person in a room charged $5. There's an all-day coffee shop. For reservations, write the motel at San Ignacio, Baja California Sur, Mexico.

The **San Ignacio Transpeninsular Trailer Park** has 20 RV or tent sites, and is located on Highway 1 behind the Pemex Station at the junction of the paved road into San Ignacio. The charge is $5 per site, which includes flush toilets and showers.

Prehistoric Cave Paintings

North of San Ignacio the land has been deeply eroded by volcanic lava flows, and the mountains rise to 5,000 feet from the desert floor. Scammon's Lagoon can be seen on the Pacific side of the peninsula, as well as the Vizcaíno Desert and Las Tres Virgenes that rise from the plain. In this mountain wilderness there are groves of palm trees in deep canyons grouped around pools of water beneath sheer cliffs of colored rock. A few small ranches survive in these mountain fastnesses. Here, and in several other interior mountain valleys, a race once lived that produced thousands of cave paintings. They are unlike other prehistoric art in the southwest, and they depict men and animals mostly in black and red colors. No one has any definite idea about what kind of people lived here, except that they probably created the paintings between 500 AD and 1500 AD. Then they disappeared. The animals are depicted in motion and are exceptionally well conceived. Why were they painted in such remote areas? There is only conjecture that the paintings describe the material and spiritual sides of these people.

In one cave, 30 feet long, 16 feet wide, 30 feet high, the paintings cover the walls and ceilings. They show men in loose shirts, coats and breaches, but with no shoes. Often their hands are raised and open. The women wear dresses, and one is shown with her hair neatly coiffed. The animals are familiar, including wild pigs and wolves. Although red and black colors predominate, some greens and yellows were used.

Father Joseph Mariano Rothea, while stationed at San Ignacio from 1759 until the Jesuits left the peninsula in 1768, was told by Indian elders that the paintings were made in ancient times by a race of giants who had come from the north. Supposedly, this race had been exterminated through their own tribal battles and by the aborigines who inhabited the region. The story of "giants" is a typical exaggeration to explain anything that is incomprehensible to people of limited knowledge. The painters no doubt used scaffolding to reach the ceilings. Giants would have had to have been 30 feet tall to reach them!

The Sierra de San Francisco has many paintings, including some of the best. The Arroyo del Parral, largest in the area, has a 26-foot mural of a deer-headed serpent with people clustered around it. Here, as in other caves, there is much over-painting by artists who came after the original painters.

The Sierra de San Francisco is deep in a series of canyons that cover 300 to 400 square miles. Only experienced backpackers can walk its difficult paths. For the uninitiated, there is grave danger. Not only is water scarce but, in many areas, it is nonexistent throughout the year.

The ranch village of San Francisco today has fewer than 20 families. It lies at the head of the Arroyo de San Pablo and contains numerous caves with paintings so similar in technique that it appears as if they were painted by the same artist.

The caves evidently were formed by erosion of volcanic layers of rock that collapsed and formed deep recesses. There is no indication that the caves were ever lived in. If they were used as places of worship, there is no evidence to back up such a theory.

Deer are often portrayed with their mouths open, as if gasping for breath. Their appearance suggests they were run down and then killed by arrows and spears. Some deer are shown with their legs broken, and the Indians may have used throwing sticks to slow down the fleet-footed animals. In all these hunting scenes, there is a graceful flow of movement that adds to their sense of reality.

Southeast of San Ignacio, and below the Bahía de la Concepción (Conception Bay), the Sierra de Guadalupe rises in a tortured mass of peaks ranging up to 5,000 feet. Early missionaries reported numerous Indian families here and cave paintings of black mountain lions and deer. In one arroyo, the animal paintings are 10 feet long.

Although no one can be certain, the race of painters who left their indelible mark on thousands of caves possibly began in the San Francisco mountains and then spread to other areas.

The Sierra de San Borja, bounded by the Bahía de los Angeles on the north and the tiny village of El Arco on the south, dominates the middle part of the peninsula. Here, in canyons carved millions of years ago by volcanic flows that covered the original granite, painted walls can still be found. There are others. The Sierra de San Juan lies along the 28th parallel that divides the peninsula. It has the smallest number of cave paintings. The Sierra de San Borja has paintings in shades of red that were applied to granite boulders.

In the high mountains above the Bahía de los Angeles, the caves have long, sloping sides and are covered with paintings – some of large size. Men in headdresses, and women, are shown either lifesize or larger, facing outward with their arms raised. The animals are painted either in motion or in silhouette. Birds are depicted with their wings spread, or in actual flight.

The paintings were done in black, white, red and yellow. Paints probably were obtained by grinding colored volcanic rocks and adding water to make a paste. In some areas, there are miles of caves. Trails are difficult to locate without an experienced guide. The ancient trails were carved out of solid rock, and small stones were moved to one side so the Indians could feel their way at night by guiding themselves with their toes touching these rocks. In places, the solid rock has been worn smooth after hundreds of years of use.

The cave people evidently departed as mysteriously as they appeared hundreds of years ago. It is known that the peninsula's climate became more arid, and quite possibly the game upon which the hunters subsisted began to disappear. These people may have been forced to migrate to the mainland to survive. As far as is known, they disappeared after the 14th and 15th centuries. They probably lived in tribes of about 100, migrating to and from the seas for food.

In these mountains, there are a few men and women still living in isolated villages. Some are six feet or more in height, and they appear to be pure Indian with no mixture of blood from other races.

It is believed that seven tribes came from the north to mainland Mexico in the 12th century and conquered the Chichimecas. They then conquered the Toltecs. These newcomers were either cliff dwellers from Arizona and New Mexico, or they may have come from Baja California. It is possible that the people who still reside in these mountains are descendants of the war-like tribes who conquered the mainland. The original race left no ruins or pottery in Baja to identify them. However, the mainland's conquering tribes created paintings similar to those in Baja's caves.

Traveling To Cave Sites

Although there is a dirt road to some of them, travel to these caves is difficult, and it is not for the inexperienced. For information about mule trips to the caves contact Oscar Fischer at San Ignacio's **La Posada Motel.** The trails permit travel on foot with pack mules, and oftentimes it takes hours to go just a few miles. Scorpions are an ever-present menace while traveling in these mountains, as are red diamondback snakes. Few people ever recover from a full bite by these six-foot-long snakes. They are particularly numerous in deep crevices in the arroyos. Pack animals rarely survive such bites.

The Lost Mission

For years after the Jesuits were expelled in 1760 searches were made for the so-called lost mission of Santa Isabel that the padres supposedly built to hide their treasures of gold and silver bars and church ornaments. This enormous wealth was believed to have been acquired since the Spanish Crown gave the Jesuits authority to Christianize the peninsula's Indians in 1697. The expulsion of the Jesuits was justified by the Spanish Court because it claimed that the priests had enriched themselves at the expense of the state.

Responsible people at the time refused to give credence to the stories about this lost mission. Rumors spread like wildfire, however, each time there was a report that an Indian had found such a mission with a cross on its adobe walls. It was usually located high in the mountains, but somehow the Indian was never able to find his way back to it.

The story of the lost mission is pure fiction. These hardworking Jesuit padres established missions by planting crops and raising livestock to feed their flocks. They had enough problems surviving in this harsh but beautiful land, and they certainly never had time to mine any of the earth's riches even if they had been available. We know, of course, that gold and silver could be found on the peninsula, but only in limited quantities.

From San Ignacio to Santa Rosalía

After leaving San Ignacio, Highway 1 winds through low hills until it reaches the vicinity of Las Tres Virgenes, whose purple volcanic cones rise majestically above a high plateau covered with yucca validas and cardóns. Then the road dips steeply and descends in sharp switchbacks for seven miles through eroded hills until it reaches the Gulf of California. There, after turning south, the road leads to Santa Rosalía six miles farther along the coast.

SANTA ROSALÍA'S PAST

Copper mining was started at Santa Rosalía after ore was discovered there in 1868 by a rancher in small balls or boleos. Geologists at France's House of Rothschild noted the richness of the ore and the house purchased the mining rights from the German company Casa Moeller of Guaymas, Mexico. A company called El Boleo Copper Company was set up in the 1880s and soon rows of frame buildings with corrugated iron roofs were built and Santa Rosalía became a company town, similar to those in the American West during this same period. Roads were constructed, wells were dug, and ranches and farms were established to provide food for the miners and their families.

After the world copper price dropped in the early part of the 20th century mining operations declined, and miners and their families became so indebted to the company that it proved impossible for them ever to break out of their indebtedness. Despite two world wars that temporarily increased the need for Mexican copper, the company continued to be hard-pressed. Workers complained of mine hazards, and left-wing labor organizers moved in, but the miners remained in financial distress. When strikes developed, several hundred Yaqui Indians were brought to Santa Rosalía from Sonora on the mainland, along with other outside workers. But the mine continued to prove unproductive.

After years of labor unrest and ore deterioration, the French company failed, although many company officials had become millionaires. Few Mexican laborers benefited from the French-operated company because of the extremely low wages it paid. After failure of the French firm, new deposits of copper and manganese were located, and a Mexican firm has given the town a new lease on life with the mining of these metals. The company is now called Boleo Estudios e Inversiones Mineras. To the residents of Santa Rosalía it is still familiarly known as El Boleo.

Jesuit Influence on the Region

Periodically through the years hurricanes have devastated the lower part of the peninsula. In 1717, immense destruction was caused to the missions of San Xavier and Mulegé. High winds and torrential rains destroyed the plantations and, even worse, stripped the land's topsoil down to bare rock.

Two years later Jesuit Father Juan de Ugarte authorized the construction of a large ship at Mulegé. He planned to obtain lumber from the mainland, but the Indians explained that suitable trees were available in the mountains north of Loreto. He was doubtful that such trees grew in Baja California – at least the areas he had explored – but he set out for the ranchería at Mulegé in September 1718, with a shipwright from Mexico and some Indians to act as guides. There he was joined by Father Sistiaga who led him to a grove of large trees less than 90 miles from Santa Rosalía. The trees were members of the poplar family, and they were called güéribo.

The shipwright said it would be impossible to get the timbers to the shore, but Ugarte was not so easily discouraged. After returning to Mulegé, he persuaded three experts in logging operations from the mainland to join him and he returned to the mountains. He directed the felling of the trees during a four-month stay, and had planks made of them on the spot. Despite the ridicule of almost everyone at Mulegé, Ugarte built a road to the gulf and, with his three loggers, five other white men and Indians from the area, he brought the planks down to the shores of the gulf where the ship was built. Ugarte called it *El Triunfo de la Cruz* – The Triumph of the Cross. It was the first large ship constructed in Baja California, and he sailed it proudly as far north as the mouth of the Colorado River. The ship later made more than 60 crossings of the gulf carrying supplies to a growing number of missions.

SANTA ROSALÍA TODAY

Away from the smelters Santa Rosalía is an unusual town, showing both its Mexican and French heritage. The blending of nationalities is especially noted in the features of its lovely señoritas. Everything about Santa Rosalía is unique. The original French company put up most of the town's frame buildings, with their corrugated iron roofs. They give it the appearance of an old western movie set.

There is an unusual church in Santa Rosalía constructed of galvanized iron sections that were shipped from France. It was originally conceived by A. O. Eiffel, designer of the Eiffel Tower in Paris. It was shipped in sections around Cape Horn in the 19th century to Santa Rosalía. The church has been renovated in recent years, and its interior is lovely.

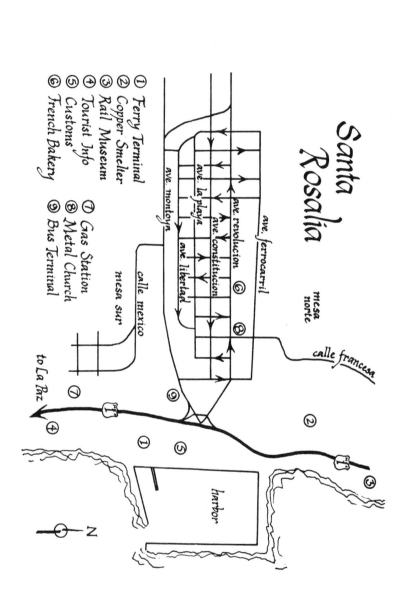

Santa Rosalia

1. Ferry Terminal
2. Copper Smelter
3. Rail Museum
4. Tourist Info
5. Customs
6. French Bakery

7. Gas Station
8. Metal Church
9. Bus Terminal

ave. ferrocarril

ave. revolucion
ave. constitucion ⑥
ave. la playa
ave. libertad ⑧

ave. montoya

mesa
norte

calle francesa

calle mexico

mesa sur

to La Paz

harbor

N

Where To Stay In Santa Rosalía

There are two modern hotels in Santa Rosalía, including **El Morro,** a mile south of the ferry terminal. It's a Spanishstyle hotel that overlooks the Gulf of California, with single rooms priced at $25 and double rooms up to $30. There are also suites available. Extra persons are charged $3, and there is no charge for children under six years of age. The hotel has an all-day dining room and bar. Reservations and a deposit are required with a seven-day notice to obtain a refund. Reservations may be made by writing Apartado Postal 76, Santa Rosalía, Baja California Sur, Mexico, or by calling 01152 (685) 2-0414. The **Hotel Francos** is on Avenida 11 de Julio on Mesa Norte. This French colonial hotel overlooks the copper smelter and the gulf. The rooms are air conditioned. The single and double rates are $18, with a $3 charge for each extra person. The hotel has a dining room and a bar. Its mailing address is Avenida 11 de Julio No. 30, Santa Rosalía, Baja California Sur. Or you can call 01152 (685) 2-0829.

Two more modestly-priced but nice hotels, one with 11 rooms and the other with 12 rooms, offer lower rates. The **Hotel Blanco y Negro,** Avenida Sarabia 1, can be reached by calling 01152 (685) 2-0800, while **Hotel Palencia** on Calle Primera is at 01152 (685) 2-0161.

South of Santa Rosalía, and 15 miles west of Highway 1, a new hotel is located on a bluff overlooking the gulf. **Hotel Punta Chivato** rents single rooms for $47 and doubles for $60, with each extra person in a room charged $11. There is also a campground for tents and RVs on the nearby beach called **San Lucas**. Each site costs $6.50. There is an airstrip that can be contacted by calling unicom on 122.8. With the excellent fishing in the gulf, this is a good spot to charter a boat. Hotel reservations for Punta Chivato may be made by writing Apartado Postal 18, Mulegé, Baja California Sur, Mexico, or by calling 01152 (685) 3-0188. For the San Lucas campground, write San Lucas RV Park, Apartado Postal 131, Santa Rosalía, Baja California Sur, Mexico.

Ferries To & From Santa Rosalía

Baja California's ferries, previously government-run, were privatized in 1989 and prices were sharply increased. Ferries depart from Santa Rosalía on Tuesday, Friday and Sunday for Guaymas at 11 p.m. and arrive at 7 the following morning. Guaymas ferries leave at 10 a.m. and arrive at Santa Rosalía at 5:30 p.m. Salon seats are $11 (up from $1.70 in the previous edition of this guide!), a roomette with bunk, $22, and a cabin $36. Vehicles up to 16.4 feet are charged $85 and those from 29.5 to 55.8 feet in total length $285. Motorhomes pay $145. The office can be reached by calling 01152 (685) 2-0013 or 0014 at the Terminal Building on Highway 1. Reservations must be made in advance for passengers and automobiles. In addition, cars brought to the mainland must have advance permits. (See Introduction for rules and regulations.)

MULEGE VIA HIGHWAY 1

Once the road turns inland again, the countryside becomes barren until Mulegé is reached. This community is at the bottom of a lush valley on each side of the Río Santa Rosalía, or Río Mulegé as it is known locally, and four miles from the gulf. Much of the village is poverty-stricken, but there is an air of tranquility along the palm-fringed river with the rustle of hundreds of palm trees, the soft murmuring of the river, and the calls of hundreds of tropical birds. It is a lovely place where date palms, mango trees and vegetables grow in profusion. Artesian wells supply fresh water, while a spring fills an artificial lake at the headwaters of the river. Downstream the water becomes brackish and mangrove trees border the river for two miles.

There is an old territorial prison at Mulegé. Quite often it has no prisoners and, when there are some, they work outside and spend only their nights inside its walls.

Hotels In Mulegé

Mulegé has excellent tourist accommodations. The **Hotel Las Casitas** is in the center of town at Callejon de los Estudientes and Avenida Madero. Its rooms rent for $23 single, and $31 double. They face an attractive garden patio and are air conditioned. There is a $5 charge for each extra person in a room. The hotel provides for guide services and can arrange fishing trips. Their mailing address is Francisco Madero 50, Mulegé, Baja California Sur 23900, Mexico, or call 01152 (685) 3-0019. The **Hotel Serenidad** is at the mouth of the river about 2 1/2 miles south of Highway 1. A ranch-style hotel on the river's shore, its rooms rent for $42 for a single room and $43 to $55 for a double, with a $9 charge for each extra person. The hotel can arrange fishing trips. Cabin cruisers rent for $220 per day for six people, or skiffs for $98 a day for three people. There's a nearby airstrip and aviation gasoline is available. An auto mechanic is furnished by the hotel in case a guest's car needs service. The dining room is open for three meals a day and provides a banquet on Wednesday and Saturday nights with live music. For reservations, write Apartado Postal 9, Mulegé, Baja California Sur 23900, Mexico, or call 01152 (685) 3-0111. East of town, overlooking the gulf, is the **Hotel Vista Hermosa** whose single and double rooms rent for up to $64 with an additional $16 for each extra person in a room. Reservations and a deposit are mandatory, with a refund notice time of two weeks. For reservations write Camino al Puerto S/N, Mulegé, Baja California Sur, Mexico, or call 01152 (685) 3-0222. In California, they have a toll-free number-(800) 829-0510. More modest hotels include the **Hotel Hacienda** whose eight rooms have a 200-year-old historic front on Calle Francisco I, Madero 3; call 01152 (685) 3-0021. The **Hotel Terrazas** has 18 air conditioned rooms downtown and can be reached at 01152 (685) 3-0009.

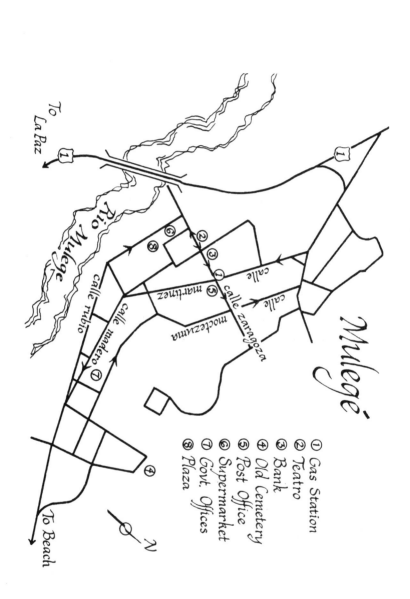

Mulegé

① Gas Station
② Teatro
③ Bank
④ Old Cemetery
⑤ Post Office
⑥ Supermarket
⑦ Govt. Offices
⑧ Plaza

To La Paz

To Beach

Río Mulege

calle rubio

calle madero

calle martinez

calle moctezuma

calle zaragoza

calle

calle

N

RV Parks

There are a number of campgrounds in the area, including **Playa Sombrerito** three miles east on an unpaved road, with an open beach area at the mouth of the river. It offers no facilities and charges up to $3 per vehicle. **Jorge's del Río Trailer Park** is a mile south on Highway 1, and then over an unpaved road to a fenced area near the river. It has 18 RV sites with hookups and charges $9 per site. Their mailing address is Apartado Postal 3, Mulegé, Baja California Sur, Mexico. **Huerto Saucedo (the Orchard) RV Park** is a mile south of town on Highway 1. It is a partially-shaded camp near the river with 46 RV sites, and 30 tent sites with hookups. There's a boat ramp and fishing privileges. The charges range up to $11.50 for two people, with $1 for each extra person. One and a quarter miles south on Highway 1, the **Villa María Isabel RV Trailer Park** is also near the river in a partially-shaded area with 25 RV hookups. They have a European-style bakery on the premises. The fee is $11 for two people, with a $2 charge for each extra person. The **Hotel Serenidad** off Highway 1, two and a half miles south of Mulegé, also has 15 RV sites on their grounds and some sites are palm-shaded. Patrons have the use of the hotel's facilities. The park charges $11 for two people, with $2 for each extra individual. They can be contacted at 01152 (685) 3-0111. Thirteen and a half miles south on Highway 1 is the **Playa Santispac** on an unpaved road. It is situated on a public beach at Santispac Cove which is part of Bahía Concepcíon. The charge here is $4.50 per vehicle. Another mile and a half farther along the highway is the **Posada Concepcíon** whose landscaped grounds overlook the bay from 13 RV sites and an open area for tents, with hookups. The fee is $11 for two people, and $2 extra for each additional person. The **Bahía el Coyote** is another public beach farther down the bay that charges $3.50 per vehicle. And the **El Requesón** is a public beach 27 miles south of Mulegé on a beautiful sandspit that connects the beach with an off-shore island. The road leading to it is unpaved. It furnishes only a pit toilet and trash cans, with a charge of $3 per vehicle.

Restaurants

There are two outstanding restaurants in Mulegé. **El Nido Steakhouse** is on Calle Romero Rubio S/N and features seafood and steaks in a ranch-style setting. It is open from 8 a.m. to 10 p.m. and dinners cost up to $16.50. Call 01152 (685) 3-0221. **Las Casitas Hotel's** dining room serves meals on a patio and specializes in Mexican foods, beef and seafood. Each Friday evening it has a fiesta buffet with a mariachi band. Dinners range up to $16. Their telephone number is 01152 (685) 3-0019.

HIGHWAY 1 TO LORETO

Proceeding along Highway 1 on the coast of the gulf towards Loreto, there are barren coastal hills to cross until the shore of Bahía de la Concepcíon (Conception Bay) is reached. The bay is deep enough for large ships. The surrounding countryside, however, is in sharp contrast to the magnificent beauty of the 25-mile-long bay. The bay's mouth, at the tip of a long peninsula (Punta Concepción), lies three miles to the east. Farther south the bay widens to nine miles. Near shore the water is turquoise in color, turning to a deep Mediterranean blue as the depth of the water increases. There are hundreds of sandy beaches, most of which have never been visited by tourists, and they remain unspoiled.

The bay teams with fish, and the bird life is fascinating to watch. Pelicans hover over the placid waters until a school of small fish ruffles the surface, trying to escape larger predators. Pelicans plunge down to grab a fish from the hurrying school, each one raising its beak to let the fish slide down its throat. Cormorants, sleek as arrows, dive into the water, each emerging with a fish. Seagulls, their strident cries filling the air, rush to snatch fish off the surface.

If one watches the beach closely, a Sally Lightfoot crab with its red, blue and brown shell gleaming in the sun like baked enamel, will tiptoe across the gleaming sand. Here, as elsewhere in the gulf, one finds the world's most fantastic sport fishing and many fish can be caught from shore.

The beaches are marvelous for long walks because they team with wild life. Blue-footed boobies waddle across the sand on large webbed feet. They are clumsy on land but, once in the air, they fly with graceful ease, diving quickly into a churning mass of fish, and always emerging with a fish crosswise in their beaks.

At the head of the bay the road climbs to a sandy plain with jagged peaks of the Sierra de la Giganta soaring on the right-hand side of the road. The hills are covered with scrub as they recede towards the gulf near Loreto.

LORETO'S OFTEN VIOLENT PAST

Loreto is the oldest settlement in Baja California. For 132 years it was the capital, but an 1829 hurricane wrecked the presidio and government buildings so the capital was moved to La Paz. Loreto has had a violent past, being devastated eight times by earthquakes, floods and pirate raids. After hurricane winds and heavy rain destroyed most of Loreto in 1959, it was stubbornly rebuilt. These storms, called chubascos, occur mainly between July and December. The hard ground is unable to absorb heavy amounts of rainfall, and communities like Loreto, Cabo San Lucas, Mulegé and La Paz have suffered extensive damage when chubascos reached hurricane velocity. Such major storms are infrequent, occuring every 25 years or so, but when they do take place they destroy almost everything in their paths. The river at Mulegé once was turned into a raging torrent as heavy rain overflowed its banks and caused enormous destruction.

At Loreto, the Misíon de Nuestra Señora de Loreto was founded by Jesuit Father Juan María de Salvatierra in 1697.

Although it has been repaired many times, some of the original church still stands.

Life Among The Early Indians

In the building of the missions, the Indians appear to have learned elementary skills quickly under the patient direction of the padres. Many Indians learned to be excellent stone masons, and excelled in the art of brick laying. Those missions that still stand give positive evidence of their skills because most of the work was done by the natives.

The guamas, or medicine men, despite the efforts of the priests, continued to maintain a strong control over the members of the tribes they represented. After a dead person was cremated, relatives and friends of the deceased decorated themselves in black and yellow paint and gathered at the guama's hut. The medicine man, with these mourners grouped around him, unrolled a red mat made of human hair that he put on. Then, with a whistle, he supposedly called the dead. With a stick in one hand, to which was attached some hair of the deceased, the guama talked to the dead person while the mourners tore their own hair and wept. The deceased was thought to have been taken to the "House of the North" and, in communicating with the departed, the guama would ask if there was anyone there as important as the guama. Of course, to keep control of the situation, the response was always negative.

The ceremony concluded with a eulogy for the deceased that only increased the weeping of his relatives. The wake continued throughout the night, and ended the following morning with a dance by all except the relatives. The latter, to demonstrate their grief, cut off their long hair. Throughout the proceedings, the guama insisted that the departed had told him that he must be given the best of the food or the dead person's spirit would refuse to depart. If the spirit remained behind it would haunt the rest of them, so food was eagerly given to the guama who departed waving a stick with some of the deceased's hair tied to it. That ended the burial ceremony.

As with most aborigines, women acted as beasts of burden when they traveled, bowed down with the family's possessions. Thus the man was free to use his weapons if they were threatened.

When a woman gave birth to a child her body was immersed in warm water. Then she lay in a pit that had been warmed by fire, and her body was covered by branches and earth, where she remained for several days. The umbilical cord was severed by a piece of flint, then bathed in warm water before it was buried in the ashes of the fire to keep it warm.

Jesuits' Relations With Indians

The Royal Council of the Indies at last decided that it was impossible to conquer Baja California's Indians because there were too many of them, and the Spanish leaders were convinced that they did not have the resources or manpower to complete the job. The Society of Jesus, or Jesuits, pleaded for a chance to convert the so-called heathen, and the council agreed to subsidize them with an annual sum of 30,000 pesos. Once that agreement was reached, the Jesuits decided to make further colonizing attempts, but to take with them only small detachments of soldiers. Father Kino and Father Juan María Salvatierra were placed in charge. They were both men of strong faith, fearless and willing to die if necessary as martyrs for Christ.

Father Juan de Ugarte was appointed procurator for the missions the Jesuits hoped to establish. An aristocrat, Ugarte was well-educated, and of immensely strong physique. In the years ahead, Ugarte proved to be a pillar of strength for the Jesuit fathers because he used all his great persuasive powers to secure the necessary donations and supplies the padres needed. For almost the next hundred years the

Pious Fund, or Fund for the Californias, supported the Jesuits.

Salvatierra was first to leave the mainland with ships manned by Yaqui sailors, with only a Spanish corporal, five soldiers and three Christian Yaqui Indians to assist him. His ship landed first at the entrance to the Bahía de la Concepción, and then turned south to San Bruno where Father Kino had tried to establish a settlement with Admiral Antillón. Salvatierra's Yaqui captain, who was familiar with the coast, suggested that they sail farther south. Kino agreed and they landed at the mouth of a large arroyo that they named San Dionisio on October 19, 1697. They were delighted with the place, in full bloom since the recent rains, and with plenty of water. An encampment was established on the shore, and a large tent was erected as a temporary chapel. A cross, intertwined with flowers, was erected in front of the chapel. The image of Our Lady of Loreto, Patroness of the Conquest, was brought ashore October 25 in a procession, and possession of the land was formally taken in the name of the King of Spain.

At first, the Indians were peaceful, but a Cochimí Indian chief by the name of Ibó – the Sun – warned Salvatierra that an attack on the encampment was imminent, probably on the night of the 31st. That night, while the colonists waited apprehensively in hastily-dug trenches, they were surprised by the sound of a cannon off-shore and musket fire. They rushed to the shore to learn that Padre Francisco Piccolo had arrived on the expedition's second ship with more domestic animals and supplies.

The attack that night did not materialize, but the Indians did attack several times during November, once with 500 men, and several were killed when the Spanish soldiers opened fire. Shocked by the deaths of their warriors, the Indian women and children pleaded for an end to the hostilities and even offered an Indian child as hostage. The youngster was accepted by Father Salvatierra.

The anxious days ended when a third ship arrived, and later Padre Piccolo returned with the second ship November 23 to bring even more supplies and five more soldiers.

Expedition leaders now strove for a permanent settlement, and began with the help of friendly Indians to build a chapel of rocks hewn by hand from a nearby quarry. In addition, a start was made on three small houses: one for Father Salvatierra, another for Captain Don Luis de Torres de Tortolera, and the last for use as a storehouse. Each was covered with thatch to make it waterproof.

All previous attempts at colonization of Baja had failed because the sites either were too poor for successful farming, or the military expeditions were unprepared for the realities of living in a new and uncivilized environment. In the past, there also had been difficulties in getting adequate supplies across the Gulf of California on a regular basis because of frequent storms.

The Indians on the peninsula proved equally frustrating. They lived mainly by hunting, fishing and the gathering of wild fruit, nuts, and plants. In the Loreto area, and along the peninsula's coasts, the Indians used primitive rafts while fishing with nets or spears. Most fish were caught in tidal pools. Such an existence, virtually always at the point of starvation, forced the Indians to eat anything available, including insects and snakes, just to stay alive. Only one animal was taboo. They would not eat the flesh of the badger because the animal's facial features and footprints too closely resembled those of humans. During periods of great hunger, when a deer was killed the Indians would tie a string to a piece of meat, chew off bits, and hand it to the next person until it was all consumed. Primarily nomads, when Indians took up residence they lived in shelters constructed of stones and branches piled one on top of the other. In this arid climate, water dictated their lives to the greatest extent. As a result, they wandered from one waterhole to another. The padres soon learned that they had a formidable task to change the lives of these primitive aborigines because they had little concept of a supreme being or a Christian God.

Father Salvatierra succeeded at Loreto where others had failed at other sites. It was the first mission to survive in Baja California. It grew each year until 200 Cochimí Indians had been baptized by 1704, and there were 70 permanent colonists including Spaniards, mestizos – people with mixed white and Indian blood – and Christian Indians from the mainland. Salvatierra learned the Indian language and it was primarily his kindness that converted the Indians. Food was used as a reward for those who would consent to take instructions in the Catholic religion. Often boiled maize, that the Indians dearly loved, was the best inducement for them to learn their Latin prayers.

Indians were frequently abused in the guise of saving their souls, and some were forced into the dangerous pursuit of pearl diving. Once some Indians stole Father Salvatierra's horse and his goats, which they promptly ate, before making an attack on the encampment. Despite their constant threats to the peace and security of the mission, the father refused to permit the soldiers to fire on the hundreds of Indians when they became rebellious, even though they outnumbered the Spaniards 50 to one. Once, when a situation got out of hand, he was forced to give his consent and the soldiers fired upon the Indian mob. After this determined show of force, the Indians quickly abandoned the field. In retrospect, it is almost unbelievable that a few armed Europeans – in this case just 10 soldiers – could frighten off 500 Indians. With the attack repelled, Salvatierra offered thanks to God, along with his most holy Mother, and to St. Stanislaus (whose festival this date was) for their intercession. To Salvatierra this was proof again of their divine protection. During this attack, most of the arrows reportedly struck in the pedestal of the Cross, and both the Cross and the tent that served as chapel remained undamaged.

Baja California's medicine men quickly saw they had serious rivals in the Jesuit priests, who viewed them as pagan sorcerers. Priests derided these medicine men when they attempted to heal their sick brethren. The guamas usually applied a tube made from a black stone to the affected part of an Indian's anatomy, alternately blowing into it or sucking the tube to rid the body of disease. The padres noted that the medicine men sometimes filled the tube with cimmaron or wild tobacco. The priests realized, with some surprise, that the treatment sometimes proved successful and the disorder was eliminated. They decided that this was due to the irritation or scarification of the skin resulting from this powerful caustic – a procedure that was also widely used at the time in civilized countries. Its effectiveness, in either case, was no doubt primarily psychological.

Growth Of The Early Missions

Father Piccolo continued to bring supplies from the mainland as the mission grew and Indian medicine men became convinced that the Spaniards this time planned to stay on the peninsula. The guamas aroused their people to resist further encroachment of their tribal lands. The muskets of the Spanish soldiers had to be used again during a number of outbreaks.

Piccolo, meanwhile, learned the Cochimí language and set up a school for Indian boys and girls. This was a shrewd move on his part because he used the children as hostages to maintain control of their parents.

After 1700, the growth of the settlement reached such proportions that food became a problem because most of it had to be imported from the mainland. By now, the Indians had been settled in four towns, with more than 600 Christians – primarily children – and approximately 2,000 adults.

Salvatierra now faced a serious problem among his own people. The garrison of soldiers, including its captain, mutinied because they had not been paid and because they lacked adequate provisions. In addition, they were incensed by the re-

straints placed upon them by the padres in regard to association with and control of the Indians. Father Salvatierra dis-
charged most of them, keeping only a few of the faithful.

Father Juan de Ugarte, procurator for the missions in Mexico City, came to Loreto the following spring along with more
soldiers and vowed to make each mission self-supporting. He
arrived April 1, 1701, after a journey of incredible mishaps.
Forced to use a shipwrecked long boat, he crossed the gulf in
a storm, with a crew of seven Yaqui Indians. He immediately
set to work to learn the Cochimí language before he accepted
the responsibility for heading the new mission San Francisco
Xavier de Viggé Biaundó. Indians had earlier visited Loreto
from their mountain hideouts north of Loreto. A youth, who
seemed especially bright and promising, had been baptized
and named Francisco Xavier. Father Piccolo had returned
the visit in March, 1699 and was received with great warmth
so he decided to found a mission there. The land appeared
suitable for farming, with nearby grazing fields and sufficient water. Before such a mission could be established, however, a road had to be built through the mountains. This
proved to be a difficult job but, once it was completed, a
chapel was dedicated on November 1.

When Father Ugarte arrived at the new mission, he found it
deserted because the Indians had fled. In seeking an answer,
he found that the Indians feared his escort of soldiers. He
promptly sent the soldiers back to Loreto and faced the Indians without arms. They quickly returned to the mission and
he preached to them.

Ugarte was an imposing figure of a man – well over six feet
in height – and when his patience was tried to the breaking
point he would seize two Indians by their long hair and whirl
them around his head, literally knocking some sense into
them. He soon became a legendary figure, and it is difficult
to sift the truth from the many stories about his exploits that
have come down to us through the years. One favorite story
tells about the time Ugarte ridiculed an Indian belief that
the mountain lion was a god. While exploring the wilds, Ug-

arte supposedly found a lion blocking his path. He stoned it and, if one can believe the legend, Ugarte strangled the beast with his bare hands. After skinning the lion, the redoubtable padre is said to have picked out the choicest parts, broiled them over a fire, and eaten them. His Indian friends evidently joined the feast, or at least the legend says they did, perhaps out of fear of this man who had so casually overcome one of their most powerful gods.

Some of the first mission orchards were started by Father Ugarte, who brought fruit trees from the mainland. He showed the Indians how to plant and harvest cotton, and even hired a master weaver from the mainland to instruct the Indians how to make cloth. The weaver, Antonio Moran, remained with the mission for several years.

Although Ugarte's actions often intimidated the Indians, he made farmers instead of gatherers out of them, and soon they had plentiful harvests of wheat, maize and other grain. Grapevines were also imported, and soon he had wineries to supply the missions and for export to mainland Mexico in exchange for other needed goods. He had brought a few sheep with him and, once they multiplied, Ugarte taught the Indians how to make woolen clothes after he personally constructed spinning wheels and looms.

Always resourceful, Father Ugarte not only supervised the work of his mission, but he worked right along with the Indians. By his example, he convinced most of them that hard work paid off. But they were not used to such hard labor and often rebelled, despite the fact they were now better fed, housed and clothed than in previous years. When a reproof for their idleness failed to get results, the padre went into physical action while his recalcitrant laborers fled in fear. Indian children received his particular attention and he personally made sure that the children were taught.

A man far ahead of his time, Father Ugarte built a hospital, and saw to it that older Indians were taken care of when they could no longer take care of themselves. Ugarte maintained an unbounded enthusiasm for what he considered was God's work.

The Jesuits soon learned that the words of the Royal Council of the Indies were not to be trusted. Despite authorization by the King of Spain that the Jesuits should receive 30,000 pesos a year to aid their colonizing efforts, the council refused to pay it. In part, they were jealous that the Jesuits had succeeded where they had failed. Undaunted, the Jesuits sought funds through charity, and they were so successful that even the Spanish soldiers assigned to their missions began to be paid by charitable contributions. Provisions and livestock came principally from the mainland missions in Sonora – a chain of missions that extended all the way to Tucson in the present state of Arizona.

Somehow, in 1706, Ugarte found time to cross the peninsula with only 12 Spanish soldiers and 40 Yaqui warriors. Upon reaching the west coast, the party turned south, and explored land never before seen by white men.

Ugarte's foresight in raising his mission's own food spared the settlement in 1707 when a drought on the mainland caused harvests to fail. Those on Baja who were dependent on the mainland's food died by the thousands, while Ugarte's mission continued to produce bountiful harvests for its tenants. Ugarte's mission, due to his insistence upon irrigating his fields despite the back-breaking labor of building ditches, never had a food shortage.

Indians frequently resisted their masters, and even Ugarte's Indians joined in protesting the dominance of the padres. Cattle were frequently stolen and the harvests often were destroyed. Some of the Indians' resistance to authority was due to the brutality of the soldiers who quickly executed Indians if they attacked the settlements. The Jesuit fathers protested such treatment, but the actions of the soldiers quelled all disturbances and there were long periods of peace and quiet. Mission Commandant Captain Esteban Rodríguez Lorenzo took matters into his own hands in 1703 when he hanged the ringleader of one such revolt.

South of Loreto, at a site first visited by Father Salvatierra, another mission was founded in 1703 by Father Pedro de Ugarte – Juan's brother. This was San Juan Bautista Ligüí or Malibát – the two names resulting from the fact that two different tribes inhabited the area.

Another site visited earlier by Juan de Ugarte was considered for a mission because of the docility of the Cochimí Indians. The mission of Santa Rosalía de Mulegé was not completed, however, until 1766 by Father Escalante.

Great changes were looming on the horizon in Baja California as new padres arrived from the mainland. Father Salvatierra was recalled to Mexico City in 1705 to serve as Padre Provincial of the Jesuit Order for New Spain. His old friend, Father Francisco María Piccolo, a Sicilian, was appointed in his place as superior for the Sonora missions of which those in Baja California were a part. Upon Salvatierra's arrival in Mexico City, he urged the viceroy to take steps to continue settling those areas that had proved suitable for agriculture, despite the barrenness of the rest of the peninsula. The viceroy agreed, new sources of money were found and further missions planned.

In the years ahead, the Jesuit fathers were most successful with Indian youths, but they had little success in changing the habits of their parents. Father Juan de Ugarte used force and inducements to get young Indians to learn their catechism. If sweets and other delicacies failed, he joined them at work. In the forming of bricks, Ugarte challenged them to make a play of kneading the clay, and joined them in treading it while raising his voice in songs until the clay was well-kneaded.

Father Jacob Baegert described Loreto after visiting it in 1768. "It is situated in the center of a stretch of sand which reaches for almost half an hour's distance up to the mountains. This land is without grass, with a tree, a bush, or any shade. Loreto bears as little resemblance to a city, a fortified place, or a fortress, as a whale to a night owl.

"The dwelling of the missionary, who also was the administrator and who had a lay brother to assist him, is a small, square, flat-roofed one-story structure of adobe brick thinly coated with lime. One wing of the building is the church, and only this one is, in part, constructed of stone and mortar. The other three wings contain six small rooms each approximately six yards wide and as many yards long, with a light hole toward the sand or the sea. The vestry and the kitchen are found here, also a small general store, where the soldiers, sailors, their wives and children buy buckles, belts, ribbons, combs, tobacco, sugar, linen, shoes, stockings, hats, and similar things for no Italian or other trader ever thought of making a fortune in California.

"Next to the quadrangle four other walls, within which dried steer and bear meat, tallow, fat, soap, unrefined sugar, chocolate, cloth, leather, wheat, Indian corn, several millions of small black bugs which thrive on the grain, lumber, and other things are stored.

"Beyond these imposing buildings a gunshot's distance away, a shed may be seen which serves simultaneously as guardhouse and barracks for unmarried soldiers. The entire soldiery and garrison of Loreto, their captain and lieutenant included, consists occasionally of six or eight, but never more than twelve or fourteen men.

"In addition, there are toward the west two rows of huts made of dirt, in which dwell about a hundred and twenty natives, young and old, men and women. About two to three and a half dozen mud huts are scattered over the sand, without order, looking more like cowsheds of the poorest little village than homes. These are occupied by the married soldiers, the few sailors, the carpenters, and equally numerous blacksmiths, and their wives and children, and serve as lodging, living room, storeroom, and bedroom. Finally, a few poles thatched with brush make up the armory or the shipyard."

Don Felipe de Neve arrived in Loreto as the new military governor March 4, 1775, with orders that would change the destiny of the Californias. New regulations, most of them suggested by Padre Junípero Serra, were established to govern all the missions. While maintaining close relations with the missionaries, without interfering with their religious instruction or upsetting their disciplining of the Indians in minor matters, they were advised that they must not interfere with the enforcement of civil or military authority. One regulation called for the branding of cattle by their owners; otherwise the cattle would be taken to feed the soldiers and their families.

Another regulation set a fee to operate all mines – the Quinto Real or Royal Fifth – that must be paid to the Spanish Crown.

The Jesuits were forced out of Baja in 1768 and they were replaced by the Franciscan order. But management of missions in Baja and Alta California proved too much for the Franciscans so their officals accepted responsibility for missions in Alta California while the Dominicans took over those in Baja.

Expansion of the missions continued despite such changes and the Dominicans in Baja methodically completed their chain of missions to meet up with those established in Alta California by the Franciscans.

By 1800, the Indian population was down to 5,000. Diseases inadvertently introduced by the Spanish continued to decimate the original native population throughout Baja. Many Spaniards considered these deaths as God's punishment for their wickedness and rebellious natures.

By the middle of the 19th century, abandoned missions were literally torn apart because of rumors that the Jesuits, following their expulsion from the peninsula, had hidden their gold and silver, along with church ornaments with a reported value in the millions – some estimates ranged up to 60 million pesos – in one of the old missions.

In the spring of 1900, a goatherd reported that he had slept beside the wall of the old Santa María church and, upon awakening in the morning, he had seen an earthenware pot in the crumbling wall over his head. He told his avid listeners that he dug it out and found 6,000 pesos in gold.

The rumor spread like wildfire and churches were destroyed by gold seekers looking for more pots of gold. No one ever found one, but thousands tried to locate one through the years.

The Jesuits left a legacy of a different kind; one of selfless sacrifice and concern for the salvation of heathen souls.

LORETO TODAY

The inscription above the door of the Misión de Nuestra Señora de Loreto is in Spanish. It says, "Head and Mother of the Mission of Lower and Upper California." The church has undergone a great amount of reconstruction after damage by earthquakes. Little remains of the original structure. Inside, there is a blue-paneled domed tower. All churches had at least three bells, but this one, like those at San Javier and San José Comondú, had up to nine. In the early days, solid silver candlesticks were used on the altars and the Loreto church still has a chalice of pure gold. The altar is gilded, and gold and silver frames hold religious pictures of remarkable quality. Priestly vestments in the old days were silk lined, and bordered with gold. Everything in the church's religious services was brought from Spain at great cost.

Loreto today lies in a palm grove on the shore of the Gulf of California. Jagged peaks of the Sierra de la Giganta form a dramatic backdrop to the west.

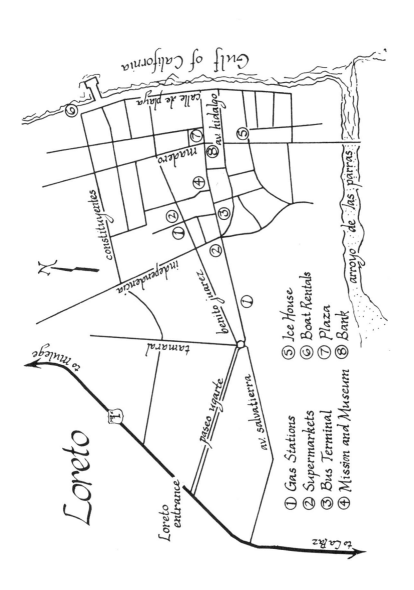

Loreto

Gulf of California

to mulege

Loreto entrance

to La Paz

① Gas Stations
② Supermarkets
③ Bus Terminal
④ Mission and Museum
⑤ Ice House
⑥ Boat Rentals
⑦ Plaza
⑧ Bank

Most major game fish can be caught in the gulf by boats from Loreto, but it is most famous for its roosterfish.

A paved runway for jet aircraft has further opened the area to more tourists and fishermen now that there are commercial flights from Los Angeles to Loreto. With the new marina, and large camp and trailer grounds to the south, development of tourism is increasing at a rapid rate.

Hotels In Loreto

The **Stouffer Presidente** is located at Napoló, about nine miles south of Loreto off Highway 1. Rooms are air conditioned. For a single person the rate is $67-$81 per day and $77-$120 for a double. Each extra person is $37. Pets are forbidden. The mailing address is Apartado Postal 35, Loreto, Baja California Sur 23880, Mexico. Or call (800) 468-3571.

La Pinta, a mile north of the plaza, has a somewhat cheaper rate but it is equally well-appointed. Some rooms have private patios or balconies and a few have fireplaces. The single rate is $44-$56 and the double rate $47-$60 with an $11 charge for each extra person in a room. Pets are permissable, and the usual fishing trips can be arranged (at $76 per day), as can other excursions. The toll-free number is (800) 336-5454. Their mailing address is Apartado Postal 28, Loreto, Baja California Sur, Mexico.

The **Misión de Loreto** is on the shore of Loreto Bay, a quarter-mile east of the town plaza with good air conditioned rooms at $40 single and $46 double. Each extra person in a room costs $5. Fishing boats can be chartered, with a guide, for $110 a day. The mailing address is Apartado Postal 49, Loreto, Baja California Sur, Mexico 23880. Call 01152 (683) 3-0048.

The **Hotel Oasis** is also on the shore of the bay, a half-mile south of the plaza, and is beautifully situated in a palm grove. The rooms are large and rent for $60 single or $77 double with each extra person charged $22. Fishing trips can be arranged and they vary in price from skiffs for three people at $85 a day to $205 a day for cruisers accommodating five. Call 01152 (683) 3-0112, or write Apartado Postal 17, Loreto, Baja California Sur 23880, Mexico.

These hotels all have excellent dining rooms. The **El Nido** chain has a restaurant a mile east of Highway 1 on Salvatierra 154 with the usual ranch atmosphere. Seafood and steaks are served, with dinners from $9 to $20. They are open from noon until 10 p.m. Reservations may be made by calling 01152 (683) 3-0284.

There are more modestly-priced hotels and motels. The **Hotel Villa del Mar** has 80 air conditioned rooms with a bar and restaurant. Reservations may be made by writing Apartado Postal 17, Colonia Zaragoza, Loreto, Baja California Sur, Mexico, or by calling their Loreto number 01152 (683) 3-0299. The **Motel Salvatierra** has 17 air conditioned rooms near the town's center, and they can be reached by calling Loreto 01152 (683) 3-0021.

RV Parks

There are four trailer parks. **Loremar RV Park,** is a half-mile south of the plaza on the beach with 45 RV or tent sites and hookups. They charge $11-$13 per site. The mailing address is Colonia Zaragoza 68, Loreto, Baja California Sur, Mexico. Fifteen miles farther along the highway is the **Tripui Trailer Park** on a paved side road near Puerto Escondido. The grounds are landscaped with 37 large RV sites. They charge up to $14 for two people, and $5 for each additional person. Their mailing address is Apartado Postal 100, Loreto, Baja California Sur 23880, Mexico, or call 01152 (683) 3-0818. The **Playa Juncalito** is a public park 13 miles south of Loreto off Highway 1 on an unpaved road. The beach setting is attractive, but there are no facilities. The fee is $2 per vehicle. There are other such public parks on sandy beaches at **Playa Napoló** and **Playa Notri.**

CANYON OF THE WILD GRAPES

Southwest of Loreto is the Arroyo de las Parras, or the Canyon of the Wild Grapes. Parts of El Camino Real, or the Royal Road, can still be seen in the area. The old road, connecting each of the missions, ranged through the mountains, across dry lakes, and rock-strewn dry riverbeds from the gulf on the east side to the Pacific Ocean on the West. Over its entire length from Baja's tip to the American border, it was 1,187 miles and provided an essential but dangerous link between the missions. There is no road today except a path through rock-strewn terrain. Underground water still can be found in the arroyos because the mountains on each side of the old road drain into them.

Occasionally one finds rusty chains attached to logs. Wild burros were chained to the logs until they were close to starvation to make them more tractable. The Mexicans who used this practice claimed that burros soon became docile after such treatment. Afterwards, the burros were fed with leaves of the dipua tree, a relative of the palo verde, that they love. Few Mexicans will eat the flesh of burros. They believe the cross of darker hair on burros is a sign of divine protection because a similar animal was used to carry Mary and the Christ child.

Wild burros are wary of human beings, and with good reason. They will congregate around a water hole, their eyes bright with intelligence, and with every appearance of good health despite their environment. Once burros are domesticated, their eyes become dull looking and they don't have much spirit.

Burros are a species of small donkey. Many are descendants of the burros that were used to carry ore from the mines at **Las Flores** and other places. There are abandoned ranches all over this area, and many of their cattle and horses went wild. The few ranchers still operating often release their mares so they will mate with wild burros. The offspring are mules that are hardy and can tolerate the hot and dry surroundings.

Burros are frequently abused in captivity. They are sure-footed and can carry heavy loads through rocky country, narrow mountain passes, or across deserts. Mexican ranchers like them because they are tough and they seldom complain.

Here and there in rock-filled arroyos there are tinajas, or large rock basins filled with water. They fill up during run-offs from seasonal rains and are lifesavers to travelers in the mountains and to wildlife. During long periods of drought, tinajas dry up and travel through wild country becomes almost impossible.

Plantlife is varied. The zalate tree is a giant bearing wild figs that are edible, but on the dry side. These trees grow out of the crevices of rocks at the bottom of an arroyo where their roots creep over rocks for a great distance in their constant search for water. It is a beautiful tree with a creamy-colored trunk and green leaves. Mesquite grows profusely, and its dark, gray-green trunks and branches seem to be everywhere. Palo verde trees are aptly named because of their green branches and yellowish-green bark. In spring, the palo verde is covered by cascades of gold flowers. The mesquite and palo verde are both members of the pea family.

After a rain, mountain passes become a riot of color as purple verbenas, golden poppies and multi-colored primroses start to bloom. With the ground carpeted in color, the palo verde trees emerge with yellow blooms, along with the pink blossoms of the elephant trees.

Foot travelers in this area are warned not to camp in low spots. Sudden rain storms at night can fill the arroyo's bed with a wall of rushing water that sweeps everything in its path. Although the arroyo is fairly close to civilization, it is still wild country that can be unforgiving to those ill-prepared to meet its sudden whims of violence.

MISSION SAN JAVIER

Southwest of Loreto there is a rough road that leads into the interior and is passable only for high-clearance vehicles. It crosses the Sierra de la Giganta that divides Baja California along the Gulf. The road is steep in places along its 23-mile route to the Mission San Javier, located in an almost inaccessible valley. There are a few ranches along the route and each has its own water supply. In one place, there is a waterfall surrounded by native fan palms. The ranches have green gardens that give an idyllic look to otherwise barren surroundings. The road is graded but it has deep ruts and is difficult to drive. Early explorers and priests must have found the Sierra de la Giganta a formidable barrier to cross. At the summit, the Gulf of California can be seen to the east, and the blue waters seem to have a vibrancy that one does not notice at Loreto. These waters normally are calm but a south wind at times brushes the surface while only an occasional small boat breaks the monotony. During chubascos, however, the waters of the gulf are rippled by white caps.

The church at San Javier nestles in a deep valley beneath towering walls of gray rocks, its dark volcanic squares set in mortar. The church was built of five-foot-thick walls in the form of a cross, with a high tower, a graceful cupola, and with recessed windows.

On the stone arch above one of the church's three doors the date of 1758 has been carved. Inside, the main altar – one of three – is covered with gold leaf, and it is surrounded by statuary and religious paintings. A spiral stairway leads to the tower and it is fashioned of stone blocks. The stairs to the tower were made of mesquite – one of the strongest and most decay-resistant woods known to man. The colored-glass windows probably are the only ones remaining from the early mission days. Those at Loreto were destroyed in an earthquake.

The valley around the church was formed by erosion of old lava flows. Outside, the church blends well with its stark surroundings. Inside, the church is a marvel of color with three high altars finished in gold. In its heyday, young boys were trained for the church's choirs. There are many accounts of their glorious voices raised in honor of the Christian God. Above the altars there are plaster mouldings and paintings with detailed religious scenes.

Father del Barco wrote his superiors after the church was completed in 1758, "The church is all of mortar and stone, with proper vaults, with its transept and cupola well made and a tower in proportion. It is adorned more than average with three retablos in its three altars, silver fixtures and decent ornaments for the divine service.

"This church is in the headquarters of the site or town called San Pablo, but to which about 40 years ago was moved the household of the missionary father because of the failure of permanent water at the site where this mission was established in the first conquest of the region. There only remains there at the first site a little ranchería or town (where no one lives all year) with the name of Old San Javier, the headquarters having been moved to the place of San Pablo, the name San Javier was moved also and that of San Pablo has fallen into disuse and that Saint remains as a Patron without a constituency."

Padre Miguel del Barco remained at his church until the Jesuits were evicted from the peninsula in 1768. Like all Jesuit priests, he was sent into exile to the Papal States of Italy. Behind him in Baja, he left an enduring monument for his efforts that will probably last for centuries to come.

The once-fertile valley around the church now is a desert without water. Only a few inhabitants remain in the area on ranches and in the village, although the church is still used for services. There's a small store used by area residents.

HIGHWAY 1 FROM LORETO
TO CONSTITUCIÓN

The road south of Loreto towards La Paz has some of the most spectacular scenery in all of Baja. On the left, the deep-blue waters of the gulf lap against glistening beaches. On the right, the reddish-brown slopes of the Sierra de la Giganta rise abruptly. There are dangerous curves and switchbacks along the coastal highway, but nothing compared to what it becomes after the road turns inland. Soon, however, it straightens out and crosses a wide valley reminiscent of upper California's Imperial Valley. Someday this may rival it in productivity now that federal water projects are turning the arid soil into a major agricultural area.

In one deep canyon the road snakes along as it descends into Villa Insurgentes and turns south. This is part of the Magdalena Plain, arid for the most part but spotted by oases of green farmland. This land is irrigated by wells whose water is recovered after being trapped for centuries deep in the earth. Several farms are quite large; cotton and produce trucks are common as they head either for Loreto to the north or to La Paz in the south.

Sixteen miles farther south is Ciudad Constitución, resembling a town in the American Old West of the 1880s. A few years ago it was only a tiny village. Now it is growing so rapidly, with more than 48,000 people, that it has become the second largest city in the state of Baja California Sur. Cotton is still the leading agricultural product, and it is ginned locally. Wheat, alfalfa and vegetables are also widely grown on newly-irrigated land that looks like a checkerboard from the air. Tourists are welcome, but the city has few facilities to satisfy a traveler's needs.

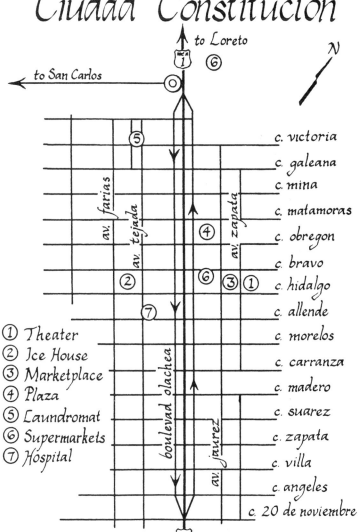

Ciudad Constitución

to Loreto

to San Carlos

N

c. victoria
c. galeana
c. mina
c. matamoras
c. obregon
c. bravo
c. hidalgo
c. allende
c. morelos
c. carranza
c. madero
c. suarez
c. zapata
c. villa
c. angeles
c. 20 de noviembre

av. farias
av. tejada
av. zapata
boulevad olachea
av. jaurez

① Theater
② Ice House
③ Marketplace
④ Plaza
⑤ Laundromat
⑥ Supermarkets
⑦ Hospital

Hotels In Constitución

The **Hotel Maribel** on Guadalupe Victoria at Highway 1 is well-equipped to satisfy travelers with single rooms priced at $30 and doubles with private balconies a dollar more. There are also some suites. There is a charge of $3 for each extra person in a room. A dining room and bar are open all day. Write them at Guadalupe Victoria 156, Ciudad Constitución, Baja California Sur, Mexico, or call 01152 (683) 2-0155. Two other places, the **Hotel El Conquistador,** Nicholas Bravo 161, 01152 (683) 2-1555, and the **Motel Casino** at Guadalupe Victoria y Juárez, 01152 (683) 2-0751, offer about the same accommodations in this price range.

RV Park

There's only one campsite. The **Campestre La Pila** has 70 sites, with hookups, a mile and a half south of the city on an unpaved road off Highway 1. The fee is $8 for two people, with an additional $2 for each extra person. You can write them at Apartado Postal 261, Ciudad Constitución, Baja California Sur, Mexico. Call 01152 (683) 2-0562.

HIGHWAY 1 SOUTH TO LA PAZ

The ever-changing nature of Baja California asserts itself again after Constitución, where you encounter a wasteland so uninviting that its annual rainfall is less than two inches a year.

Traffic is heavier through this area, and more roadside shrines appear. Hundreds of such shrines have been placed along Baja's highways by relatives of loved ones who were killed at the spot marked by each. Some are simple shrines with dried flowers, while others are more elaborate. One is a replica of a cardón cactus made out of concrete.

The road south traverses a seemingly endless terrain with chalk-covered hills and eroded gullies. This is Baja California's worst wasteland. Usually, the only sign of another living creature is a vulture soaring high in the sky. They appear to float on motionless wings. A motorist is often startled as a vulture plummets from the sky to snatch a dead rodent off the road. On the ground the large bird is clumsy, running along the road flapping its wings until it can become airborne. In the air, however, the vulture's five-foot wings carry him gracefully as he rides air currents to some distant hideaway.

In Baja, as elsewhere, vultures are the scavengers of the world, living primarily on dead animals. They patrol the skies for hours and can spot carcasses of animals miles away. Their eyesight is so keen that a human being can equal it only by using binoculars. All vultures, including the Upper California Condors, have broad wings with slotted tips to give them stability in flight. They can regulate the size of these slots, rotate the tips of their feathers, and bend their wings to change the flight angle. Vultures are much more efficient aerodynamically than anything man has ever created. They date back to the earth's Ice Age when their ancestors had wings 17 feet wide – probably the largest birds that ever lived on planet earth.

The blue waters of the Gulf of California make their appearance again as the road reaches a bluff. For miles the waters of the gulf spread to the north and south, with the crescent-shaped Bahía de La Paz in the middle. La Paz, or the City of Peace, is farther east than Tucson, Arizona, or Salt Lake City, Utah, because the peninsula curves toward the east. It is only 50 miles north of the Tropic of Cancer.

The road descends to the wide coastal plain that is farmed to feed a growing population. La Paz lies on a narrow shelf between the barren foothills and the curving line of the bay. It is a city of old Spanish colonial charm and, at night, along the Malecón or sea wall colorful promenades by the young of both sexes add a touch of glamour. Although La Paz is a growing city, it still maintains a small-town atmosphere.

This area is much like the south of Italy in climate, and it has attracted admirers from all over the world. It is best in winter when the sun is less oppressive than during the summer. Sunsets are so magnificent that they have to be seen to be appreciated. La Paz faces northwest so it gets the maximum impact from its sunsets.

La Paz's Incredible History

The history of this "City of Peace" dates back more than 450 years to the time when one of Hernán Cortés's pilots explored the area in 1533. Two years later Cortés took possession of the land for the Spanish Crown. He named the first settlement Santa Cruz in honor of the festival day on which he claimed the land. This is the area now known as La Paz. This event occurred 85 years before the Pilgrims landed at Plymouth Rock.

A freebooter, William Walker, in 1853 tried to take over Baja and to establish a new nation. This self-styled general sailed to La Paz with approximately 300 men from San Francisco on the bark *Caroline* to take over the city, and ultimately the peninsula. With him, he had a staff of secretaries that he hoped to appoint as cabinet members in a new government.

Walker and his men reached La Paz November 3, hauled down the Mexican flag from the defenseless city, and hoisted his own. He proclaimed Baja California a separate republic, announcing he would act as president and that civil and military power would be held by his men. Baja California and the mainland state of Sonora were proclaimed part of this new nation to be known as the Republic of Sonora.

While Walker was busily forming his new government, he secretly sailed from La Paz to meet with his co-conspirator Colonel Watkins. Watkins had sailed from San Francisco December 7, 1853 with 100 armed men to join the new republic. The two men met south of San Diego.

Meanwhile, the Mexican Government sent troops into Baja and the state of Sonora to oppose the invasion, and Walker and his men left precipitously for the United States. Military officers at San Diego arrested them and accepted Walker's parole to appear later at a trial for breaching the neutrality laws of the United States. At the trial, nothing could be proved against Walker, and the charges against him were dropped.

Walker edited several newspapers in California during the next two years, but he could not resist the call to continue his freebooting ways. This time he went to Nicaragua and Honduras to foment trouble. When the British resisted his efforts in Honduras, he was captured and executed.

Early Pearl Fishing

Pearl fishing first attracted the Spaniards to La Paz but now is largely a thing of the past, although some limited pearl fishing is still conducted. There are residents who believe that Japanese fishermen, who often came to these waters prior to World War II, did something to destroy the beds. There is no truth to these allegations, and the beds probably died out because of a disease or, more likely, due to over-fishing. In its heyday, pearl fishermen extracted thousands of black, green, pink and white pearls from the bay's oyster beds.

Indians had been diving for pearls for years but, after the Spaniards settled La Paz, their dives were regimented in a way that they intensely disliked. A mother ship was used over the beds, and divers carried a pointed stick to dig the oysters from the bottom. They remained below as long as humanly possible before surfacing and placing their oysters in bags hung around the ship. Once the bags were filled, divers joined the ship's crew in a circle around the ship's owner or armador, who selected two oysters from each bag for himself, two for the busos or divers, and one for the king. After the bags were emptied, with piles of oysters on the deck, the process of opening began under the watchful eyes of the armador. The owner remained in the center as each oyster was opened to make sure that the divers, in swallowing the meat of each oyster, did not also swallow a valuable pearl. Oysters included in the king's fifth were opened the same way, and his pearls were deposited separately. The pearls belonging to the divers generally were sold to the armador on the spot. Normally, the Indians were so indebted to him for their outfits that they had little left over for the basic necessities of life. They managed to hold out some pearls to sell on shore to traders who gave them in exchange metal knives, liquor, cigars, sweets, and cheap articles of little value – often for pearls of great worth.

During the pearl-fishing season, normally July until October, divers frequently ruined their health because they remained too long in the ocean's depths. Generally, though, owners tried to limit their underwater activities to short periods.

Spanish and British scientists both realized that a diver with a mask and a flexible tube might remain below for longer periods and be more productive. Tests also were tried in both countries with primitive diving bells that were constructed to supply a reservoir of air and even furnish divers a refuge if they suffered from a lack of oxygen. This was a sound idea, developed centuries later, but technology had not advanced in this age to the point where such a bell could be successfully developed.

Shark And Shrimp Fishing

Shark and shrimp fishing has replaced the taking of pearls as a lucrative trade. Germany's occupation of Norway in 1940 cut off a major source of cod liver oil, and Mexicans made up the shortage by fishing for sharks. The livers of many gulf sharks contain a hundred times more Vitamin A per gram of oil than cod livers. Shark fishing boomed during the war years, and the shark population was so huge that there was no noticeable reduction in their numbers. In the late 1940s, a synthetic Vitamin A was developed that replaced the natural variety in fish livers so Mexican fishermen lost a major business to science. Although sharks are no longer economically a major resource for Mexicans, shrimp fishing is most lucrative.

Father Serra's Supply Ship

Father Serra's supply ship, missing for more than 200 years, was located in the gulf north of La Paz. A shrimp fisherman dredged up a bronze mission bell that matches the description of the three known to have been on the 72-foot Spanish packet ship bound for the San Diego mission in 1769. On one side of the bell the inscription reads "San Agustín," and it weighs 150 pounds.

The *San José* was lost while en route from La Paz to San Diego carrying relief supplies for the mission there. In addition to the bell, it also carried 10,000 pounds of dried meat, eight casks of wine, two casks of brandy, 1,250 pounds of dried figs plus beans, raisins, dried fish, trading goods for the Indians and vestments for the padres.

LA PAZ TODAY

The city is growing at a spectacular rate and its present 176,000 population rises yearly. From November through May the days are ideal, with warm temperatures and balmy nights that defy description. In summer La Paz can be uncomfortably hot between noon and four o'clock, and children and older adults suffer from the stifling heat. The waters of the bay turn a dull gray, and there isn't a ripple to mar the surface.

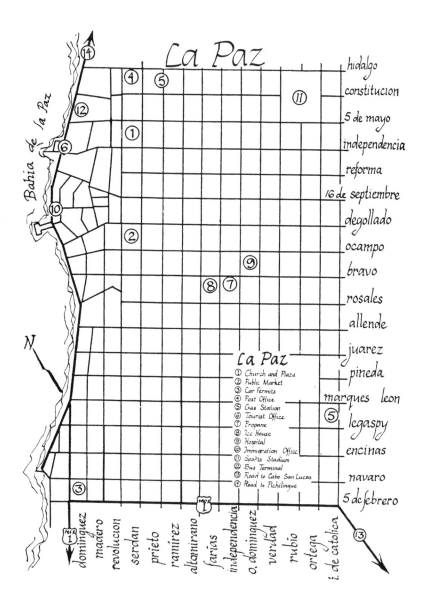

La Paz

① Church and Plaza
② Public Market
③ Car Permits
④ Post Office
⑤ Gas Station
⑥ Tourist Office
⑦ Propane
⑧ Ice House
⑨ Hospital
⑩ Immigration Office
⑪ Sports Stadium
⑫ Bus Terminal
⑬ Road to Cabo San Lucas
⑭ Road to Pichilingue

Bahia de la Paz

N

hidalgo
constitucion
5 de mayo
independencia
reforma
16 de septiembre
degollado
ocampo
bravo
rosales
allende
juarez
pineda
marques leon
legaspy
encinas
navaro
5 de febrero

dominguez
madero
revolucion
serdan
prieto
ramirez
altamirano
farias
independencia
o. dominguez
verdad
rubio
ortega
i. de catolica

The people of La Paz have a saying that "only gringos and dogs will venture forth at midday, and in La Paz even the dogs know better."

After four o'clock, a breeze called the *coromuele* blows down the bay from the land and the city comes slowly to life. No one is sure how the name was derived, and there are several explanations. One is that *coromuele* is a corruption of the word Cromwell. Oliver Cromwell was lord protector of England between 1653 and 1658. Early English privateers were known as men of Cromwell. There is also the story that Cromwell was the name of a pirate in the 18th century who set his sails to this breeze and rode into the bay on marauding expeditions. There is no historical record that such a character existed. It is more likely that the daily breeze is named for a type of sail that fishing boats once used.

The streets of La Paz are shaded by coco palms and Indian laurels. In early spring, some of the streets are a riot of color as jacarandas, flame trees and acacias provide blue, red and yellow splashes of color until late in the fall. Nestled beneath these trees are adobe homes coated with plaster and placed flush with the sidewalks. Inside most homes are flower-filled patios.

The broad street or Malecón that parallels the sea wall is bordered by coconut palms on the bay side, and Indian laurels on the other. In the evening, strolling members of both sexes enliven the Malecón with their happy laughter and colorful apparel. Many a romance started on the Malecón, so its attraction is multi-faceted.

Opposite La Paz is El Mogote, a narrow sandspit that separates the main part of Bahía de La Paz from inlets on the west known as Ensenada de los Aripes. These inlets are almost hidden by bright green mangrove bushes. In the gulf east of La Paz is a basin 10,800 feet deep. It was formed when Baja split from the mainland 20 million years ago, leaving volcanic peaks as islands when the sea rushed into the huge trench created by the cataclysm. The city is noted for its excellent beaches, and it is world-renowned for its sport fishing. There are excellent modern accomodations for tourists, and the duty-free shops lure people from all parts of the North American continent.

Chubascos have long plagued this end of the peninsula, and La Paz suffered widespread loss of life and property from one in 1976. The city recovered quickly, and many of the ramshackle homes that were destroyed were bulldozed and replaced by modern apartments. This is an old story for La Paz, and each time the city has risen from devastation to become more modern and livable.

Hotels In La Paz

The **Hotel de los Arcos** opposite the Malecón, or sea wall, at Alvaro Obregón is located on La Paz's waterfront, and it's a colonial-style hotel with single rooms at $58 and doubles $5 more. Each extra person has to pay $5. There are suites available. Pets are forbidden, and a deposit is required with a normal three-day refund notice (15 days for holiday occupancy). The mailing address is Apartado Postal 112, La Paz, Baja California Sur, Mexico. Call (800) 421-3772 or, in California, (800) 352-2579.

The **Cabañas de los Arcos** is a wing of the hotel with 52 units, including 16 garden bungalows at the same rate as the hotel. Reservations can be made at the above numbers.

La Concha Beach Resort, formerly the El Presidente, has 110 air conditioned rooms on the beach about three miles north of the city on Calle Rangel S/N. Depending on the season, single and double rooms are $45 to $55. Call (800) 347-2252.

The **Hotel Palmira** is two miles northeast of the city's center on a paved road to the Pichilingue Ferry Terminal. A modern hotel, nestled in a lovely setting across from a beach, it charges $49 for a single room, $65 for a double, and $5.50 for each extra person in a room. Pets cannot be accommodated. There are various family plans that should be explored by calling 01152 (682) 2-4000, or write Apartado Postal 442, La Paz, Baja California Sur, Mexico.

La Posada de Englebert Motel is a lovely older place on the beach of Bahía de La Paz, 2 1/4 miles southwest of the city's center off Highway 1. Suites are available. Single rooms rent for $44 and doubles for $50, with extra persons charged $10 each. Pets are not welcome. Reservations and a deposit are required with a three-day cancellation notice for a refund. You can reach them by mail at Apartado Postal 152, La Paz, Baja California Sur, Mexico, or by calling 01152 (682) 2-4011.

There are several less expensive places to stay. The **Hotel Perla** has single rooms at $35 and double rooms for $36. Each extra person is charged $16. No pets are allowed. Their mailing address is Paseo Obregón, 1570, La Paz, Baja California Sur 23000, Mexico, or call 01152 (682) 2-0777. The **Club El Morro** is two miles northeast of the city across from Palmira Beach. This is a small Moorish-style hotel with attractive landscaping. The single and double rooms are $66. Apartments with kitchens rent for $66 with one bedroom and $88 with two bedrooms. A refund notice of seven days is required. Reservations may be made by writing Apartado Postal 357, La Paz, Baja California Sur, Mexico, or by calling 01152 (682) 2-4084. The **Hotel Aquario** at Ignacio Ramírez 1665 has 60 air conditioned rooms. Reservations may be made by calling 01152 (682) 2-9266. The **Hotel Calafia** has 28 rooms at Km. 4 on Highway 1 north. For reservations call 01152 (682) 2-5811. The **Hotel Guaycura** has 40 rooms in the same area and can be reached at 01152 (682) 2-6700.

Restaurants

Most hotels serve excellent food but two independent restaurants are noteworthy. **El Taste** is a half-mile southwest of the city's center section on Paseo Alvaro Obregón at Juárez.

Overlooking the Malecón and the bay, it specializes in Mexican food based on beef and seafood recipes. Dinners range in price up to $18. For reservations call 01152 (682) 2-8121. **La Paz-Lapa de Carlos 'n Charlies** is in the same area, at Marquez de Leon. Diners eat in a patio on the waterfront. This restaurant specializes in Mexican food and charges up to $18 for dinner. It is open from noon to 11 p.m., Wednesday through Monday. For reservations call 01152 (682) 2-6025.

RV Parks

Trailer parks are numerous and generally excellent. The **Oasis Los Aripez** is on La Paz Bay, 9 1/2 miles north on Highway 1 in the small town of El Centenario. It has 29 RV or tent sites on the beach with hookups and a restaurant and bar. The charge is $11 for two people, and $2 for each extra individual. Write Km 15 Transpeninsular Norte, La Paz, Baja California Sur, Mexico. The **Aquamarina RV Park** is two miles southwest of the city's downtown, just off Highway 1 on Calle Nayarit. The landscaping is superb, and the park is on the bay offering 19 RV sites with hookups, a marina, boat ramp and a storage area. They charge $15 for two people, and $1 for each extra person. Write Apartado Postal 133, La Paz, Baja California Sur, Mexico, or call 01152 (682) 2-3761.

A mile south of the city's center is **La Paz Trailer Park** in a residential area with 56 RV sites and 40 RV or tent sites with hookups. The fee is $13 per site for two people, and $2 for each additional person. There's a three-day deposit refund notice requirement. Write Apartado Postal 482, La Paz, Baja California Sur, Mexico, or call 01152 (682) 2-8787. The **El Cardón Trailer Park** is 2 1/2 miles southwest of the city on Highway 1. It's in a partially-shaded area at the edge of the city. It has 90 RV or tent sites with hookups and a $10 fee for each site. Their mailing address is Apartado Postal 104, La Paz, Baja California Sur, Mexico. Or call 01152 (682) 2-0078.

There are two public campgrounds. **Puerto Balandra** is four and a half miles north of the ferry terminal by way of an unpaved road. It is located on the shore of a lovely inlet surrounded by mangrove trees. The fee is $2 per vehicle, for which you receive only trash cans. Another mile farther north is the **Playa Tecolete** near the northern tip of the peninsula. It also has a $2 fee and provides no facilities.

Shopping

Travelers will find shopping in La Paz a treat, with the usual imports and Mexican goods, and their first chance since Ensenada to stock up on food at reasonable prices in the city's large supermarkets, bakeries and fruit markets. "La Perla de La Paz" is a huge department store where you can buy almost anything, including auto parts and sporting goods.

Night Life

La Paz is not noted for its nighttime entertainment although the major hotels provide some. The popular discotheques at the **Hotel Palmira,** the **Gran Hotel Baja,** and **La Cabaña** in the Hotel Perla on Paseo Alvaro Obregón satisfy some of this desire for live entertainment, as does **El Bucanero** across from the beach at the end of Calle Salinas.

Ferries To & From La Paz

There is extensive ferry service from La Paz to mainland cities such as Topolobampo, Mazatlán and Puerto Vallarta. They are located at Pichilingue, 10 miles from La Paz via the paved Highway 11. This is the northward extension of Paseo Alvaro Obregón along the city's bay and is its main street. This highway ends at the ferry terminal.

Ferries leave for Topolobampo Monday, Tuesday, Wednesday, Thursday, Saturday, and Sunday at 8 p.m., arriving at their destination at 4 a.m. Passengers are charged $11 for a salon seat. Vehicle fares are determined by length, varying from $73 for lengths up to 16.4 feet, and up to $246 for cars and trailers with an overall length of 29.5 to 55.8 feet. Motorhomes are charged $120.

Ferries from La Paz to Mazatlán and back operate every day, leaving at the same hour of 5 p.m. from each port, with arrival time the following morning at 9 a.m. Passengers pay $16.50 for a salon seat, a roomette with bunk is $33, a bedroom with a bathroom, $50. Vehicles up to 16.4 feet are charged $122 and the rate increases to a maximum $450 for a car and trailer with a total length of 29.5 feet to 55.8 feet. Motorhomes are charged $206.

The Baja Express uses a catamaran to carry passengers (no vehicles) to Topolobampo. It leaves the commercial wharf near downtown La Paz at 10 a.m. Tuesdays through Sundays. The Express departs Topolobampo at 3 p.m. Rates are $35-$48, which includes ground transportation to Las Mochis, Sinaloa. Call 01152 (682) 5-6311 in La Paz or toll free in California at (800) 829-0510.

Heading South from La Paz

BIRDS & FISH OF THE GULF

The port at La Paz, and the warm waters of the Gulf of California, has always attracted anglers from all over the world. There are many protected areas on both sides of the gulf where fish are spawned. Larger fish have been coming from the tropics for thousands of years. Many of the biggest, along with small whales, migrate to the gulf in season. Dolphins and porpoises, as well as sea lions on the islands, are common. They visit the gulf at certain times of the year and some even stay the year around. Shell fish are abundant, and they provide valuable food for the Mexican populace as well as for the large bill fish.

Birds and animals have adapted to the special conditions in the Gulf of California. There is a type of bat that lives on rocky islands and eats only seafood instead of insects like other bats. At dusk, these bats are a familiar sight as they skim the water, catching small fish with their claws.

San Pedro Mártir Island in the gulf's mid-section is home for large colonies of boobies. The brown booby, and the blue-footed booby, are large, handsome birds with fierce eyes and topknots resembling crewcut hairdos. They are strong fliers and can career seaward from a height of 60 feet in pursuit of a fish, disappearing entirely into the water. When they emerge, the booby will have a small fish in its long, yellow beak. After swallowing the fish quickly, the booby rises a few feet off the water to search the area. Soon, it will spot a school of fish and strike again and again, capturing a fish each time during dives from just a few feet above the water. The blue-footed booby has dark brown feathers, except for a portion of its underbody which is white.

The booby is not afraid of people, but fears the frigate bird and it will drop its catch if it is pursued by one. Early Spanish sailors called the bird a bobo or dunce, and the name became anglicized to booby. He may be stupid-looking on the ground, but the booby is a marvel of graceful precision in the air.

Pelicans lurk around fishing boats in the gulf. Like the booby on the ground, the pelican is squat and awkward on the shore with its enormous beak pointing down. In the air, it is a creature of dignity and charm. In their natural element, their powerful wings seem to barely move as, in rhythm with a leader, they sweep across the water. It is a thrilling sight to see a pelican dive from 50 feet as it spots a fish, dropping to the water's surface with half-closed wings. During his free fall, the big bird twists in the air as his target maneuvers beneath the surface until, with a splash, the pelican hits the water almost on his back and slides beneath the surface. The large air sac under his skin serves as a cushion and helps him to pop back to the surface.

The frigate bird is the terror of the skies. When it folds its huge wings and forked tail and hurtles at another bird rising from the surface with a fish in its beak, the other bird normally drops its catch and hurries away. If the other bird tries to get away by streaking across the wave tops, the frigate bird spreads its seven-foot wings and, uttering a harsh, chattering cry of rage, takes off after the fleeing bird, who frantically ends the pursuit by dropping the fish. Frigates are the pirates of the sea, and they are aptly named man-o'-war birds. Their wings seem out of proportion to their small bodies, which normally weigh less than three pounds. Actually, their skeletons weigh only four ounces and they have two sets of flight muscles attached to their breast bones. One set provides the power stroke on the down beat of its wing while the other acts like a pulley to pull the wing up. Their feathers overlap like shingles on the roof of a house, giving their bodies great flexibility in flight.

Frigate birds are skilled robbers. Sometimes several will gang up on a booby, bite him, and force him to drop his fish. They are not true sea birds because their feathers are not waterproof. If their bodies ever get soaked, they will drown. They nest on rocky heights or in tree tops. During the breeding season, the male's throat turns crimson and puffs up so it resembles a balloon under its beak.

Gulls follow fishing boats, their noisy chatter irritating at times as they wheel gracefully above the incredibly blue waters of the gulf. Cormorants are numerous, diving headfirst into the water, and hardly ever failing to make a catch. They usually avoid frigate birds who dare not go into the water, but who hope to snatch a fish from their more aquatic brethren.

Chuckwalla lizards, up to two feet in length, inhabit some of the gulf's islands. These odd creatures store fresh water in sacs that become so heavy they gurgle when they walk. If fresh water is not available, the chuckwalla has the unique capacity of converting salt water to its use.

There is another unusual lizard that has only two front legs and moves across the ground much like a worm.

Flying fish are common, leaping out of the water to escape one of their numerous predators. Albacore will vault clear out of the water to catch one of them. These 75-pound yellowfin tuna can make surprising leaps when they spot a flying fish.

Isla Espíritu Santo, or Holy Spirit Island, spreads across the outer reaches of the bay of La Paz. Manta rays are frequently seen here, and these huge creatures rise with breathtaking speed from the depths, looking like some bat-winged monster. They often fly above the surface for some distance before plopping down with a resounding splash and disappearing. A giant manta ray weighs a ton or more. There are a greater number to the south around Cabo San Lucas. They are harmless to humans, but smaller sting rays can be painful if stepped on in shallow water.

The waters around La Paz, and throughout the gulf, abound with game fish in season and they provide hours of untold delight for those who enjoy deep-sea fishing. Sadly, the once-plentiful bill fish have been depleted in recent years and people are encouraged to release them once they have been brought up to the boat. Bill fish are not particularly good eating and, to insure years of game fishing for the future, more and more people are heeding the pleas of conservationists.

Sharks are still plentiful and these raiders of the deep will snatch a catch as it comes alongside a boat, their rows of teeth showing all too vividly as they slash chunks out of helpless large fish. At times, a shark seems to have a macabre grin as it moves in close with its long snout and murderous teeth.

Fishing For Marlin

Cruising through the serene waters, with two lines on outriggers trailing lures or bait fish far behind, everything will be quiet until a line sings and becomes taut after leaving its outrigger. The slap of the skipper's bare feet lends excitement as he races back to give the fisherman a hand. The first sight of a marlin rearing out of the water hundreds of feet behind the boat is a sight no one will ever forget. While the captain races the motor to set the hook the marlin will seemingly stand on its tail while it whips its head trying to dislodge the hook. Then the battle is on, with the fisherman reeling frantically as the line goes slack and the marlin heads toward the rear of the boat, or to one side. Soon, the marlin sounds and the pole seems about to break. There is nothing the fisherman can do except keep the pressure on, and hang on while the line goes out.

With the boat's canopy pushed back, the sun bears down and the battle between fish and fisherman becomes an ordeal, often lasting an hour or more depending upon the size of the fish. An experienced captain can make the difference between success or failure as he maneuvers his cabin cruiser adroitly, putting pressure on the marlin when it is needed, and relieving the fisherman of some of his back-breaking, arm-twisting chore. For minutes, the blue water erupts as the fighting-mad marlin shakes its head and long bill in hopes of getting the tormenting hook out of its mouth. For the marlin, it is a fight for life as it rises high above the surface only to splash back into the water, sending cascades of spray 20 feet into the air.

After 20 minutes, even the most avid fisherman feels that his or her arms are turning numb. At times, the pole bends almost double as the marlin dives deep, and one has to let him go even deeper because brute force would snap the line. Suddenly the line goes limp, and you have to reel madly as the marlin heads back up. Otherwise the hook will be dislodged. Even the strongest fisherman – or woman – soon has beads of sweat on the forehead because the marlin strains their strength to the utmost.

Now it becomes a matter of endurance – who will outlast the other? Most times, the marlin loses because he is unable to overcome the expertise of the person with the rod combined with the pull of the boat's powerful motor dragging him through the water despite his powerful muscles and fins. Once the marlin gives up, he can be brought alongside. He deserves another chance, and the wise fisherman signals for release of this magnificent creature.

In the past, bill fish were not wasted, and if the fisherman did not want to take it home to be mounted, it was given to one of several orphanages where its flesh was appreciated. Today, in releasing the billfish they are not harmed because the hook is carefully removed. Then the fish slowly swims away and disappears into the depths.

There are many commercial fishermen in the gulf, and cormorants can be a nuisance to them. Oftentimes these fishermen will find a large school of fish only to have them scattered by cormorants. Fish will panic whenever a cormorant is overhead because they are such good fishers.

During the mating season, cormorants put on a show that is almost unbelievable. The male bird pounds his wings on the water near a female bird, then hurtles himself along the surface, jumping in and out of the water. Both birds then toss bits of seaweed at each other, while one spins away and goes round and round in a madcap merry-go-round, swinging its orange throat pouch and hook bill. They are beautiful birds, with bronze-colored heads and necks, merging to black lower down and becoming intermixed with shiny green feathers.

Hooking A Dolphinfish

Among the non-bill game fish, the dolphinfish is the most exciting once it is hooked. The dolphinfish should not be confused with the porpoise to which it bears no resemblance. It is related to the Hawaiian mahimahi-a, one of the tastiest eating fish of all. They are difficult to catch, and one of the most vicious fish in the gulf. The dolphinfish tears tackle apart and makes incredible leaps into the air once it is hooked. It has a stubby head and narrow fins extending down its spine.

When a dolphinfish is hooked, it rears out of the water and savagely shakes its head to dislodge the hook. An average of 20 pounds in weight, it puts up a fight out of all proportion to its size. Each time tension is applied to the line the dolphinfish seems to career off the wave tops, pulling on arms that soon begin to ache. At times, when the dolphinfish explodes out of the water, all the hard-won gains to bring the fish closer to the boat are lost and one must begin again in a contest to determine who will wear out first. With persistence, the battle is eventually won and the beautiful fish with its gold belly, iridescent sides, blue fins and emerald-green dorsal fin is alongside the boat. In death, the shimmering rainbow colors quickly fade and their beauty with it.

SIDE TRIP TO SAN JUAN DE LOS PLANES & ENSENADA DE LOS MUERTOS

While visiting in La Paz, a side trip to San Juan de los Planes will prove to be a delightful 29-mile jaunt where tourists seldom go. On the city's southern outskirts a road marked "BCS 286" leaves Highway 1 and travels through a lush farming area. On a summit 16 miles from La Paz the Bahía de la Ventana is visible on the left while straight ahead is San Juan de los Planes. A graded road to the left travels seven miles to El Sargento and La Ventana. These fishing villages are on the lovely bay's western shore. If you remain on "286" it takes you first to an intersection with a new road that goes off to the right about 15 miles to the village of San Antonio on Highway 1. But traveling farther brings you to San Juan de los Planes, a town of 1,000 people and a cafe, several stores and a health center. The town is set in a rich agricultural region. Although the pavement ends here you can take the dirt road for another 13 miles to Ensenada de los Muertos or Deadman's Bay. The bay curves gently to the north and the area is incredibly beautiful. There's a small fishing camp here because the fishing is superb.

Where To Stay

There are some good campsites at the bay, although they are primitive, with limited facilities.

The **Hotel Las Arenas** is just south of Punta Arena de la Ventana by way of Highway 286. It is a modern resort hotel whose private balconies overlook the gulf of California. It's expensive, at up to $95 for a single room, $164 for a double, and $50 for each extra person in a room. There are special rates for children under 12. A 6,000-foot airstrip is nearby and it can be contacted on unicom 122.8 by incoming aircraft. A full range of boating/fishing reservations is available. Their mailing address is Hotel Las Arenas, 16211 E. Whittier Blvd., Whittier CA 90603 for mandatory reservations and deposit. You can call toll free from anywhere in the United States at (800) 423-4785.

HIGHWAY 1 SOUTH FROM LA PAZ

There are isolated ranches on each side of the road as it heads south for Cabo San Lucas and motorists are warned by signs that cattle freely range across the road. Most cattle and horses are gaunt, seeking constantly for something edible to sustain them. People who have settled here have learned to live off the land, and they have few modern conveniences. They cultivate crops, raise cattle and goats, and are as independent as any people on earth. Their homes are built with what nature provides. They use palo de arco wood in six-foot lengths, and weave it together to form walls that are covered with adobe. Fences are made of the same material, along with ocotillo that is woven between the rods. For a tight roof they rely upon thatch.

Mesquite is frequently used to make boats, and this wood is fitted together in pieces with great skill. What metal is used comes from scraps that are formed in an open-air forge. Joints are held together with bolts instead of rivets and they are fashioned in the same way.

These ranches live in isolated independence. They are a self-confident group, contented for the most part with their lives because, having learned to live off the land, their wants are few. Doctors are few in number, and ranchers have learned to be self-reliant during periods of ill health.

Even during months when the desert is bright with flowering trees and shrubs there is a monotony to this land as one vacant mile follows another until the road seems endless.

Desert Vegetation South Of La Paz

On Highway 1 south of La Paz the desert springs to life once the rains start to fall. Trees and shrubs that had been drab-looking now burst into bloom, and the desert becomes gay with color, where only a few weeks earlier it had looked half dead. Cirio trees now dangle sprays of pale yellow blossoms at the end of their arm-like branches. The flowers are small, but they fill the area with a sweet odor.

Every twig of the gnarled and distorted branches of the elephant trees is covered with clusters of tiny flowers that have a faint, but pleasant odor. They resemble peach trees in bloom, and many are covered with pink blossoms. Others have salmon-colored or yellow blossoms. They bloom heavily to assure survival of the species.

Palo blanco trees grow wild throughout much of this area. They are small, related to the acacia family, with bark that is white on the outside, somewhat similar to the more familiar birch tree in northern climes. Towards the center, the wood of the palo blanco is extremely hard, and it was used by the Indians to make sculptures, often inlaid with mother of pearl, that are now highly prized. Their bark is thick and dark brown beneath an outer covering of white. Leather goods made in La Paz are noted for their quality, due in large part to the chemicals taken from the palo blanco to tan the leather. In the old days, bark was removed from half of the tree frequently resulting in the tree's death. Today, trees are cut off four feet above the ground so that all the bark can be used for tanning leather. The trees sprout again from the stump and are ready for harvesting in approximately five years.

Twelve-foot cardón cacti are common on the southern part of the peninsula. After heavy rains they turn a deep green in color, but they can live for months with no water. They store moisture in their pulpy stalks to use during prolonged droughts.

Also common is a form of yucca called the candelilla. It has a gum or wax that the Indians once used to waterproof their baskets. Today this wax is used to make candles. The sap looks somewhat similar to the juice of the milkweed. If taken internally, a small amount acts like a large dose of castor oil. Other yuccas provide materials for mattresses, carpets, cords and horse blankets.

A variety of trees and shrubs have been useful for hundreds of years. The huizache is a spiny bush that belongs to the legume family. Its beans once were used to make ink. It also has some unpleasant properties. Cattle or wild game that feed on this bush develop meat with a distasteful flavor. If it is used as firewood to roast meat, the meat will be inedible.

In the arid foothills of Baja California the jojoba bears oblong berries that look somewhat like almonds. The oil once was used as medicine, but it has the excellent qualities of sperm oil and is rapidly becoming a commercial crop in deserts in the United States and Mexico where few other crops can be grown successfully.

Hair brushes once were made by Baja California's Indians from the spines of the hecho plant, but more modern materials are used today. Other common shrubs include the palo-hierro or ironwood, the uñagato or cat's claw, and the wild fig.

Barrel cacti, often six feet tall, are not only pretty in bloom with their orange-yellow blossoms, but they provide a life-saving source of water to the desert traveler who has been foolhardy in not bringing enough water with him. Desert dwellers chew the white pulp to quench their thirst if their water runs out. These barrel cacti have saved many a man's life. Ranchers also boil the flesh to eat as a vegetable, or to make cactus candy.

The ocotillo, or candelwood cactus, grows in profusion throughout the southern interior of the peninsula. Each plant sends out long twisted shoots covered with green leaves, thorns and branches with red tassels. Outlined against the sky on the western hills at sunset, they form an intriguing contrast to other desert plants.

The sour pitahaya is a multi-stemmed cactus, whose dark gray branches sprawl across the desert floor. Its lovely white blossoms appear at times along with ripe fruit. The spiny red fruit tastes like a sour orange and it is no match for flavor with the sweet pitahayas. It is frequently used to surround corrals because its thorns form a protective barrier.

The sweet pitahaya often grows in clumps, with organ-like trunks. In season, it has waxey, pink-tinged white flowers. The crimson fruit is spiny, and one has to move the spines aside to bite into it. Each fruit is about the size of a hen's egg with red pulp and black seeds. The sweet pitahaya is juicy and delicious-in taste – a cross between watermelon and strawberry, with a pungent tang all its own. It is easy to understand why the aborigines loved pitahayas, gorging themselves until they became so bloated they could barely walk. They also believed the fruit was an aphrodisiac.

According to reports left by the padres, when the pitahayas were ready to harvest there was little work done by the Indians because they had such a hunger for the fruit. "Young and old thronged our thorny forests, eating juicy, red pitahayas as large as a horse's hoof." According to the priests, the Indians ate and danced continually during the harvest season, sleeping only when tired of dancing, and eating again as the languor of sleep passed,

Father Johann Jakob Baegert, who later wrote extensively about Baja California, said pitahaya seeds were passed by the bodies of the aborigines in an undigested state. He said the Indians collected their dried excrement during the fruiting season, removed the seeds, and roasted them. After grinding the seeds, Baegert said they ate the meal with much laughter and gusto. The padre was mystified as to why they gorged themselves on the seeds and called their love of pitahayas a "filthiness."

HIGHWAY 19 BRANCHES OFF
TO TODOS SANTOS

South of the village of San Pedro, Highway 1 turns to the left towards the gulf of California while, 19 miles south of La Paz, Highway 19 turns off to the right heading toward Todos Santos on the Pacific Ocean's side. Highway 19 also continues on to Cabo San Lucas at the tip of the peninsula, and it is a more scenic route, passing a succession of west coast beaches that are largely unpopulated.

This is flat cactus country – miles of it until you reach Todos Santos, a farming community with 6,000 residents, which also provides good fishing. There are stores, including a gasoline station, a bank and a medical clinic, in Todos Santos.

Hotels In Todos Santos

The community has three hotels. The **Hotel California** is a block north of the highway in the center of town near the Pemex station on Calle Juárez. Single rooms rent for $27, doubles for $32, with a $6 charge for each extra person. The mailing address is Todos Santos, Baja California Sur, Mexico. The **Todos Santos Inn** is in an historic brick building in the center of town with single rooms up to $35 and double rooms for the same price, with a $5 fee for each extra person. The hotel can arrange a three-day guided pack trip into the

Sierra de la Laguna for $400 per person. The Inn requires reservations that can be obtained by writing 17 Calle Obregón, Todos Santos, Baja California Sur 23300, Mexico. The **Hotel Misión de Todos Santos** has 15 rooms with private baths. For reservations call 01152 (682) 2-7173.

RV Parks

There are two campsites. **El Molino Trailer Park** is at the southern end of Todos Santos with 21 RV sites and hookups. The fee is $9. Their mailing address is Rangelo Villarino y Verduzco, Todos Santos, Baja California Sur 23300, Mexico, or call 01152 (682) 4-1856. In the United States there is an agent who can be contacted at (213) 828-1856.

The **San Pedrito RV Park** is four miles south of Todos Santos off Highway 19 on a dirt turnoff. Drive 2 1/2 miles on the dirt road to an open area on the beach where there are 51 RV or tent sites, all with hookups. Tent sites are $3 and RV sites $11. For reservations write Apartado Postal 15, Todos Santos, Baja California Sur, Mexico, or call 01152 (682) 4-0147.

Highway 19 passes through the small farming community of El Pescadero which has 1,500 residents with a number of stores and cafes.

RV Parks South Of El Pescadero

There are two public parks in this area that have no facilities but charge a fee. The **Los Cerritos RV Park** is four miles south of El Pescadero by way of Highway 19 and then another 3 1/2 miles southwest over a dirt road to a sandy beach on the Pacific Ocean. Fifty RVs can be accommodated, and there are tent sites but no hookups. Each vehicle is charged $4. The **Playa Los Cerritos** charges $3 per vehicle and is located six miles south of El Pescadero. There are no hookups.

The **Playa Gasparina** is 3 1/2 miles south of Colonia Plu-tarco Elias Calles, another small farming community. It charges $2 per vehicle and there are no facilities. This park is spectacularly beautiful with few tenants – if any.

FROM SAN PEDRO,

HIGHWAY 1 HEADS SOUTH

Highway 1 continues straight towards the foothills of the Si-erra de la Laguna by descending to the bottom of a narrow valley before climbing up through the mountains via a can-yon walled on each side with steep cliffs.

San Bartolo is distinguished only by the microwave relay station that provides a telephone link with La Paz and the people at the tip of the peninsula.

Once the road returns to the gulf after winding through the mountains, the shore of Bahía de Palmas, or Bay of Palms, emerges on the left.

BAY OF PALMS

This is one of the finest deep-sea fishing spots in Baja Cali-fornia; particularly at Buena Vista where even yellowfin tuna can be found. Some of these tuna weigh 100 pounds or more. Golden beaches along the bay, with the incredibly blue waters of the gulf lapping gently along the shore, spread for miles in curving arcs.

Hotels In Bay Of Palms

Along this beautiful coastline there are a number of out-standing places to stay. Many of them, by the way, add at least a 10 percent service charge to your bill. The **Hotel Punta Pescadero,** eight miles north of Los Barriles on an unpaved road that leaves Highway 1 at the El Cardonal exit, is the most secluded resort. The road to it should not be attempted by wide vehicles. It's on a sandy beach and the rooms have private balconies. There is a full range of equipment for sportfishing, boating, and skin diving. The rooms rent for $46 to $60 single and up to $82 double, with each extra person charged $22. There are special rates for children. The 3,500-foot airstrip can be contacted through unicom on 122.8. Reservations and deposits are required, with a 15-day cancellation notice required, or twice that for holiday accommodations. Write Apartado Postal 362, La Paz, Baja California Sur, Mexico, or call toll free in the United States (800) 426-2252.

There are several other fine hotels, including the **Hotel Palmas de Cortés,** open year round. It's on the beach a half-mile from Highway 1 and caters to fishermen in this angler's paradise. Single rooms rent for $60 and double rooms for $93. Fishing cruisers rent for up to $220 a day and skiffs for $110. There's a 3,000-foot airstrip that can be contacted on unicom 122.8. The meals here are especially good. Reservations and a deposit are required, with a 30-day refund notice. Write Hotel Palmas de Cortés, PO. Box 9016, Calabasas CA 91372. Call (818) 887-7001 or toll free (800) 368-4334.

A mile north of this bay, and three quarters of a mile east of Highway 1, is the **Hotel Playa Hermosa** where the rates are $60 single and $88 double, with each extra person charged $25. Fishing cruisers are $200 a day, with skiffs priced at $110. Reservations and a deposit are required with a 30-day cancellation notice requirement. Their American agent can be contacted by writing Hotel Playa Hermosa, PO. Box 1827, Monterey, CA 93942, or by calling (408) 375-4255. In California, they have a toll-free number: (800) 347-6847. The **Hotel Spa Buena Vista** at Buena Vista on Bahía de Palmas is on the beach a quarter of a mile from Highway 1. A converted mansion, its rooms rent for up to $92 single, and up to $145 double, with a $30 charge for each extra person – although children under 12 are charged $13. Fishing cruisers rent for as much as $310 per day and skiffs are $110. For mandatory reservations and deposits, with a 30-day refund notice requirement, write Hotel Spa Buena Vista, P.O. Box 218, Placentia, CA 92670, or call (800) 752-3555. The **Hotel Rancho Buena Vista,** a half-mile east of Highway 1, is also on the bay and their rates are determined by the time of the year – from 4/1 to 11/30 the single rate is $76 and the double is $130; from 12/1 to 3/31 the single rate is $61 and the double $105. Each extra person in a room is charged $49. Their 2,800-foot airstrip can be contacted by unicom on 122.8. Fishing cruisers are $174 to $203 a day, plus equipment and bait. Reservations and deposit can be arranged by writing Hotel Rancho Buena Vista, PO. Box 673, Monrovia, CA 91016, or by calling (818) 303-1517. The **Rancho Leonero** is on the bay four miles southeast of Highway 7 on a dirt road. Their single rate is $65 and double $100, with a $35 charge for each additional person in a room. Fishing and hunting trips can be arranged, and there is a 3,200-foot airstrip available for private planes. For a mandatory reservation and deposit, with a refund notice requirement of 30 days, write Rancho Leonero, 223 Via de San Ysidro, Suite D, San Ysidro CA 92143. Call (800) 696-2164.

Further south on Punta Colorado is the **Hotel Punta Colorado** that overlooks the gulf. It is 10 miles east of Highway 1 on an unpaved road (La Rivera exit) and charges $60 for a single room, $93 for a double, with $35 for each additional person. It is closed during September and early October – the area's storm season. Hotel employees can arrange hunting or fishing trips, with sportfishing cruisers and a skipper priced at up to $265 a day, or skiffs at $110. There is a 3,200-foot airstrip with the usual 122.8 on unicom for contacting the hotel from incoming aircraft. For mandatory reservations and deposit, with a 30-day refund period, write Hotel Punta Colorado, PO. Box 2573, Canoga Park, CA 91306, or call (818) 703-1002. You can also call toll free at (800) 340-3745.

RV Parks

There are two trailer parks at Bahía de Palmas. The **Martin Verdugo** is a half-mile east of Highway 1 in an open area with level sites for 65 RVs or 25 tents – with hookups. Groceries are available, and fishing trips can be arranged. The fee is $7.70 to $9 per vehicle. Write Apartado Postal 536, La Paz, Baja California Sur, Mexico. The **Playa de Oro RV Resort** is a half-mile east of Highway 1, north of the bay. It's an open area with 54 RV sites and two tent sites, with hookups. The fee ranges from $9 for two people, and $1.50 for each additional person. Deposits are required with a seven-day refund period. Write Apartado Postal 4, Santiago, Baja California Sur, Mexico, or Playa de Oro RV Park, 3106 Capa Drive, Hacienda Heights, CA 91745. Their telephone number is (818) 336-7494.

HIGHWAY 1 TURNS INLAND

As Highway 1 turns inland again it crosses a cactus-covered plain with the Sierra de la Laguna rising high in the west. This is what botanists mean when they talk about a tropical thorn forest. Soon the village of Santiago appears off to the right, almost hidden by trees in a deep arroyo that was once a drainage bed for the nearby mountains.

With the road steadily bearing towards the center of the peninsula, a large concrete ball appears designating the Tropic of Cancer. This is the point on the earth's surface that is exactly 23 1/2 degrees north of the equator and the northernmost latitude reached by the overhead sun.

It takes only another 15 minutes or so before the road swings south again towards the community of San José del Cabo on the shores of the gulf of California, and near the peninsula's tip. The highway skirts the mountains on the right but runs, for the most part, in straight stretches. Cattle, burros and horses attempt to share the middle of this unfenced road so drivers must beware of the sudden appearance of animals.

As Highway 1 turns inland again, a paved road takes you to San José del Cabo. It was founded in 1730, and today has a population of about 7,000 people.

Hotels In San José Del Cabo

The **Hotel Aquamarina** is on the beach a mile and a half west of town. It charges $50 for a single room and the same for a double, with a $5 charge for each additional person. Pets are strictly forbidden. For reservations and deposit information (there is a 72-hour cancellation notice requirement), write Apartado Postal 53, San José del Cabo, Baja California Sur, Mexico, or call 01152 (684) 2-0110. The **Hotel Posada Real Los Cabos** is a mile and a half west of town with singles and double rooms priced at up to $80, and an $11 charge for each extra person. Suites are also available. No pets are allowed. You can charter a fishing boat at up to $360 a day for three people. There's a 72-hour cancellation notice requirement and you can make reservations by calling 01152 (684) 2-0155, **or** through Best Western in the United States on their toll-free line (800) 5281234. The **Stouffer El Presidente** is a mile and a quarter west of town with single and double rooms priced from $92 to $152, and an extra-person charge of $16. Pets are not allowed. A deposit is required with a 72-hour cancellation notice requirement. Write Apartado Postal 2, San José del Cabo, Baja California Sur 23400, Mexico. Or call toll free (800) 468-3571.

Five miles west of San José del Cabo, the **Hotel Palmilla** is situated in one of the most beautiful spots in Baja California. Palmilla is a place of enchantment with its blooming many-colored oleanders, while cascades of brilliant red bougainvilleas cling to the white walls. The driveway is paved, and at the entrance there is a two-tiered fountain. Palmilla is a place of old-world charm with cemented stones leading to a large swimming pool. Surrounding the pool are date and co-

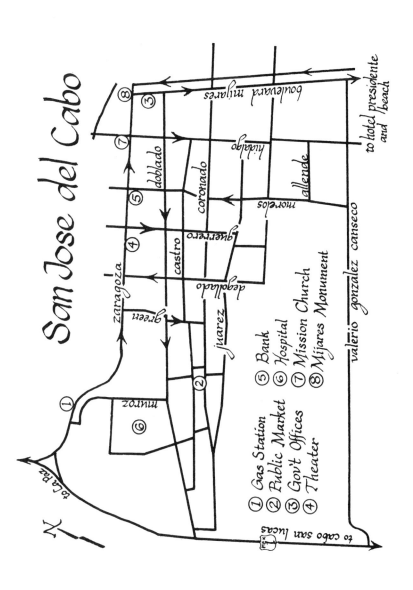

San Jose del Cabo

① Gas Station
② Public Market
③ Gov't Offices
④ Theater
⑤ Bank
⑥ Hospital
⑦ Mission Church
⑧ Mijares Monument

boulevard mijares

to hotel presidente and beach

zaragoza

green

doblado

castro

guerrero

degollado

juarez

coronado

hidalgo

morelos

allende

valerio gonzalez canseco

munoz

to cabo san lucas

to la paz

N

conut palms, whose fronds rustle in the light breeze. Beyond the hotel the deep blue waters of the gulf are visible through the trees and, along the shore, the water turns from a deep blue to a lighter color, ending in foamy white swells that dash against jagged rocks.

In the dining room there's a vaulted ceiling with wide windows so one can see along the sandy shore far to the east. There are mounted marlin and dolphinfish over the bar because this, too, is an angler's paradise. The food is excellent, and expertly served by vivacious young Mexican girls from the local orphanage.

The Palmilla charges according to the season. From 6/1 to 10/31 it is $130 to $145 for a single or double room. From 11/1 to 5/31 single rooms are $185-$220. Extra persons cost $25 each, but there are special rates for children. There is guide service available for hunting, fishing, skin diving and horseback riding. Fishing cruisers are $395 per day. The 4,500-foot lighted airstrip, reachable on unicom 122.8, is available for private pilots. You can expect to have a 15 percent service charge added to your bill, but the service here is superb. For reservations and deposit, call Koll International (800) 637-2226, or write Palmilla Reservations, 4343 Von Karman Ave., Newport Beach CA 92660-2083.

Restaurants

Each of the hotels serves fine food but two independent restaurants are worthy of notice. **Da Georgia's** is near the Hotel Palmilla on a hill overlooking the gulf. It serves Italian dishes from 11 a.m. to 10 p.m. with prices from $9 to $18. **Damiana** is near the center of San José del Cabo at Boulevard Mijares No. 8 across from a church. The atmosphere in the patio or inside the restaurant is delightful and the Mexican dishes and seafood are equally so. It is open from noon until 11 p.m. and dinners are priced from $9 to $19.

RV Park

There is only one trailer park, the **Brisa del Mar**, two miles southwest of the center of town on Highway 1. It's on a south-facing beach in a fenced area with 110 RV or tent sites with hookups. Fishing trips can be arranged. The fee is $7-$11 for two people, with a $1.50 charge for each additional person. Their mailing address is Apartado Postal 45, San José del Cabo, Baja California Sur, Mexico.

EN ROUTE TO CABO SAN LUCAS

North of San José del Cabo, Highway 1 turns almost due west and the waters of the gulf can be seen on the left through hills dotted with scrubby growth totally lacking in appeal. Lovely beaches, without a sign of humanity, now begin to appear, with the azure waters turning to white foam as the sea reaches the shining sand.

Land's End

Land's End, where the Gulf of California meets the Pacific Ocean at the southernmost tip of Baja California, is only a few miles from Hotel Palmilla. The first sight of it is the familiar picture-postcard scene of sculptured rocks. These huge piles of stone, some with large openings at their bases where great swells have battered the weaker sections for thousands of years, rise majestically from the sea. To the right a small bay, filled with fishing boats, forms a harbor for Cabo San Lucas.

SPANISH GALLEONS AND PIRATES

Here, centuries ago, Spanish galleons from Manila stopped to take on food and water before proceeding home with silks and spices from the Philippines. Some made it safely. Others did not because of waiting privateers like Sir Thomas Cavendish who seized the galleon *Santa Ana* in 1587.

During the reign of Queen Anne in England, a company of adventurers was organized in Bristol in 1707 to carry the war between England and Spain to the Pacific Ocean.

France had long been using privateers to prey upon Spanish possessions, and Spain's ability to protect her Manila galleons and other ships became a matter of grave concern to her leaders. The situation worsened in the early part of the 18th century when a growing number of British privateers began to take an increasing toll of Spanish ships.

Captain Woodes Rogers secured a commission from Prince George, Lord High Admiral of England and husband to Queen Anne. Rogers set out from Bristol with the frigate *Duke* that he personally commanded with the noted navigator William Dampier as his chief pilot. The *Duke* had 30 guns and was manned by 117 men. Another frigate, the *Duchess,* was of equal size but carried only 26 guns and 108 men. Dampier, who had been to Mexico's west coast on earlier voyages, led the two ships to a landfall at the island of Juan Fernandez, 400 miles off the coast of Chile, after sailing around the Horn. On the island they rescued a man called Alexander Selkirk who had been marooned on the island four years earlier by Captain Stradling of the ship *Cinque Ports.* Selkirk's experiences as a lonely exile later provided the basis for *Robinson Crusoe* by Daniel Defoe. Selkirk was appointed second mate under Rogers on the Duke, and he joined in the sacking of several towns in Peru, Chile and Mexico, and also participated in the capture of several Spanish treasure ships.

Rogers led his two ships to Baja's Cabo San Lucas to await the arrival of the Manila galleon due to stop there in November, 1709 on her way to Acapulco. The *Nuestra Señora de la Encarnación y Desengaño* was late arriving at Cabo San Lucas but she was captured December 23 without a fight when she sailed into the bay. She was a large ship, carrying 20 big guns and 193 sailors in addition to her passengers, and she was commanded by a chevalier of France, Sir John Pichberty. The galleon was a rich haul for Rogers, worth millions in the currency of the times.

Questioning some of the people on board the Manila galleon, Rogers learned that the ship's escort, the *Begonia,* had not been seen for the past three months. He was advised by informers that she carried an even richer cargo. The *Begonia* was a much larger ship, and carried 60 big guns, with 450 crew members plus the passengers.

Rogers put to sea to search for the *Begonia,* He found her but was beaten off in a fierce battle. Rogers was wounded and the Spanish ship proceeded safely to Acapulco.

Meanwhile, the first Spanish ship was repaired and Rogers renamed her the *Bachelor,* ordering her to sail for Guam in the Marianas under Captain Thomas Dover, with Alexander Selkirk as sailing master. Rogers's two ships followed later and they finally reached England in 1710, three years after their departure.

Although other mariners had expressed their convictions that the peninsula of Baja California was an island, Rogers reported to his superiors that he believed it was indeed a peninsula and attached to the mainland.

EARLY INDIANS

AND THEIR JESUIT PADRES

Padre José de Echeverría, appointed Visitador General of Missions in 1729, with responsibility for all missions in Mexico and Baja California, went first to Loreto to inspect the peninsular missions and reported on his findings to his superiors in Mexico City. "All the inconveniences of the journey are well compensated when noting the fervor of this new Christianity." He was pleased to report that 6,000 Indians had been baptized by these missions and that most of the children had been taught the Christian doctrine.

Through the years the Pericué Indians south of La Paz had caused problems for the Spanish so Echeverría decided to found two new missions among them. Padre Nicholás Tamaral, who had been stationed at La Purisíma 75 miles northwest of Loreto, and one of the most prosperous of all the missions – only a mound today marks the spot – was selected to go along with Echeverría. En route south by ship, they stopped first to pay a visit to Padre Guillermo Gordon at La Paz, taking a long side trip south by mule to see Padre

Lorenzo Carranco at Santiago Apóstol de los Coras, a mission inland from Bahía de Palmas.

After these visits, they re-embarked and sailed further south where they anchored near Bahía San Bernabé north of Cabo San Lucas. They selected a mission site on a little mesa overlooking the gulf, and constructed shelters of bamboo poles covered by palm fronds with a reed roof.

Except for a few Indian families, the others refused to visit them. They claimed that most of their tribe had recently died of smallpox. Echeverría stayed for three weeks. After his departure, the Indians came in large numbers. They told Padre Tamaral that they had not come earlier because they feared the soldiers.

The industrious Tamaral built his first mission at San José del Cabo and it is now known as San José Viejo. Today, there are no remains of the original mission because the foundation stones were later incorporated in a nearby ranch house. Mosquitoes became such a problem that Tamaral moved the mission to a site now known as San José Nuevo further south and more inland from the coast. There, he gathered the tribes around the mission and proceeded to indoctrinate them in the mysteries of the Catholic faith. He later reported to his superiors that the natives were remarkable for their dullness. As savages, he complained, they are steeped in tribal superstitions and are more inclined to take part in murderous acts than to offer themselves to the service of God.

Tamaral was not alone in condemning the immoral lives he believed the Indians led. To the padres, with their strict interpretation of morality, all savages were abominations in the eyes of God and must be made aware of the errors of their ways. The padres particularly objected to the Indian practice of taking multiple wives. Even the poorest, they said, had two or three wives. Tamaral understood some of their feelings, knowing that women outnumbered men, but he was strongly opposed to the practice. He wrote his superiors that if a woman were rejected by one man, she found it difficult to establish a new relationship because there were so many more women than men available. "The men" he said, "if reduced to one wife according to our holy law, would find themselves compelled to go in search of food." Among the Indians, he explained, this was by tradition a woman's job. They have been raised in absolute idleness, Tamaral said of the men, and they will lie in the shade of a tree rather than forage for food. He claimed that it was impossible to induce such lazy and indifferent men to lead more productive lives. "They are so accustomed to have a number of women at their service that they cannot see how they could exist with only one wife. To submit to everything that is disagreeable to savage people, and to resolve to embrace the Christian life, will require a miracle of Divine Grace."

Despite his dire predictions, Tamaral succeeded in baptizing 1,036 Indians the first year. To his superiors, he wrote, "Thanks be to God, they now recite in their rancherías the Doctrina at night before they go to sleep, and sing the Benedicto three times." He was pleased to report that they observed the same custom each morning.

Mission lands remained primitive, but Tamaral had planted a cross on the highest elevation in each ranchería and brush huts were constructed in which to instruct his flock.

Despite his best efforts, after two years Father Tamaral had to admit to his superiors that the Indians still used incredible wiles to deceive him and he claimed they still could not be trusted, relying upon revenge to gain their ends.

At first, Tamaral believed that the Indians had prior to his arrival some vague ideas of Christianity. Actually, such ideas probably came from the crews of Spanish galleons that had been visiting the cape for a hundred years. Negroes, most of them slaves on visiting ships, frequently had escaped from their masters and had taken up life among the Indians. As a result, many Indian leaders were of mixed blood.

For centuries, Baja California's Indians had been isolated from the rest of the world, and so they had not benefited by the higher civilizations on the mainland of Mexico and in Central and South America. They were true primitives whose basic instinct was survival in an unforgiving land. From the beginning, the Spanish were convinced that all Indians were cruel and treacherous with disgusting personal habits. They were convinced at the start that, being non-Christians, they had no redeeming qualities. This one-sided viewpoint has come down to us because the Indians themselves left no written description of their lives. We see them only through the eyes of white men who often were bigoted and cruel. Balancing the negative aspects reported by the Spaniards, there are many reports that the Indians were quick to laugh, and that they enjoyed a joke on themselves as much as anyone. No doubt they also possessed many other good and endearing characteristics.

Spanish priests, who suffered untold hardships in establishing missions throughout the peninsula, had one primary goal and that was to explain to the tens of thousands of Indians the mystery of the trinity and the promised salvation through baptism in the Catholic faith. In their attempts at salvation, although the intentions of the priests were honorable, the end result was the virtual annihilation of the aborigines who had no immunity to the diseases the white men brought with them.

Before his departure, Echeverría had planned another mission at the tip of the peninsula. It was named Santa Rosa de Todos Santos in honor of a noble lady who donated the money for its construction and support. Doria Rosa de la Peña, sister-in-law of the Marquez de Villapuente, generously gave 10,000 pesos to the new mission. The son of the distinguished Lieutenant General of the Armies of the King of Spain in Lombardy was named to head it in 1733. With service at La Purisima and San Ignacio, Padre Sigismundo Taraval was well equipped to deal with the founding of the new mission. Initially, a mission was planned at the Bahía de Palmas on the gulf side, but instead it was located on the Pacific side because of the availability of water from springs to irrigate the fields for farming.

In his first year, Taraval baptized the greater number of the Pericués in the area, although the tribe had been drastically reduced by a smallpox epidemic.

Each year the missions chose one of their Indians to serve as their liaison with the tribes. Padre Carranco at Santiago Apostol de los Coras made the mistake of recommending the appointment of a mulatto named Boton who appeared to be more intelligent than the rest. Instead, the mulatto proved to possess a vicious temper and the padre was forced to discipline him with a whip. Boton moved away and lived with another mulatto chief by the name of Chicori. This chief had been reprimanded by Father Tamaral for stealing an Indian girl from the San José del Cabo mission after she became a Christian. They immediately began to plot Tamaral's murder, but the first attempt failed when the father was warned by faithful Indians. They marched to Santiago, where Tamaral was visiting with Padre Carranco, and escorted him safely back to his own mission.

Relative calm descended upon the missions for the following year, but the plotters were still at work and they planned attacks on all the southern missions. While Padre Gordon was visiting Loreto, the rebellious Indians killed the only soldiers at La Paz during a raid. This raid was reported to Padre Clemente Guillón, who headed the southern missions, at his Mission Dolores del Sur headquarters. He immediately wrote letters to each of the missions advising them of their danger, and recommending that they come to his headquarters for their own safety. Before the letters could reach their destinations, Father Carranco at Santiago sent some faithful Indians to San José to bring Tamaral back with them. He refused to abandon his disciples and was murdered at San José del Cabo.

CABO SAN LUCAS TODAY

Modern Cabo San Lucas has grown from a small community of 1,500 people in 1970 to today's population of 11,000, and the area's growth is spreading beyond the immediate cape. It has always been a superb fishing spot, both for sportsmen and for the local commercial fishermen. The ferry formerly connecting Cabo San Lucas and Puerto Vallarta has been discontinued.

Hotels

The hotels and motels vary in quality and price. The colonial-styled **Hotel Cabo San Lucas** is 10 miles east of town on Chileno Bay at Highway 1. It overlooks the Gulf of California, which you can see from your balcony. Single and double rooms rent for $80 to $100, with a $25 charge for each extra person. Three- to seven-room villas rent for $1,000 to $1,500 a night while a few one- and two-bedroom apartments rent for $285 for four people per night, plus a 15 percent service charge. There's a 3,600-foot airstrip (122.8 on unicom) and a yacht anchorage. Pets are forbidden. Trips can be arranged for fishing or hunting, and there is tennis and horseback riding available. Reservations and deposits are required with a 14-day cancellation notice to get a refund. Write Hotel Cabo San Lucas, P. O. Box 48088, Los Angeles CA 90048 or call (800) 733-2226.

The **Hotel Calinda Cabo San Lucas** is four miles east of town via Highway 1 and then a paved side road. The complex is built Pueblo-style and overlooks the Gulf of California. The rates vary by season from $77-$120 for single and double rooms, with an extra charge of $15 for each additional person. Suites are available. For reservations and deposit information write Apartado Postal 12, Cabo San Lucas, Baja California Sur, Mexico, 01152 (684) 3-0044. Their toll-free number is (800) 228-5151. The **Giggling Marlin Inn** is in town at Boulevard Marina and Matamoros. Their single and

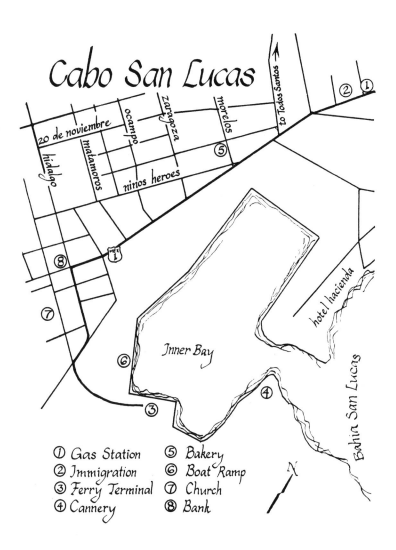

Cabo San Lucas

20 de noviembre

ocampo

zaragoza

morelos

to Todos Santos

hidalgo

matamoros

niños heroes

MEX 1

Inner Bay

hotel hacienda

Bahía San Lucas

① Gas Station ⑤ Bakery
② Immigration ⑥ Boat Ramp
③ Ferry Terminal ⑦ Church
④ Cannery ⑧ Bank

N

double rooms are priced at $93 to $120. There's a 30-day notification requirement for a deposit refund. Call 01152 (684) 3-0601 or write Giggling Marlin Inn, 13455 Ventura Boulevard, Suite 207, Sherman Oaks, California 91473. Their California number is (818) 907-7219. The **Hacienda Beach Resort** is south of Highway 1 on Cabo San Lucas bay with rooms overlooking the Gulf of California. Their rooms rent for $120-$187 for singles or doubles, with up to $25 charge for each additional person. There are also a number of one- and two-bedroom apartments. Sportfishing cruisers cost $300 to $475 per day. A reservation and a deposit are required with a 14-day refund notice needed (30 days for holidays). Write Apartado Postal 34, Cabo San Lucas, Baja California Sur, Mexico 23410, or call 01152 (684) 3-0123. In the United States you can write Hotel Hacienda, PO. Box 48872, Los Angeles, CA 90048. Outside of the 213 area you can call toll free (800) 733-2226.

There are more modest accommodations including the **Los Cabos Inn,** a half-mile west of town in the residential area at Abasolo and 16 de Septiembre. The rooms aren't air conditioned, but they have fans and showers and their single and double rates are $27 with a $4 charge for each extra person. No pets are allowed. For reservations call 01152 (684) 3-0510. There's a seven-day notice requirement for a deposit refund. Near the center of town on Highway 1 is the **Hotel Mar de Cortés** with single rooms for $22-$42, double rooms for $33-$46 – all with private baths. Sportfishing cruisers rent for $325 a day. For reservations and deposit information (15-day notice required for a refund) write Hotel Mar de Cortés, PO. Box 1827, Monterey, CA 93942 or call (408) 375-4755. From California, dial toll free (800) 347-6847. Condominiums that provide full hotel services in three- and seven-storey buildings on the bay can be rented at Marina Sol between Boulevard Lázara Cárdenas (Highway 1 is the same here) and 16 de Septiembre. The single rate is $120 and the doubles are $120-$175. Kitchens have refrigerators and there are private balconies or patios. Each extra person in a room is charged $15. For a refund, notice must be given 30 days in advance. Write Apartado Postal 119, Cabo San

Lucas, Baja California Sur, Mexico, or call (706) 843-0151. In the United States, call (800) 348-2226.

There's a resort hotel on the beach at the southernmost tip of the peninsula – **Hotel Solmar** – and most rooms face the Pacific Ocean. Single rooms are $90, doubles $100 and there is a $14 charge for each additional person. Suites are also available. Fishing cruisers are priced at up to $350 per day. Reservations and a deposit are required with a seven-day notice for cancellation. Call 01152 (684) 3-0022, or write Hotel Solmar, PO. Box 383, Pacific Palisades, CA 90272; or call the California number, (213) 459-9861.

Seven miles before you reach Cabo San Lucas the **Twin Dolphin Hotel** has private balconies overlooking the Gulf of California. This luxurious resort charges a hefty $245 a day for a single room, and $330 for a double, with a charge of $165 for each additional person. There are special rates for children. Suites are also available. Fishing cruisers rent for $300 a day. For reservations and information about a mandatory deposit – refundable only with notification 14 days in advance – write Twin Dolphin Hotel, 1625 W Olympic Boulevard, Suite 1005, Los Angeles, CA. 90015 or call (213) 386-3940. Outside of California you can call (800) 421-8925.

There are many fine hotels in Cabo San Lucas, but the most enthralling is the **Finisterra**. Solid rock was blasted to level a promontory at Baja's tip, and the rocks were used to construct the hotel. As a result, it blends perfectly with its surroundings. The road to it leads up a steep driveway from the town. The hotel's rooms have balconies overlooking the ocean. Singles range from $100 to $110, doubles from $110 to $125, with an $11 charge for each additional person. For reservations and information about a mandatory deposit (seven-day notice is required for a refund, 30 days for holidays), write Apartado Postal 1, Baja California Sur, Mexico. Call 01152 (684) 3-0000 or toll free (800) 347-2252.

The view from the Finisterra is so spectacular that one gasps with pleasure. Far below, a crescent of beaches extends for miles on each side. To the left, below the rocky peninsula, the Hotel Solmar nestles against the rocks with a sandy beach in front. Most of the time there are only one or two people walking those golden sands that stretch for miles.

For those conditioned to life in cities, the stillness at night is so profound that one is reluctant to break it, even to whisper to one another.

Late at night, the millions of stars overhead are overwhelming. They seem to shine more brightly than at any other place on earth because of the clarity of the atmosphere. Here, the Milky Way is a brilliant splash of light illuminating the night sky. The setting at the cape is a fairyland of incredible beauty, bringing Baja California to an abrupt end where the waters slope sharply down to a depth of more than 9,000 feet.

Cabo San Lucas's RV Parks

There are three campsites in Cabo San Lucas. The **El Arco Trailer Park,** two miles east of town on Highway 1, has 35 RV or tent sites with hookups. The charge is $18 per site. Call 01152 (657) 7-1215. The **Faro Viejo Trailer Park** is a mile northwest of Highway 1 on Calle Matamoros. It is in a residential area that is fenced with 50 RV or tent sites with hookups. The fee is $8 for two people, and $2 for each additional person. Write Apartado Postal 64, Cabo San Lucas, Baja California Sur, Mexico. Two miles east of town on Highway 1 is the **Vagabundos del Mar RV Park,** offering 95 RV sites with hookups for $16 per site for two people, and $3.50 for each additional person. They insist on a deposit, with a refund notice requirement of 10 days. Write Apartado Postal 197, Cabo San Lucas, Baja California Sur, Mexico or call 01152 (684) 3-0290.

Restaurants

Most of the larger resorts provide excellent dining facilities. **Villa Alfonso's Restaurante** is located above the Marina Sol Condominiums and offers an international cuisine with six-course dinners starting at approximately $33. They are open every day Monday through Saturday from November through June. You can call them at 01152 (684) 3-0739. Beef, chicken and seafood dinners are served at the **Marina Sol's Acuario Restaurant.** Prices range from $8 to $15. They are open every day. For reservations call (706) 843-0151.

There are a number of private restaurants that serve quality food. **Candide's,** which is a half-mile northeast of the center of town at the beach, serves chicken, seafood and steaks. They are open Tuesday through Sunday during the period from October through June. Dinner prices range from $15 to $25. Call 01152 (684) 3-0660. The **Restaurant Galéon Italiano** is a half-mile south of the center of town on Boulevard Marina. Mexican cuisine is featured, including seafood, in their dining room with a view of the bay and the town. Dinners range from $6.50 to $18 and they are open all day. Call 01152 (684) 3-0225. The **Coconuts Restaurant** is a mile northeast of town center at the beach in **Club Cascadas de Baja.** This is a tropical setting for dining on chicken, seafood and steaks with meals from $11 to $18. For reservations call 01152 (684) 3-0738. The **Romeo y Juliete Ristorante** is a quarter-mile south of the center of town at the entrance to the Pedregal condominium district where one can dine from 4 p.m. until midnight in an old hacienda setting. Dinners range in price from $5.50 to $17. Call 01152 (684) 3-0225 for reservations.

Getting To Cabo San Lucas

You can fly to Cabo San Lucas in jet-age luxury but it is more fulfilling by far to drive the length of the highway and to see this fabulous land by car, trailer or camper. Only by personal contact with the land and its people can you fully appreciate Baja California's enchantment, as yet unspoiled by man. There are few such places left on earth. Sadly, with the growth of tourism by land, sea and air Baja will someday lose its charm. Until then, by meeting Baja California's people in their own communities, you can still share an experience like no other. Baja is a land pulsating with hope for the future, whose people today are finally reaping the rewards that their ancestors, with survival their preoccupation, long sought but seldom achieved.

Baja Atlas

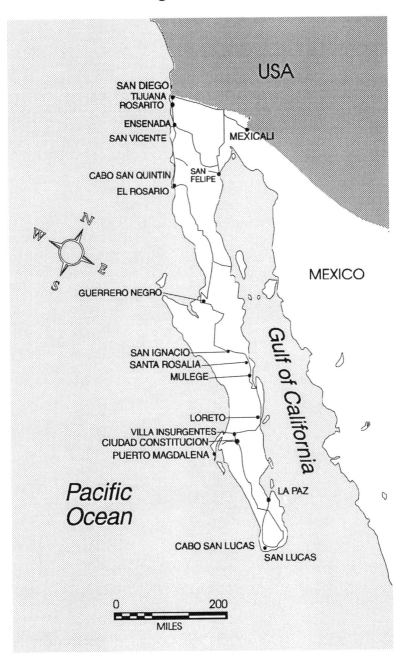

SAN DIEGO TO ENSENADA

Pacific Ocean

SAN DIEGO
CORONADO
IMPERIAL BEACH
ROSARITO
TIJUANA
TECATE
GUADALUPE
ENSENADA
MEXICALI

LAKESIDE
LA RUMOROSA
ESCONDIDO
SAN FAUSTINO
LA HECHICERA
VALLE DE LAS PALMAS
LA MISION
EL SAUZAL

U.S.A.
MEXICO
(CALIFORNIA)
(BAJA CALIFORNIA)

Laguna Salada

MILES
0   20

N
W   E
S

Ejido Vallejo
NEJI
LAS JUNTAS
VIEJO

SAN ANTONIO
PLAYA GUIJARRO
PLAYA ENCANTADA
LOS HERMANOS
POPOTLA
EL DESCANSO
Punta Mesquite
La Burrita de la Mision
La Salina
Punta Salsipuedes
Viewpoint
Salsipuedes

COSTA AZUL
EL VIGIA
ESTERO
DEL MAR
Toll Gate
SAN YSIDRO
LA MESA
LA PUERTA
EL MEZQUITO
SANTA ALICIA
site

MEXICO
BAJA
GULF OF CALIFORNIA
PACIFIC OCEAN
U.S.A.

MEXICALI-
YUMA AREA

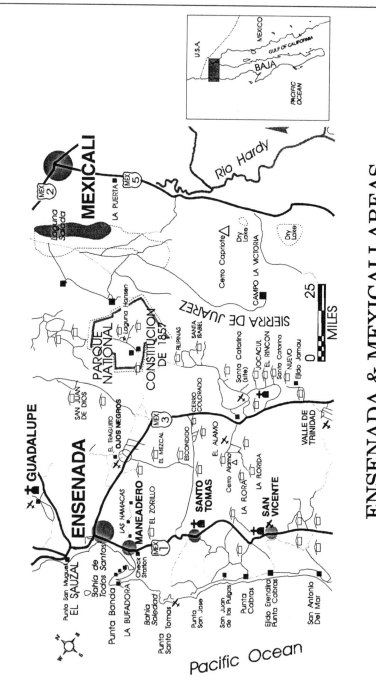

ENSENADA & MEXICALI AREAS

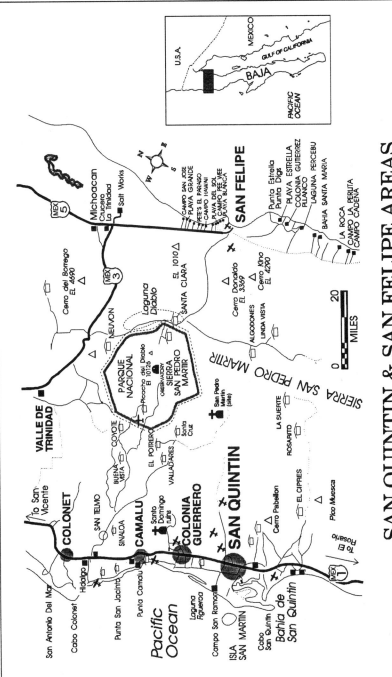

SAN QUINTIN & SAN FELIPE AREAS

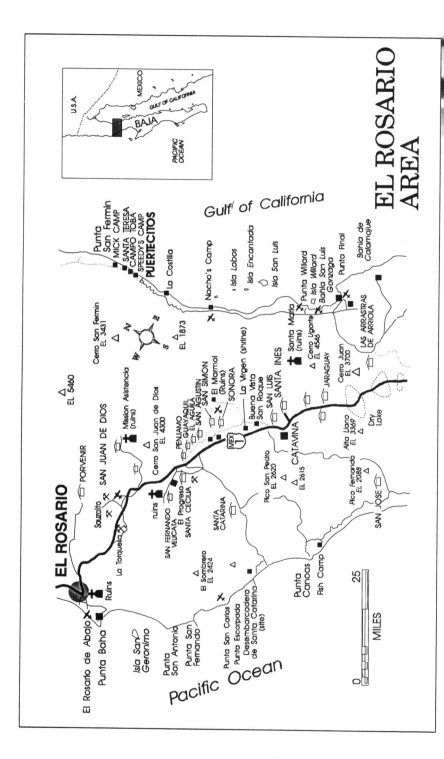

EL ROSARIO AREA

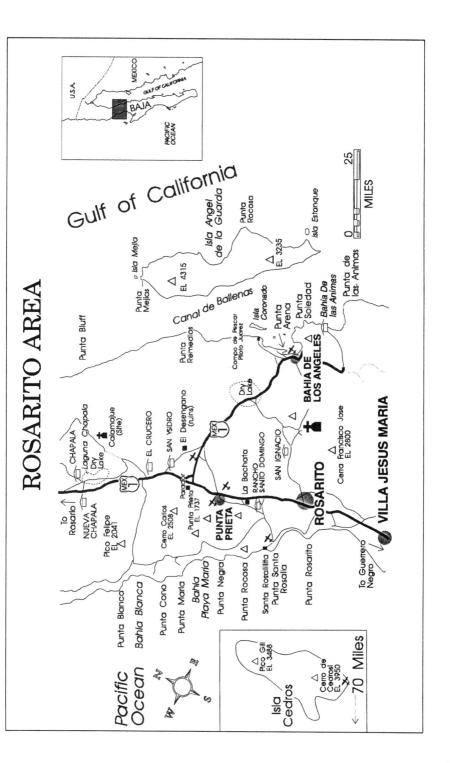

GUERRERO NEGRO TO SAN IGNACIO
Punta Eugenia
Punta Falsa
Bahia de Sebastian Vizcaino
Punta Sargazo
BAHIA TORTUGAS
Laguna Ojo de Liebre
To Rosarito
GUERRERO NEGRO
Cabo Tortolo
Morro Hermoso
Pico Vera Cruz EL 2233
BAHA CALIFORNIA
EL CANON
LA UNION
EL ARCO
Isla San Lorenzo
Punta San Gabriel
Punta San Teresa
Whale Watch
Monte Azul EL 2836
Cerro Roberto
Cerro Mesa EL 2047
El Barril
Bahia de San Cristobal
Scammon's Lagoon
EL 2866
Cabo San Miguel
EL 3067
BAHA CALIFORNIA SUR
EL 3504
Punta San Juan Bautista
Punta San Pablo
BAHIA ASUNCION
Pico Doctor EL 1302
LA CANTINA
MEX 1
Dry Lake
Bahia San Juan Bautista
Cerro Mateas EL 4485
Gulf of California
Ejido Vizcaino
Ejido Diaz Ordaz
TABLON
SAN RAFAEL
Punta Trinidad
LOS ANGELES
Pacific Ocean
Bahia Asuncion
Cerro Mesa
Pico Santa Monica EL 6905
Pico Doble EL 2349
Pico Reffer EL 3068
Pico Bartlett EL 2874
SAN ANGEL
Punta Santa Ana
Punta San Hipolito
Pico Aspero El 1763
CAMINANTE
EL 2881
To Santa Rosalia
Bahia San Hipolito
Pico Dobles EL 1996
EL 1800
Monte Piano EL 1833
SAN IGNACIO
0
20
MILES
N
E
S
W
U.S.A.
MEXICO
BAJA
GULF OF CALIFORNIA
PACIFIC OCEAN

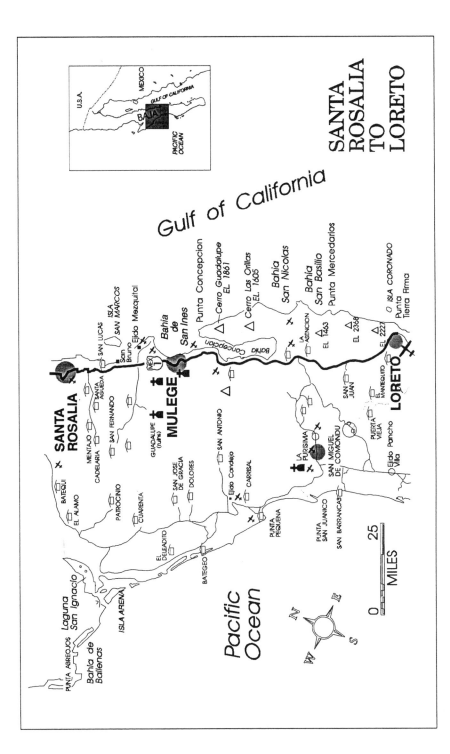

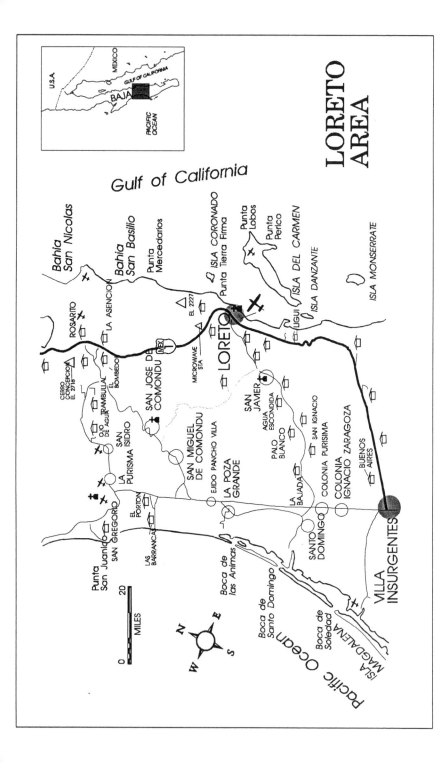

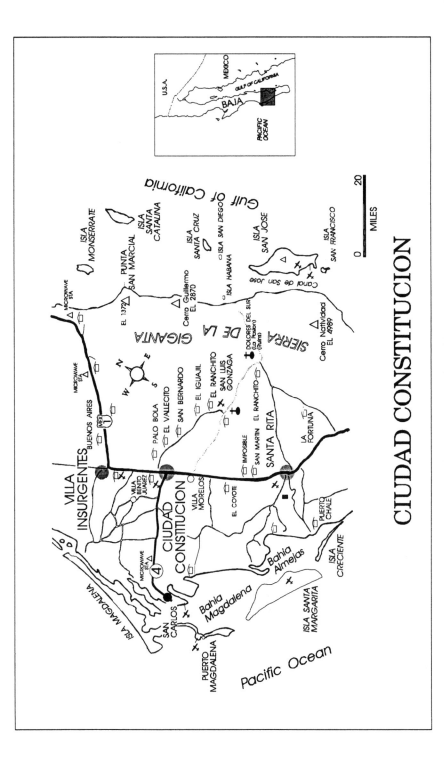

CIUDAD CONSTITUCION

CABO SAN LUCAS & SAN JOSE DEL CABO

0   25

MILES

LA PAZ AREA

0 ——— 25
Miles

LAS POCITAS
EL CIEN
R. Guadalupe
GUADALUPE
△ Microwave Sta.
EL CONFIO
Punta Conejo
LA BALLENA
EL CERRITO
ARROYO SECO
Punta Marquez
CUNANO
EL REFRESO
Microwave Sta.
TEPETATE
SAN PATRICIO
CAJEME
SAN PEDRO
To Cabo San Lucas

Gulf of California
ISLA PARTIDA
ISLA ESPIRITU SANTO
Ferry to Topolobampo
PICHILINGUE
Ferry to Mazatlan
EL MOGOTE
Punta Coyote
EL COYOTE
LA PAZ
LA FORTUNA
Canal de Cerralvo
ISLA CERRALVO
Punta Perico

Pacific Ocean

N W E S

U.S.A.
BAJA
MEXICO
GULF OF CALIFORNIA
PACIFIC OCEAN

Bahia de La Paz

COMMERCIAL WHARF
TOURIST WHARF

SINALOA
ABASOLO
PASEO ALVARO OBREGON
FRANCISCO I. MADERO
BELIZARIO DOMINGUEZ
REVOLUCION DE 1910
TOURIST INFO. P.O.
FRANCISCO I. MADERO
REVOLUCION DE 1910
MARQUEZ DE LEON
ALLENDE
DEGOLLADO
INDEPENDENCIA
IGNACIO ALTAMIRANO
IGNACIO ALTAMIRANO
SALVATIERRA

LA PAZ
0 ——— 4
MILES

5 DE FEBRERO
BRAVO
16 DE SEPTIEMBRE
5 DE MAYO

W N E S

SPORTS STADIUMS

CAMINO A LAS GARZAS
ISABEL LA CATOLICA
TO CABO SAN LUCAS
Government Offices

Index

Additional Reading

Hundreds of other specialized travel guides and maps are available from Hunter Publishing. Among those that may interest you:

HILDEBRAND'S MEXICO TRAVEL MAP
1:3,000,000 scale. Full color map shows all roads, with practical travel information on the reverse. Map measures 2 1/2 x 3 feet/$9.95

INSIDER'S GUIDE TO MEXICO
Lavish all-color guide to every part of the country, what to see & do, where to stay, how to get around. Maps and photos on virtually every page. Large fold-out map included. *5 5/8 x 8 3/4 paperback/290 pp./$17.95*

MEXICO BY RAIL
by Gary A. Poole
How to see the country by train, the cheapest and easiest way to get around. Complete details on where the rail routes take you, costs, reservation procedures, passenger stops and excursions, characteristics of the various trains, what to see along the way. Includes over 50 maps. *5 5/8 x 8 paperback/350 pp./$13.95*

THE MAYA ROAD
by Jim Conrad
Through Yucatan, Belize, Guatemala & eastern Mexico, past Maya ruins, traditional villages, and virgin forests. This guide gives an understanding of the region's natural history and Maya culture for the traveller. *5 1/2 x 8 paperback/288 pp./$15.95*

ADVENTURE GUIDE TO BELIZE
by Harry S. Pariser
With some of the best diving in the world, 1000-foot waterfalls, virgin rainforest, 500 bird species, this is a naturalist's paradise. The latest and best guide. Hotels, food, maps, color photos. *5 1/2 x 8 paperback/288 pp./$14.95*

ADVENTURE GUIDE TO COSTA RICA
by Harry S. Pariser
The biggest, most detailed guide available. Exhaustive coverage of the history, people, customs, unique wildlife, restaurants, transport, where to stay. The best hiking trails, the national parks, a complete guide to San José and all other towns, with maps and color photos. Offbeat, unusual adventure possibilities as well. *5 1/2 x 8 paperback/380 pp./$15.95*

GUIDE TO VENEZUELA
A new guide to travel in all regions, including the mountains, coast, savanah and rain forest, with an emphasis on ecotourism and the excellent national parks. *5 1/2 x 8 paperback/272 pp./$16.95*

BACKPACKING & TREKKING IN PERU & BOLIVIA
by Hilary Bradt
Walks in the Andes, including Cuzco & Macchu Picchu. "All a backpacker needs to see as much as possible with minimum hassle" *(South American Explorer).*
5 x 8 paperback/150 pp./$17.95

BACKPACKING IN CHILE & ARGENTINA by Hilary Bradt
The best book on the subject, now revised and updated. *5 x 8 paperback/204 pp./$17.95*

CLIMBING & HIKING IN ECUADOR by Rob Rachowieki
A complete guide to the mountains and trails. Ascents of all the major peaks, walks along the Inca Trail, the Pacific Coast.
5 x 8 paperback/160 pp./$18.95

BICYCLING MEXICO
by Eric Ellman & Ericka Weisbroth
The best routes, the places to seek out (or avoid at all costs), with a wealth of practical tips. The authors cycled the length and breadth of Mexico.
5 x 8 paperback/288 pp./color throughout/$16.95

•HUGO'S SPANISH IN 3 MONTHS
•HUGO'S EL INGLES SIMPLIFICADO/
** ENGLISH FOR SPANISH SPEAKERS**
•HUGO'S LATIN-AMERICAN SPANISH IN 3 MONTHS

These are intensive cassette-based courses in conversational speech. Each course comes in a vinyl album containing a 190-page book and four 1-hour cassette tapes designed to speed learning and to teach pronunciation. Together, the tapes and book take the absolute beginner to a good working knowledge of the language. These are more intensive than the "At the Wheel" course described above. The book and cassettes are priced at $39.95. The books are also available without the tapes at $7.95 each.

The above books, maps, and tape courses can be found at the best bookstores or you can order directly. Send your check (add $2.50 to cover postage and handling) to:

HUNTER PUBLISHING, INC.
300 RARITAN CENTER PARKWAY
EDISON NJ 08818

Write or call (908) 225 1900 for our free color catalog describing these and many other travel guides and maps to virtually every destination on earth.